CHANGE AND DEVELOPMENT
IN NOMADIC
AND PASTORAL SOCIETIES

INTERNATIONAL STUDIES
IN
SOCIOLOGY AND SOCIAL ANTHROPOLOGY

General Editor
K. ISHWARAN

VOLUME XXXIII

JOHN G. GALATY AND PHILIP CARL SALZMAN (EDS.)

CHANGE AND DEVELOPMENT
IN NOMADIC
AND PASTORAL SOCIETIES

LEIDEN — E. J. BRILL — 1981

CHANGE AND DEVELOPMENT IN NOMADIC AND PASTORAL SOCIETIES

EDITED BY

JOHN G. GALATY AND PHILIP CARL SALZMAN

LEIDEN — E. J. BRILL — 1981

Change and development in nomadic and
pastoral societies / ed. by John G. Galaty and
Philip Carl Salzman. — Leiden : Brill. —
(International studies in sociology and social
anthropology : vol. 33)

UDC 397

ISBN   90 04 06587 3

PRINTED IN THE NETHERLANDS

CONTENTS

Preface

THE International Congress of Anthropological and Ethnological Sciences was held in New Delhi, India, in December 1978, and represented a typically clamorous, rich and colorful occasion at which the bazaar-like diversity of Anthropology was enthuasiastically acted out. The event marked the first time that an International Congress has been held in a Third World setting, and its significance was highlighted by both the warm welcome given to participants by the Indian National Committee of the Congress, and the opening of the meeting by the Prime Minister of India, His Excellency, Shri Morarji Desai. Substantial Third World participation and a thematic emphasis on social change in the developing nations gave the Congress weight as another significant step in the growth of a World Anthropology, the directions of which are increasingly defined by the needs, values and sensibilities of those societies which are of academic and practical concern.

In the same year, the Commission on Nomadic Peoples was founded as an agency of the International Union of Anthropological and Ethnological Sciences, due in large part to the foresight and encouragement of the IUAES Secretary-General, Professor Cyril Belshaw. Under the chairmanship of Philip Salzman, the Commission was charged with drawing to the attention of anthropology the problems of contemporary nomadic peoples, and with developing a world network of scholars concerned with the study of the dynamics of change in nomadic and pastoral society. The Commission began a program of activities which included the synthesis of existing knowledge and theory on nomadic societies, the facilitation of research on problems of change, and the communication of the results of research and its practical implications. Through the distribution of NOMADIC PEOPLES, the Newsletter of the Commission, the organization of a network of persons concerned with academic and practical aspects of social change among nomadic peoples was begun.

Because of his role as chairman of the Commission, Professor Salzman was asked by the Indian National Committee of the International Congress to collaborate in the organization of a session on "Nomadism". Members of the Commission were encouraged to submit papers on "Change and Development in Nomadic Societies", and conference support for part of the Commission delegation of twenty participants was procured through the Smithsonian Institute. The session on Nomadism included a total of over thirty participants, from fifteen countries on five continents, with major contingents from India, the Soviet Union and the United States. Despite the remarkable range of diversity in emphasis and theoretical orientation of the papers, not to mention their number, the entire session took place within a three-hour time period, as a result of a timetable set in advance of the Conference. In response to the high level of interest expressed in the subject matter of the session, and frustration over lack of time for complete presentation and discussion, an informal session was spontaneously arranged at the close of the formal period, for the purpose of round-table discussion and commentary. Held at a nearby hotel, this informal session drew a remarkable number of the contributors and audience from the original session. At its close this group issued a heart-felt articulation of their primary point of commonality: their shared concern for the plight of contemporary nomadic peoples—whether in India, Central Asia, Africa or the Middle East—caught by the indifferent forces of social change, and their single plea for a sympathetic and constructive involvement of social scientists in this process of change, an involvement above and beyond academic functions. That evening, a third session of the day was arranged for the participants from the Commission on Nomadic Peoples, during which the institutional roles the Commission might possibly play were discussed.

While the number and variety of contributions to the session on Nomadism represented both a stimulating, lively and staccato overview of the situations of nomadic peoples around the globe as well as the varied perspectives of scholars from around the world, it was not clear that they could be organized into a single coherent volume for publication. Hence, the present volume represents a selection of papers submitted after the Congress by participants who had been sponsored by the Commission on Nomadic Peoples. Each submission focuses on a case or offers an overview of nomadic *pastoral* societies, a narrower but central category within the overall class of "nomadic" peoples. Geographically, this collection centres on the processes of change and development among nomadic pastoral societies of three crucial areas of concern: East Africa, West Africa, and South-West Asia. The studies concern some of the most well-known and influential pastoral societies, such as the Maasai, Fulani and Bedouin, from each of the three areas. The proceedings thus represent an accessible set of apt cases, which will communicate to the interested reader the contemporary situations of groups best known through literature on their traditional social and cultural institutions. At the same time, the volume elucidates, in an analytically useful fashion, and through several general and theoretical papers, the processes of change and the programs of development which typify the contemporary nomadic pastoral condition.

We are appreciative of the help and assistance of individuals and institutions which made possible both the Delhi Symposium and this publication. Philip Salzman and Walter Goldschmidt carried out all pre-conference arrangements, including those for travel and conference support. We are most grateful to the Smithsonian Institute for providing the Commission with a Foreign Currency Grant, which made a substantial Commission participation in the Congress possible. Due to the absence of Professor Salzman at the Congress, the session was Chaired by Dr. John G. Galaty and Professor Walter Goldschmidt, and was Co-Chaired by Dr. P. K. Misra, of the Survey of India. For permission to publish these proceedings, the Commission acknowledges the Indian National Committee of the International Congress. For their support of the translations into English of French contributions to this volume, we are most appreciative of the cooperation and help of La Fondation de la Maison des Sciences de l'Homme in Paris, continuing the constructive support of members of Equipe Ecologie et Anthropologie des Societes Pastorales for the activities of the Commission. Specifically, we thank Elizabeth Ritchie for her work on these translations through MSH, and Elizabeth Linn, at the Department of Anthropology of McGill University, for editorial assistance including review of the translations. Part of the cost of editorial and publication processes was funded by the Graduate Faculty of McGill University (through general support of the work of the Commission on Nomadic Peoples at McGill), and part by the International Social Science Council in Paris (through support for institutional operations of the Commission), and for this assistance we are grateful. For secretarial assistance, we wish to thank Thea Pawlikowska and Anna Verilli, at the Department of Anthropology at McGill.

McGill University   J.G.
Montréal, Canada

Introduction

Nomadic Pastoralists and Social Change
Processes and Perspectives

JOHN G. GALATY

McGill University, Montreal, Canada

Nomadic and Pastoral societies have long served anthropology as prototypes of the 'traditional', since by virtue of their distant habitats and apparent resistance to change, they seemed to maintain social practices lost to groups occupying the geographical and political mainstreams of Third World nations. Due to their periodic and regularized spatial movement and their specialized economies, they were attributed a high degree of social autonomy. These characteristics made them ideal subjects for a social science of small-scale, pre-industrial, non-Western societies, the avenue of the development of anthropology in its own 'traditional' form. As understanding of the operation of subsistence economies and the social and cultural dynamics of small-scale societies has been advanced, in part through study of pastoral societies (*vide* Evans-Pritchard 1940), one question which anthropologists have recurrently posed concerns apparent pastoral 'conservatism' or imperviousness to forces called 'modernization' (Dyson-Hudson, 1969; Gulliver 1969; Schneider 1959).

It is noteworthy, in the light of this academic history, that the present collection of essays on nomadic pastoral societies is concerned with "change and development", for it represents a collective investigation of themes and problems quite distinct from those which concerned analysts during a thirty period from the 1930s through the 1960s. In this introduction, I will address the question, "Just what has changed?" The question is more complex than it might appear at first glance, since during the same period that nomadic and pastoral societies were undergoing fundamental social transformation—the century which saw the spread of Western influence and control over much of the Third World, its colonization, de-colonization and Independence—anthropology itself had changed. Thus, our assessment of the way things were is in part confounded by the orientation of the literature of the time, which was in large part uninterested in questions of change and dynamic social processes. But while these two processes of social and intellectual change are quite different, they are not entirely independent, for social change in the Third World in part shaped the development of dynamic social theory, while academic concern with change has revealed previously invisible social processes and has to some extent influenced their course of development. This reverse influence has been most evident in the programs of planned change and development generated by both capitalist and socialist perspectives, which puts into practice a set of implicit social theories of change and progress.

For the purpose of developing the themes elaborated through the contributions to this volume, I will temporarily put aside this perspective on the reciprocal influence of social theory and social action, by posing two exclusively defined responses to the question of change: first, that the 'change' being studied represents an historical 'state-of-affairs', and, second, that 'change' represents a theoretical 'way-of-looking-at-things'. In conclusion, I will try to tie the two threads of thought together in a discussion of the dialectics of change, a discussion in which the duality of 'tradition' and 'change' will be related both to the interaction between social change and our knowledge of it, and to the parameters of a dynamic paradigm related to the indivisibility of the social environment of nomadic pastoral people, whose worlds, though complex, are whole.

A Changed State of Affairs?

The received literature on nomadic pastoral societies articulates a fairly coherent view, wholly applicable to East Africa, of a rural-based and relatively autonomous set of often shifting homesteads, dependent to a large extent on the food products of livestock, and related to each other by means of a conceptual scheme of social and political identity and a set of social networks usually mediated by the exchange of animals. The very institutions which generate internal cohesion, integration and unity—a segmentary political system, pastoral commitment, and shared language and culture—act to differentiate the society from other similar societies, other dissimilar societies, and the national state and market sector (Evans-Pritchard 1940; Southall 1976; Sahlins 1961). Most remarkable to outside observers has been the intense and vociferous assertion of their own superiority by pastoralists, and the apparently related rejection by them of innovations considered desirable by various agents of change. Whether assumed at the outset of inquiry, or observed as a matter of fact, the classical view has always rested on several analytical elements: that 'nomadism' and 'pastoralism' largely converged in these societies; that the societies were largely static in form and impervious to history; that as social systems they were relatively autonomous and closed; that they could be characterized by a collectivist and egalitarian ideology largely manifested in practice; that their attitudes towards production and exchange of livestock were marked by values born outside of the economic domain; and that they represented a degree of equilibrium which reasserted itself following disruptions of various sorts (c.f. Dyson-Hudson 1980, Herskovits 1926).

Admittedly, this description represents a stereotype of a stereotype, a schematic rendering for the purposes of contrast of a much more complex set of views in the extant literature, views which themselves represented attempts to typify complex social realities, including indigenous images surprisingly similar to this description. I will return to the question of whether this schematic depiction is 'true', 'valid' or 'useful'. At present I want only to emphasize that this view is, to a large extent, *not* put forth in the geographically diffuse contributions to the present volume. Explicitly or implicitly, it is assumed that *things have changed*, and that if the classic description was once valid, it is no longer so.

Processes of change are widely thought to have significantly accelerated during the decade of the 1960s, following the Independence of many nations inhabited by nomadic pastoralists. But it was the widespread African drought and famine from the late 1960s through the early 1970s, extended across the breadth of the continent from the Sahel to East Africa, which precipitated a decisive break with past conditions and past perceptions (Swift 1977). A medical metaphor was drawn from the human casualties of the resulting economic collapse—whose pathetic photographs appeared in feature articles of the Western press—and was applied to the apparently disintegrating societies themselves. Famine relief and—finally—long awaited rainfall ultimately moved the 'patient' off the international critical list, but it was widely agreed that remission at the end of such an acute attack offered an opportunity for national and international communities to reconsider the nature of the underlying chronic malady: the apparent non-viability and persistent vulnerability of continuing nomadic pastoralism.

There was some agreement on the symptoms of the pathology, notably thousands of refugees, massive emigration from stricken areas, the deaths of countless livestock, and the emergency importation of foodstuffs to feed the destitute population. But deep disagreement emerged between the assessments of national governments and the international social science and aid communities regarding the specific diagnosis of the condition and the underlying forces which caused it, both of which were crucial for determining the recommendations for treatment. Each etiology located the problem at a different level. In one view, nomadic pastoral societies were seen as victims of their own indigenous traditions, as described above. Their retention of pastoral economic structures based upon the maximal increase of herd size, under new conditions of limited movement and growing dessication because of rainfall failure, were seen to have led to overgrazing of pastures, environmental degradation, and the physical decline of livestock. Eventual economic collapse and famine were thus seen to follow the logic of the 'tragedy of common', the inevitable outcome of lack of individual restraint on livestock production in the face of collectively owned pasture resources (Ferguson 1979; Konczacki 1978). In this view, 'change'—in the sense of economic failure—was not only the prognosis, but was also the recommended treatment—in the sense of 'development'.

In another view, pastoral societies were seen as victims of national and international forces of change. While their own production systems were viewed as sound, since they were based on principles of internally-regulated semi-arid-land animal husbandry, their plight was thought to have resulted primarily from the inopportune coincidence of relatively severe but not entirely unprecedented drought and a decade of confiscation and appropriation of pasture lands by expanding horticulturalists and commercial ranchers. Rural-based subsistence pastoralism was further weakened by the spread of commercial relations and international market forces, which stimulated the over-exploitation of pastures through production for export and the market. In effect, the growth of herds and the expansion of animal husbandry was seen as being due not to the indigenous subsistence-based system but to the distortion of that system by international market relations, which benefited the few at the cost of many (Copans 1975; Dahl and Hjort 1979; and Bourgeot in this volume). Here, change is seen as the cause of the pastoral affliction, hence a return to greater autonomy is the most desirable therapy.

Despite their differences, these two viewpoints on the etiology of the crisis in nomadic pastoral society share an important assumption: that there is a qualitative break between the 'traditional' system and that system in 'change'. Further, the power of the traditional analysis to account for the Sahelian crisis has been generally questioned and the need to focus on forces of change recognized. This widespread sea-change in emphasis over the past decade of study represents the single most important point of coherence underlying the present volume. Each essay emphasizes and investigates dimensions of *change*, in explicit or implicit departure from the study of the way things *were*. But since 'the past' is never really past, this temporal contrast is often transformed into a division between sectors concurrently though loosely articulated in contemporary society, such as between urban and rural inhabitants, market and subsistence producers, or, to repeat contrasts with some currency within some areas of the Third World, between the 'traditional' and 'modern' sectors.

For the purpose of this discussion, I would like to describe themes of change developed in the following essays under the three headings, of economic, political, and social processes, within the context of the market and the state.

Economic Processes and the Market

Pastoralism is subsistence strategy; however, the corollary which has been inadequately appreciated is that such systems are based primarily upon milk and not meat production. The husbanding of large herds and the practice of nomadism, in order to best exploit pasture resources, can to some extent be explained in terms of the exigencies of subsistence production, as can a degree of the social autonomy and a measure of the independence of pastoralists. The fact that, in Africa, livestock exchange is the primary medium of social relatedness complements rather than opposes the subsistence argument; both aspects together render a quite plausible account of the notorious reluctance of pastoralists to sell their cattle on the commercial market, as is developed here by Schneider. First, the number of livestock necessary to supply a largely milk-based subsistence, and the role of non-milk-producing animals in constituting and reproducing a 'herd' as such, belies the notion of large surplus which could be marketed (c.f. Dahl and Hjort 1976). Second, the multiplicity of roles played by cattle, such as those of capital and social investment, belies the notion of a strictly subsistence argument; in effect, pastoralists are involved in

a total system of investment and exchange in terms of which commercialization
is not only irrelevant but perhaps incommensurate (Schneider 1979).

    Given this view of pastoralism as a mode of subsistence, it is of significance
that the contributions to this volume generally depict a set of pastoral processes
well integrated in commercial exchange and the market. This has long been
asserted for Middle Eastern cases. Balikci, for example, notes for the Lakenhel
of Afghanistan, that they are ''absolutely and fully part of a monetized market
economy'', with the entire herd being sold each year at prices determined by
national and international markets. This is increasingly true, moreover, for
African cases as well. Frantz describes the wealth and status acquired by the
Fulbe of Nigeria through increased production of livestock for market, under
conditions of rising demand for meat and greater national income. For the
West African Sahelian pastoralists, Bourgeot sees a relationship between the
pre-drought involvement in the market economy and the growing tendency to
form commercial ranching units by a pastoral and national elite. The Saudi
Arabian case, while representing a case somewhat analogous to that of recent
Nigeria—the combination of oil revenues and growing demand for the luxury
of meat—actually may be contrasted to it. While the Bedouin are not able to
fully subsist on their herds, they do not tend to sell their animals because subsidies are received from the government and because they have access to other
sources of income, often through wage labor or government service. This
makes a market subsistence possible without the commercialization of the
livestock sector! Saudi demands for meat are thus projected onto the international market, leading to significant importation of animals from North-east
Africa. The East African evidence is more equivocal, for while Hjort and
Galaty describe pastoralist involvement in the East African market, their sale
of animals is limited and kept within the limits of the requirements of the subsistence economy. The general tendency, however, is towards greater commercialization. Even though there is great variation in the degree to which
livestock production is commercialized, or directed to the end of the wider
market, there are few—if any—systems which have not been affected in some
way by the commercialization process, for the increase in offtake in one sector
necessarily influences the subsistence sector through the appropriation of
resources for that purpose (whether between ranching enterprises, between
neighbors, or within the same herd).

    The obverse of production *for* the market is consumption of goods acquired
from the market. One motivating force for the sale of livestock, bypassed in the
Saudi Arabian case, is the need to acquire the means for purchase of necessary
commodities including subsistence. It is not surprising, then, that pastoralists
who produce for the market also consume from the market; indeed, the two
features motivate each other, for subsistence needs may generate livestock
sales, in order to acquire money for necessary purchases, while greater commercialization of livestock production undermines the subsistence base of the
domestic unit, making greater reliance on the market necessary. To a large extent, 'change' in the pastoral sector is often accompanied by the acceleration of

this feedback cycle between the market and the domestic unit. While there are various degrees of dependency upon the market for subsistence, some involvement in market consumption would appear to be ubiquitous in pastoral societies today, if only for the provision of maize or wheat flour to supplement the milk diet among the most autonomous cases in East Africa. But for each subsistence-oriented sector of a pastoral society, the market involvement of which is narrowed to a few essential commodities, there exists a non-subsistence-oriented sector, with more dense and intense market interest, mediated by livestock marketing, wage labor, or both. The linkage between these sectors, and thus the indirect influence of the market, is developed in the contributions by Cole, Hjort and Galaty.

The use of the market entails the use of a medium of exchange, invariably a national currency. The commercialization of *livestock* raises particular problems, since livestock represent not just stores of particular 'use values' for which certain demand might exist, or even 'exchange values' of certain worth assessed in terms of the local currency, but in Schneider's words function themselves as 'money' for which there is intrinsic demand, in pastoral and non-pastoral societies alike. It would appear that currency itself serves pastoral societies in ways beyond market transfers, for exchanges previously assessed in 'livestock terms', such as bridewealth, bloodwealth or stock-partnerships, are now assessed in currency terms, if currency does not actually replace the items actually transferred. This monetization of pastoral economies has profound implications for social relations built upon local exchange. But the reverse case must be recognized, for livestock *continues* to serve as a repository of value and medium of exchange, and, indeed, undermines national currencies insofar as it retains its intrinsic strength. It is not only the subsistence pastoral sector which invests in cattle rather than national currencies through the market, for urbanites and elites often get 'out of' currencies and 'into' livestock through various forms of investment. The control of meat and stock prices by governmental bodies may exacerbate this tendency, for insofar as pastoralists 'stay in' livestock for financial reasons, this alternative financial system is strengthened.

In summary, it appears that market forces and the process of monetization have left no pastoral society untouched, but the extent to which the societies described in this collection have been 'captured' (c.f. Hyden 1980) by the market appears to vary. Certainly the passive image of pastoralists *being* captured is an inadequate rendering of the active stance of pastoral managers who use the market to certain ends, one of them being the strengthening of the subsistence herd through careful adjustments of herd structure, drawing on the livestock market. It would appear that any *general* description of the impact of the market on pastoral societies must take account of the *specific* historical and cultural context of the groups in question. For instance, authors have pointed to certain historical conjunctures to describe the setting in which greater use of, incorporation into, or resistance to the market was found, for example, various colonial policies and different religious and ethnic combinations for Fulbe (Frantz), post-colonial agricultural expansion and the great drought for the

Sahel (Bourgeot), herd losses and problems of gaining secure access to pastures for the Lakenkhel (Balikci), the opening of an army post and trading center for the Samburu and Turkana (Hjort), alteration of land tenure policy for the Maasai (Galaty), and the dramatic rise in oil prices for the Saudi Arabian Bedouin (Cole). Such factors of history are mediated by specific structures in place which also bear on the form of interaction with the market—most importantly economic structures in the subsistence sector. The extent to which rights in animals are individuated or dispersed and the degree of pastoral specialization bear on the ability of pastoralists to use the market with impunity—that is, without disruption of the subsistence systems. One major factor relating to the increase in livestock marketing is the process of livestock development, which places the economic domain clearly within the appropriate context of the state.

Economic Processes and the State

Most proposals for pastoral development tie together two aims through the mediation of the market: the serving of national needs with regard to food production and export commodities by stimulating the livestock industry; and the serving of conservation requirements by reducing pressure on pastures through regularizing offtake and reducing total stock numbers (Konczacki 1978). Pastoral development, however, serves, for many national governments, the much more general and ideologically compelling end of social, political, cultural or human development. For those at the center of the process of 'nation building' or 'national development', pastoral peoples represent a constant rebuke, in that the task has barely begun, for pastoral societies are notoriously difficult to 'deliver' government services to, by virtue of their spatial mobility, independent wealth, rural base, relative social cohesion, and low population densities (Sandford 1976). But in addition to this intractability of pastoralists due to their mode of life, their positive and active resistance to forms of state control and intervention has been documented for cases in which nomadism itself may serve the political role of avoiding encapsulation by state institutions (Irons 1975; Salzman 1980a). Thus two quite divergent but mutually supporting motives have impelled state intervention into the reaches of pastoral lands: first, the aim of strengthening the state through the pacification (in the first instance), incorporation, and assimilation (in the last instance) of nomadic peoples, and exploitation of their resources, especially land; and, second, the aim of serving its mandate and meeting its responsibility to deliver the benefits of citizenship and the fruits of national independence and development to all of its peoples. While the core of 'development' is economic, one should not underestimate the political nature of that process, or the aim of radically transforming the cultural and social institutions of target peoples.

Change generated by the state can, for the purpose of exposition, be divided into the government provision of services, and government implementation of programs of land reform and organizational innovations. While few, if any, nomadic pastoralists exist outside the influence of some government services, many pastoral societies can be found which have not yet experienced fundamental institutional change, regarding land and organization. The provision of 'administration' and such services as health clinics and schools are primarily identified with small trading centers, villages or hamlets by pastoral peoples. No completely adequate solution has been found to the continuous problem of providing traditionally sedentary services to mobile people, whose mode of subsistence requires dispersal of livestock and thus of centers of human habitation (Gorham 1978). The inadequacies of health, educational and administrative services provided to nomadic peoples, can—as Cole does for the Bedouin—be used to identify them as deprived, underprivileged and subordinated within the national context. However, one can conversely emphasize the fact that nomadic pastoral societies have been profoundly influenced by these services, and that the acquisition of medical advice and treatment, the maintenance of a child at school, or the pursuit of a case of litigation, not to mention the procuring of goods in shops, decisively inflect and determine patterns of movement and activity by individuals and domestic units. Despite lack of equity, needs are served and activities are influenced.

More aggressive are extension services rendered by government agents placed at localities far from urban centers and near points of pastoral movement or watering, or mobile units which carry medical or veterinarian services to the people, either by brief forays with land-rovers or longer-term cycles dependent on larger convoys and camping facilities. Periodic or sporadic treatment of livestock or human beings, for example, innoculations, may be little apparent for the remainder of a yearly cycle, but may have decisive consequences for mortality rates and the health and nature of nomadic populations.

In many cases, several reported in this collection, national governments have altered the legal relationship between pastoralists and pastureland through programs of reform. In the Maasai case, discussed here by Galaty, a reserve system in which the two districts of Maasailand were held for the collective use of the entire group, within traditional limits, was transformed into a free-hold system, composed of adjudicated parcels under the private ownership of both individuals and groups. While the primary governmental aim was to change land-use patterns by providing direct responsibility for land through entitlement, the primary Maasai aim in accepting the plan (albeit with little choice and through fear of alternative possibilities) was to legally inscribe and thus consolidate their rights in the land (Galaty 1980). For pastoral groups such as the Fulani and the Lakenkhel, scattered amidst horticultural peoples, such processes of individuation and privitization of land have often led to their legal loss of customary rights of access to and use of pastures at various times of the year. In the reverse process, specific customary rights to pastureland have been voided through nationalization. In Iran, nationalization was aimed in part at confiscation of lands by the state, for the development of agro-industries (Digard n.d.). However, the process described by Cole, by which the Saudi Arabian government attempted to halt tribal conflict over land rights by nationalization, was designed to make all pasture available to all citizens. The result has been less control over the pastoral process and dramatic overuse of resources due to the use of trucks to transport animals and water to areas of grass (thus improving productivity of pastoral units at the cost of land degradation) and the removal of internal systems of constraint and limited access. The re-introduction of select aspects of the traditional *Hema* system of resource allocation and land-use by government agencies is aimed at halting these negative affects of nationalization (Chatty n.d.).

It would appear that the implications of programs of land reform vary with the implicit aims of the government, whether to ultimately transform pastorally-utilized land into agricultural land, to change subsistence production into commercial production, to work through pastoral units or introduce commercial units, or to strengthen or refurbish local livestock production processes by the use of land allocation (Galaty 1981). In short, the fact of privitization or nationalization of land, alone, does not seem a sufficient basis for predicting whether pastoral structures will be used or replaced, improved or undermined. This question is often answerable in terms of the organizational structures the government attempts to put into place.

Several papers discuss forms of organization for pastoral development forms which have been developed and implemented, often for commercial aims. Elsewhere Goldschmidt provides a detailed overview of significant programs of pastoral development in Sub-Saharan Africa, including model ranches among the Maasai and Fulani, the Ankola ranching scheme, commercial ranches in Angola, and Maasai individual and group ranches in Kenya and ranching associations in Tanzania (Goldschmidt 1981). His conclusion, reflected in the title "The Failure of Pastoral Development Programs in Africa", is that such schemes have rarely suceeded, primarily through attempting to implant foreign and often misguided patterns of animal husbandry in areas where they were ill-suited, or where traditional means were superior and thus continued. He states that, "Ranching schemes constitute both the most extensive and the most creative efforts at altering pastoral economies, but each of the instances cited indicates their essential failure". But where commercial ranches have been established, negative effects are often experienced by neighboring pastoralists and small-scale livestock producers, whose resources are diminished for the sake of the commercial industry. For the Sahel, Bourgeot further shows that increased market production may result in total increase rather than decrease of livestock numbers on the range, exacerbating the problem it was meant to solve. As with the question of government services, it would appear that emphasis can appropriately be put on the deficiencies of the government role in the pastoral sector, here a question of over-delivery rather than under-delivery. However, organizations and schemes have had their impact, both in transforming the organization of pastoral production for those directly concerned and in indirectly influencing those outside their direct purview. Whether successes or failures, in their own terms or judged from without, they are representative of the 'changed' state of nomadic pastoral societies and form part of the contemporary equation through which these societies must be understood.

Students of pastoral societies have often pointed out the impunity with which pastoralists cross national boundaries, or, put simply, how little ranch boundaries influence their stock movements. While true, it is often left unstated that nomadic pastoralists *know* when they are crossing frontiers and boundaries and, hence, they calculate their degrees of freedom. For the Maasai, the division between Kenya and Tanzanian sections is as often regarded in national, as in indigenous, segmentary terms and national loyalties and state policies often act as principles of controversy and differentiation within the group. Even if pastoralists have not, indeed, been 'captured' by the state, and actively and passively resist imposition of measures they deem against their interests, the state still represents a changed framework within which political positions, assertions and activities occur. In the extreme case, governments (often composed of members of agricultural background), enact policies of 'sedentarization', aimed to make nomads 'settle down' (Salzman 1980a). However, forced sedentarization inhibits efficient continuation of pastoralism, an undesirable outcome for nations trying to develop livestock industries (Aronson 1980). Some of the *aims* of sedentarization may be achieved through the sole means of individuation of land, which establishes an intrinsic connection between people, livestock and territory, through forming what are often quite extensive land units within which degrees of nomadism may continue to be practiced. Further aims may be achieved by the establishment of sedentary centers in which market and government services are found and to which pastoralists come and go. Thus there are ways that the state may be effective short of imposing a mode of sedentarization which is increasingly being seen as incommensurate with the fullest use of semi-arid land resources. Such an obvious case of 'capture' is primarily seen in the case of refugee resettlement schemes, such as those founded in Somalia following the drought and the Ogaden war. Often, however, these serve merely as way stations and are abandoned when sufficient stock is built up to allow return to pastoralism.

Social Processes

Change engendered by and associated with the market and the state has been widely seen to have had rippling effects across nomadic pastoral societies, producing alterations in their social fabric and cultural role. The papers in this collection deal with many such effects, but let me focus on just three aspects: ethnicity, inequality and ideology.

For groups noted for local autonomy, greater contact with market centers and greater use of government services at regional crossroads have led to increased contact with members of neighboring groups and various forms of linkage between them. Cole describes the intermingling of Bedouin tribes due to the elimination of tribal-based territory, and Frantz depicts the increased linkages between Fulbe and Hausa in Nigeria, mediated in part by their Islamic commonality. Among the Maasai, ingression by neighboring groups has resulted in enclaves of people known as 'mixed'; Hjort's depiction of the genesis of an ethnic group through the admixture of Samburu and Turkana is instructive, as is the convergence of their liminal ethnicity and their name, *Ilgira*, the "ones-who-are-silent". In this context of increased interaction between groups, several distinct and apparently contradictory ethnic phenomena are emerging. The first is the increased emphasis on ethnicity in new settings of interaction and competition. Increased inter-marriage and the genesis of new interstitial categories of people are dealt with through an ethnic paradigm which uses old symbols in innovative ways. Such emphasis on ethnicity may create complex ties between groups with novel rules of action and demeanor, or may open up new opportunities for exchange or use of resources in the complex economy. The second phenomenon is the lessened emphasis on ethnicity altogether, because of the growing importance of national and regional identities and also the increasing significance of identity with a 'sector'. Cole suggests that for the Bedouin to be *a* 'tribesman' is now of greater importance than the question of *which* tribe, and this great blurring of identity into the urban-rural contrast will probably increase, with pastoralists in general forming a uniquely rural group of greater autonomy than other rural people.

This process confronts us with the phenomenon of class formation and inequality, since the emerging category of *'the* tribesman' or *'the* pastoralist' represents that of a rural peasantry, whose identity is constituted by a tenuous link to land resources, on the one hand, and a tenuous link to the state and the market, on the other (c.f. Asad 1979). The description of incipient class formation represents a consistent theme carried out by the cases offered here. Bourgeot describes the classical two-fold division between those who provide pastoral labor within traditional understandings, and the emerging 'national bourgeoisie' which, in the Sahelian pastoral case, profits from that labor at little cost. In the Afghanistan case, Balikci notes five "recognized" socio-economic classes, those who are rich land and flock owners, those who are self-sufficient and without debts, those who are dependent upon the rich for work, those with debts, and those who are hopelessly poor. Similar to the Bedouin case, those who are said to "hang on the tail of the sheep" are the poor, while those who acquire land at a crucial time, are the rich. Such a distinction is also noted in the Maasai case by Galaty, who describes the acquisition of individual ranches by the rural elite, while the bulk of pastoralists are relegated to group ranches. Thus land, rather than livestock, represents the crucial division between men in the developing class system, a division related to the one created by government salaries and political posts in the state-market context. We find, here, a predicament, since the increased pace of change and programs of planned development appear to be generating increased inequality and class formation, which for the bulk of the rural pastoral society implies the emergence of a rural elite and the peasantization of the rest. However, the determined withdrawal from involvement in the wider system may only heighten the problem, as those linked the most tenuously to the market and the state become the most deprived.

Fundamental shifts of ideology are not separate from this process and predicament. Bonte describes the growing individuation of rights over animals together with the increase in the productivity of pastoral labor, a process brought to a height with the commercialization of livestock. With the shift from an egalitarian ethos to an implicit system of rural inequality goes a similar shift from an ethos of collectivism—most pertinent in attitudes related to pastures—towards an ethos of individuation, applicable to the emerging concept of 'land', a legal notion of exclusive entitlement. Many African pastoral peoples manifest a well-developed and pervasive ideology of the superiority of 'pastoralism' as a way of life, and 'pastoralists' as persons of grace and favor (Goldschmidt 1979); in the Middle-East, emphasis is often placed on 'tribal' images exemplified by the Bedouin. In the context of change, a counter-ideology promoting the superiority of urban and literate culture is becoming influential even in rural areas, and tokens of wealth increasingly are manufactured consumer items rather than livestock. Without claiming that the two ideologies are mutually exclusive, or the forms of wealth and prestige not complementary, I can suggest that the moral center of rural-based pastoral ideology is now ambivalent and is shifting towards the political and economic standards of the nation, away from the singular values of the sector-based society or 'tribe'.

As has been seen in the preceding discussion of the influence of the market, of control by the state, and of general social change in nomadic pastoral societies, most authors conceive of the contemporary situation in essentially dualistic terms, in contrast to the way things were until relatively recently, and composed of a present distinction between a 'traditional' and a 'modern' sector. In effect, history is seen as overtaking structure, with the result that the final retreat of tradition, small-scale society and conservatism, is being swept into the path of global culture and industrial society.

Based on this division of sectors is a dualism of analytical interests on the part of investigators of such societies. Two views hold that it is possible to focus either on the 'traditional' sector, which persists largely intact due to the continuing practice of nomadic forms of stock raising, or on the 'modern' sector, primarily clustered around small towns, rural industries and transportation networks. Extreme advocates of the study of either tradition or change will assert either that the trappings of change hide basically traditional orientations, or that the pervasive (and often insidious) forces of change have transformed rural society, despite the appearance of traditional continuity.

A point of resolution might be to consider the two sectors as, in effect, figure and ground, each prominent with respect to different issues and questions, and, by assuming the foreground, relegating the other domain to a background of context, for that purpose. For instance, a study of ethnic classification or ethnobotany might focus on traditional factors, while introducing aspects of changes in ethnic dominance or pasture use as context. Conversely, a study of labor migration or livestock marketing would focus on the sector of change, while making use of traditional aspects of labor utilization, work values, or livestock imagery as setting. The assumption on which such a dualistic typology of social elements is based is that change in pastoral societies is a function of at least the last few decades, and at most follows the influence of colonialism, and is thus a 'state-of-affairs', the manifestations and channels of which can be identified and traced.

A 'Changed' Perspective?

The problem in assessing just what has changed in pastoral state-of-affairs during the last 20-30 years, or even the last ten years, is that the social scientific fields on the basis of which such judgments might be made have themselves changed, with old issues and concepts being pushed aside as new ones emerge. 'Change' represents a present way of looking at things, as well as the nature of social attitudes themselves. In this volume, one finds an interest in problems such as the role of class and inequality, ethnic genesis, multiple adaptations, state influence, regional multi-ethnic fields, urban-rural dynamics, and trade. The development of anthropology has itself occurred within the context of Third World transformations and the link between Western nations and newly Independent nations forged out of new realities in the 1960s. In the pastoral field, the great Sahelian drought made new demands on social analysts for help in explaining the traumatic process, and charged them with the moral obligation of addressing issues of planned change and government-sponsored and internationally-supported development. The contributions to this volume represent an academic facet of the anthropological response to these demands, as they reveal some of the dynamic aspects of pastoral societies today, through the application of concepts, problems and theories predicated on change.

But the real test as to whether 'change' represents an identifiable state-of-affairs or a way-of-looking-at-things would be to scrutinize the state of pastoral societies in conditions prior to the historical rupture of Third World change from the perspective which has recently emerged, using this triangulation to assess the validity of the generalized and stereotypic description of 'traditional' pastoral systems. Such exercises recur implicitly throughout the papers, and such results will now be reviewed through convenient categories, paralleling those applied in the last major section, of economic, regional-political and social processes.

Economic Processes

Based on the anthropological description of non-economic attitudes towards material resources held by pastoralists, a traditional view of the 'irrational' character of pastoral economics arose. Unfortunately, the notion, born out of an implicit contrast with the 'rationalizing' of production through the application of methods of strict means-ends calculus and involvement in the capitalistic market, reverberated as well with out-dated anthropological theories of the non-rationality of non-Western peoples, and lent the idea a

loubly pejorative connotation. More recent contributions have focused either
on the means-ends relations implicit in the apparently non-economic practices
of pastoralism, or on the outright rationalization of the economy despite a non-
market context.

In the present papers, aspects of the 'traditional' picture may be found in
the contributions by Bourgeot and Cole. Bourgeot contrasts the subsistence
and commercial sectors of today and traces the transition in the revaluation of
livestock from 'use values' to 'exchange values', the latter based on a universal
assessment in monetary terms within a global market. But, contrary to this
view, the 'exchange value' of livestock has been described apart from the
market context within a system of its own, with cattle being denominated
by small-stock, and being compounded to form camel equivalents. This
indigenous livestock monetary system, so well described by Schneider, was
then used as a means of carrying out a multitude of other transactions, from
bridewealth and bloodwealth exchange, to trade for iron products and
agricultural goods, in the East African area. In West Africa, such a system was
related to units of gold and salt and used to transact long-distance caravan
trading. The essay by Galaty notes that the nature of pastoral 'ownership', like
the contemporary 'stock' market, is itself built up of 'exchange values' and
processes of investment in people, through animals.

Two other issues of importance are the degree of production maximization
and the use of pastoral labor. In a peculiar reversal of the traditional criticism
of peasant forms of production, as aimed at sufficiency rather than at the most
efficient use of resources through maximization, pastoral forms of production
have been criticized for over-producing livestock, for what were seen as the
non-economic reasons of simple accumulation or even religious ends. Cole
develops the applicability of Sahlins' notion of the 'domestic mode of production' (Sahlins 1972) to account for the apparent under-utilization of available
labor by Saudi Arabian Bedouin for production aimed at supplying partial
subsistence rather than for the market. This case seems to form an
exception to recent observations that pastoral societies do not fit the domestic
mode of production model, for the motive of production resembles that of early
capitalism, by aiming at production maximization through the most efficient
use of labor and material resources (Spencer n.d.). The case for viewing
livestock as capital, and pastoralism as involving capital production,
accumulation and investment, is elaborated by Schneider. A complementary
point of view was developed by Dahl and Hjort (1976), that optimal production
for pastoral subsistence would require herds of the magnitude often cited as
wasteful, or involving 'surplus'. Contrary to the Bedouin case, other authors
have asserted a much tighter relation between productive capacity (i.e. herd
size) and labor availability. In this volume, Bonte, for instance, describes a
form of reciprocal feed-back between increased pastoral specialization
(measured as the number of animals/person) and the productivity of pastoral
labor. It would appear, then, that pastoral systems may form a special
pre-capitalist case, for in providing a dynamic means for capital production

and accumulation, the conventional subsistence ceiling on domestic production is removed; indeed, it would appear that pastoralism expands in many cases at the expense of more limited forms of peasant agriculture.

Such arguments do not necessarily imply that pastoral systems are capitalistic in the historical sense, but merely that concepts developed in the cultural domain of the West may be of more general descriptive value; specifically, the observation that production is optimized or maximized in pastoral systems does not necessarily imply that these motives or functions are universal. One deduction from such a universalistic assumption has been the logic of the 'tragedy of the commons', which maintains that under conditions of private ownership of the outcomes of production combined with collective ownership of productive resources, competition will dictate the maximum use of the latter by each individual, in order to best maximize private benefit (c.f. Hopcraft 1981). Ironically, this 'capitalist' analysis which depicts so well forms of corporate resource-use in the Western world is used to support notions of pastoral 'irrationality', a supposed token of pre-capitalist orientation. However, much evidence has been adduced to support the view that pre-market pastoral resource exploitation was regulated by various social mechanisms of control, such as the Hema system of the Middle-East, wherein pasture access was rotated and dry-season pastures conserved (Horowitz 1979, 1981). In effect, such conservation measures were part of sophisticated pastoral technologies and existed at a social rather than simply at the voluntaristic level of regulation (Kjekshus 1977).

In conclusion, it would appear that various concepts derived from the contemporary market domain and the study of change may be usefully applied to a 'traditional' epoch and a subsistence-oriented sector, previously considered to be marked by an essential 'irrationality'. The argument is made more powerful because it does not imply that pastoralists are simply one more case of 'Economic Man', but that a specific production rationality characterizes the pastoral system, which combines dynamic maximal production and accumulation with societal control and regulation, and—as Bonte points out—avoids the development of indigenous forms of class by transforming individual maximization into societal accumulation through the mechanisms of exchange and redistribution.

Political Processes

The suggestion was made earlier that the relative autonomy of pastoral societies was progressively qualified in the context of the emerging state and market system. An earlier picture of the pre-contact situation posited a rupture between different societies, each characterized by its mode of subsistence, culture and language, the relations between them likely to be minimal and hostile. Nomadic pastoralism characterized a type of society, which embodied the cluster of features stereotypically presented at the beginning of this Introduction.

The essays in the collection articulate a quite different set of assumptions about the 'traditional' situation. A much greater intensity of relations is seen to have existed between pastoral and non-pastoral groups, including relations of inter-marriage, sociability and trade. In the East African setting, regional markets provided a setting for the exchange of pastoral, horticultural and specialty products, primarily through the mediation of women. Rather than characterizing the exclusivity of groups, social institutions—such as clanship, age-sets, or territorial political affiliations—provided the mechanisms for universalizing social ties and linking groups through individuals (Galaty 1977; Horowitz 1972). Hjort's essay describes the relations between Samburu pastoralists and agricultural and hunting peoples of the surrounding area, relationships which provided channels of refuge and assimilation in times of deprivation (c.f. Spencer 1973). Similarly, Galaty's scheme of socio-economic categories among the Maasai represents, in effect, an indigenous model for regional relations, between pastoralists, groups pursuing alternative modes of subsistence, and specialized craftsmen. From this perspective, pastoralism is not just an autonomous subsistence technique but is a symbolic form emerging in opposition to contrasting forms (such as hunting, agriculture, craft-specialization, etc.), which are mapped onto the geography of regional relations. Frantz describes a complex set of different relations which obtain between Fulbe and their neighbors, including domination/subordination in both directions, the service by Fulbe as herdsmen for horticulturalists, the use by Fulbe of horticulturalists as herdsmen, links between town Fulbe and pastoral Fulbe, the interdigitation of Fulbe pastoralists among horticulturalists, and vice-versa. Bonte depicts the function of Sahelian Fulbe as trading agents linking horticultural groups, and Balikci sketches a view of Lakenkhel as combining activities of village-dwelling agriculturalists and transhumant pastoralists, making mountain treks.

Several of these cases lead us to criticize the assumption that the conceptual ideal types of 'nomadism' and 'pastoralism' converge and characterize whole societies. As variables, both constructs represent dimensions along which cases—of individuals, sectors and groups—may range (Salzman 1980b). The contrasts of nomadic/sedentary or pastoral/agricultural/hunting/wage labor rarely characterize states, but rather processes of interchange and contextualized variation. But this realization should lead not to a dismissal of these categories but to a revised interpretation of their nature (c.f. R. Dyson-Hudson 1972; N. Dyson-Hudson 1972). They are 'ideal types' in the most useful sense, of symbolic paradigms through which human action is interpreted and directed. It is of great consequence that, despite the range of variation in subsistence activities from relatively pure pastoralism to forms of irrigation-agriculture and hunting, Maa-speakers identify themselves largely with the symbol of cattle and the activity of pastoralism. This is not simply of ideological consequence, for if subsistence activities represent forms of response to variable conditions and opportunities, they are also inflected by value hierarchies, preferences and processual trajectories. For Africa,

'pastoralist'; for the Middle-East 'tribesman'—such 'types' represent not simple markers for empirical reality but value clusters which motivate opportunity
and codify the directions of change and social transformation.

One function served by such constructs is to order the complex processes
of sedentarization which have been at work in pastoral societies long before
'settlement schemes' were organized. In the Middle East, the urban/rural and
Townsman/Bedouin/Farmer contrasts represented poles between which individuals moved, and families allocated their members. While a somewhat
similar situation obtained for Sahelian West Africa, East Africa had to deal
primarily with movements between communities of differing subsistence activities. Clearly, in such cases, an appropriate unit of analysis is not the 'group'
or the 'ethnicity' but the regional field, which might differentiate ethnic units
into divergent sectors, or integrate divergent ethnic units as differentiated sectors. Both processes are described for the Fulbe, the Maasai and Samburu, and
the Bedouin. Thus a dynamic perspective renders a quite different image of
indigenous pastoral societies than does that of autonomous and closed systems,
since it focuses on relations *between* productive sectors and ethnic groupings,
rather than taking those units as the horizon of inquiry (c.f. Asad).

Social Processes

The preceding discussion suggests how the nature of social relations in
pastoral society can be understood from a perspective on social dynamics and
change. First, the self-contained and socially explicit nature of 'ethnic' groups
or 'tribes' needs to be qualified. If symbols of praxis and language often anchor
ethnic identity, it is evident that persistent processes of inter-marriage, multi-
lingualism, and movement between subsistence forms loosen these anchors,
while the notion of ethnic integrity persists. In effect, the 'ethnic' construct
functions as an ideology of substance, continuity and simplicity of identity,
providing a fixed point around which subtle and contextualized variation occurs in the use of pragmatic ethnic 'shifters' (Galaty 1982). If recent processes
of change have made us aware of the polyvalent and contextual quality of
'ethnicity', these same insights elucidate similar qualities at work in the indigenous setting. The constructs of 'Fulbe' or 'Maasai', as described by Frantz
and Galaty, are, to be sure, problematic today, but no less than yesterday, as
they serve functions of social demarcation in complex regional settings, and
thus take on a heightened if more subtle importance in dynamic analysis than
they did when the 'ethnic group' was considered as non-problematical.

Second, the unqualified notion of pastoral egalitarianism comes into question when regional linkages are considered. The relations between pastoralists
and horticulturalists are often marked by various forms of domination and
ideological subordination, often conceived in terms of the value contrast
between the superiority of pastoralism and the inferiority of non-pastoral
activities. This ideology may correspond to a prevalent regional domination by
pastoralists, often of a military nature, as well as a determination of terms of

trade favorable to pastoralists. Of very general incidence, but described here for the Maasai, is a caste-like attitude towards indigenous blacksmiths and craftsmen, with whom marriage is forbidden and who are considered to be generally polluted and dangerous. In the strongest case, pastoral egalitarianism appears to obtain primarily between independent pastoralists themselves, and to rest in part on the radical symbolic distinction between themselves (conceived in practical and ethnic terms) and the globally subordinated and often disparaged 'others', whether non-pastoralists, clients, women or children. Such global class distinctions have seemed of less importance than the remarkable absence of centralized pastoral authority, lack of individual or family-based surplus production and accumulation, and avoidance of stratification or objectified inequality in the pastoral sector (Rigby 1979). However, these facts, significant from a comparative perspective, should not be allowed to obscure the existence of pastoral 'big men', who transform individual accumulation into political power and influence, and who may function as patrons to pastoral clients. While these *Olkitok*, or 'big men' in Maasai, may find it generally difficult to transmit such accumulation of influence to children, due to the structural predicament that wealth generates offspring and its own dispersal through inheritance, still family lines of affluence and power may be traced. Thus inequality is not simply the creation of state and market influence, although today, when state power can be mobilized for the exercise of exclusive rights over land and pasture (the ultimate pastoral resource), consolidation of privilege and its pervasive influence on a total system of relations are certainly of a qualitatively different nature.

Thirdly, the monolithic nature of pastoral ideology, previously contrasted to contemporary nationalistic ideology, is in actuality more complex, subtle and many-sided. If on the one hand, pastoralism is equated with wealth, then on the other hand the possibility of improverishment and the commonality of the human condition before God is put forth. If generalized pastoral superiority is asserted, the specialized talents of subordinate groups are granted. In particular, well developed ideologies exist which represent transformations of pastoral ideology from the perspective of non-pastoral groups, which validate their own worth and position. If at one level generalized values of collectivism, egalitarianism and generosity are asserted, at another level the specific values of individualism, differential human worth and competition may be manifested, and either or both may be used to constitute or explicate action depending on context and conditions. In short, the multiplicity of ideologies in the present day does not represent a unique situation, but one which is continually generated out of the nature of symbolic transformation and societal multiplicity.

Within each of the three domains, of economic, political and social processes, dynamic factors were seen to operate in a complex regional setting during the pre-state and pre-market period of pastoral society. Many processes of change, such as sedentarization, multi-ethnicity and ethnic genesis, regional inequality and ideological multiplicity, may be more appropriately considered as analytical problems and perspectives, rather than historically specific states of society. Certainly, by considering 'change' as a 'perspective', the continuity between the past and the present in pastoral society appears stronger. The duality of traditional and modern sectors may appear somewhat attenuated, as well, for many features of the latter have been seen to hold for the former. Indeed, one may be led to ask whether the great Sahelian drought and the political transformations of the last twenty years have not had more lasting and profound impact on the orientations, commitments and concepts of a social science of pastoralism, than on those societies themselves.

This suggestion may go too far. Complexity, dynamism and change are constructs, used to constitute and organize various social phenomena, and through highlighting their forms, to provide means for their explanation. And, like any constructs, once created and applied, they gain power, range and scope, and outdistance the limited horizons of their makers. A sociology of social scientific knowledge about pastoralism need not lead to a conclusion that change is more of the same, or that science is influenced while society is not. It seems clear that unidirectional change has occurred in nomadic pastoral societies, in large part generated by a global setting of societal transformation and development, in the context of the market and the state. One object of change has been anthropology itself, which has gained a certain perspective on indigenous societies in complex, dynamic contexts, and in a dialectical fashion changes our grasp of the past because of the nature of the present. 'Change' is *both* a 'state-of-affairs' and a 'way-of-looking-at-things', and if the interplay between the two makes it difficult to practice a science of society, at the same time it makes it possible.

Conclusion: The Dialectic of Change

An assumption underlying the foregoing discussion has been the duality of 'tradition' and 'change', most extreme in the section on change as a state-of-affairs, attenuated in the section on change as a perspective. In both moments of discussion, the contrast has been seen to have a temporal facet, distinguishing past and present, and a sector-based and spatial facet, distinguishing a modern and a traditional sector, or urban and rural processes. But if such dualism is primarily specified in terms of a contrast of theoretical perspectives, a structuralism of tradition and a processualism of change, the preceding section has established the ground-work for an overcoming of the difference through a perspective on a processualism of tradition and a struc-turalism of change. In short, if structure and process represent two angles on the same subject matter, tradition and change represent not two sectors or epochs, but two forces simultaneously at work on the same material of society.

The angle of change does not invalidate or supersede the angle of tradition, but encompasses it and puts into perspective. For instance, the giveness of ethnic categories or the construct of 'pastoralism' are not falsified by the analysis of ethnic shifters or productive variability, for the ideological nature of the former constructs are only elucidated and the nature of that 'giveness' made clear by the context of the latter. This type of tension is not different in nature if projected onto the contemporary dialectic between ethnicity and nationality, or between pastoralism and wage labor or the market. If one category assumes the foreground, as in production for the market, the other category is not rendered irrelevant but recedes to the background, as subsistence production is for that occasion deemphasized. It is the assimilation of both forms of production to a structure that renders contemporary pastoral life coherent, while it is the tension between them which represents the process of dynamic change within the structure. The notion of 'tradition' as such merely replicates certain aspects of whatever is in actuality done, but it is not explanatory. Such notions represent ideologically constituted values and needs, asserted for reasons other than their own sake. In this sense 'tradition' is alive and well, and will always be, for it is generated out of the need to assert the way things should be done, by evoking continuity where it may be lacking. Thus functions the 'pastoral tradition', whether seen today as the way things once were, or seen before as the way things should have been done in opposition to the way others did them. In this way the 'past' is a mode of creation in the present (c.f. Lévi-Strauss 1966; Sahlins 1976).

Pastoralists today do not live between two times, two places, or two sectors, but live in a single field of complex qualities and relations. If a pastoral elder received no schooling when he was young, still 'the school' represents a part of his social field, applicable to the activities of children, and appropriated to the pastoral process as competition for children needed for pastoral labor, yet as providing access to additional resources and prestige. Similarly, use of 'the market' involves no switch of sectors, but emerges from a decision regarding the allocation of animals within a total process of husbandry. The 'government' may be understood as representing the unity of ethnic groups within a given nation, in contrast to neighboring nations, but signified in another context as just another mechanism of a neighboring ethnic group, whose members dominate the civil service. Symbols we may consider as appropriate to tradition or change are simply amalgamated to form the various significant components of a single situation, characterizing pastoralism today.

Cultural codes in pastoral society do not fit neatly into a 'traditional' or 'modern' sector, but provide the means for their synthesis. In Hjort's paper, a description of Samburu and Turkana institutions of marital exchange and bridewealth payment provides a symbolic framework within which the strategies of inter-ethnic marriage make sense. The bridewealth codes articulate with each other and with the novel conditions of wage labor, providing a key to the asymmetry of *Ilgira* relations to the Samburu. The articulated codes provide the means of conceptualizing contemporary conditions of 'poor men' with access to money through 'wage labor', and in turn the codes are given a new specificity in a complex economic setting. Shifting between codes does not necessarily signify ambivalence or tension between sectors, but rather the contextualization of meaning. For instance, if, in ritual, cattle remain sacred objects, in the market they are commercial values. That no contradiction is seen or experienced is not a token of a separation of sectors but a contextual distinction between functions and codes. Such a combination and synthesis of elements of 'tradition' and 'change' into a single dynamic yet coherent social space is seen in many of the contributions, including those of Bourgeot, Frantz, Cole, Hjort, Balikci and Galaty. Here we find the ingredients for a non-dualistic investigation of pastoral change.

An anthropology of change should beware of underestimating the often underprivileged objects of their concern, by conceiving of them as tradition-laden objects of state and market forces, without motives and orientations of their own. An urban- and development-centrism quickly leads to a depreciation of the powers and perspectives of rural-based peoples, such as nomadic pastoralists, with two undesirable outcomes. First, an understanding of pastoral change is radically prevented, by ignoring the indigenously generated perceptions and understandings which modulate and direct action and response. But, further, the programs of development aimed at the improvement in the quality of pastoral life are thwarted from the outset if they are based on premises foreign to the people they purport to serve. In advocating an anthropological approach to pastoral development, Goldschmidt (1981) emphasizes the use of the knowledge of pastoralists in formulating programs of planned change, and recommends that the legitimate interests and aims of the pastoralists, including their use of livestock as factors in their social relationships, be taken into account. If forces of change from without are general and without form, as they impinge on pastoral peoples they are specific and given significance within a systematic melange of elements of multiple derivation. Pastoralists have perspectives on agencies of change, and we would do well to try to understand change from within, as part of a complex field of symbols and significant events in multiple domains and sectors, rather than from without, in just another monologue of national 'development' within an academic social science.

REFERENCES

ARONSON, Dan
    1980   "Must Nomads Settle: Some Notes Towards Policy on the Future of Pastoralism".
            In: P. Salzman, ed., *When Nomads Settle*.
ASAD, Talal
    1973   "The Bedouin as a military force: notes on some aspects of power relations between
            nomads and sedentaries in historical perspective". In: *The Desert and the Sown*, C.
            Nelson, ed., Inst. Intl. Stud. Berkeley: University of California.
    1979   "Equality in nomadic social systems? Notes towards the dissolution of an an-
            thropological category". In: *Pastoral Production and Society*, L'Equipe écologie et an-
            thropologie des sociétés pastorales. Cambridge University Press.
CHATTY, Dawn
    n.d.   "The Current Situation of the Bedouin in Syria, Jordan and Saudi Arabia and their
            Prospects for the Future". Forthcoming in: *Nomadic Peoples in a Changing World*, P.
            Salzman & J. Galaty, eds., Philadelphia: ISHI Press.

COPANS, J., ed.
1975 *Sécheresses et Famines du Sahel*. Paris: Maspero.
DAHL, Gudrun & Anders HJORT
1976 *Having Herds: Pastoral Herd Growth and Household Economy*. Stockholm Studies in Social Anthropology 2: Univ. of Stockholm.
1979 *Pastoral Change and the Role of the Drought*. Stockholm: Swedish Agency for Research Cooperation with Developing Countries.
DIGARD, Jean-Pierre
n.d. "Problèmes et Interprétations de L'Evolution du Pastoralisme Nomade en Iran depuis 1960". Forthcoming in: *Nomadic Peoples in a Changing World*, P. Salzman & J. Galaty, eds., Philadelphia: ISHI Press.
DYSON-HUDSON, Neville
1972 "The Study of Nomads". In: *Perspectives on Nomadism*, W. Irons & N. Dyson-Hudson, eds., Leiden: E. J. Brill.
DYSON-HUDSON, Rada
1972 "Pastoralism: Self Image and Behavioral Reality". In: *Perspectives on Nomadism*, W. Irons & N. Dyson-Hudson, eds., Leiden: E. J. Brill.
DYSON-HUDSON, R., DYSON-HUDSON, N.
1969 "Subsistence herding in Uganda". *Sci. Am.* 220 (2): 76-80.
1980 "Nomadic Pastoralism". *Ann. Rev. Anthropol.* 9: 15-61.
EVANS-PRITCHARD, E. E.
1940 *The Nuer: A Description of the Modes of Livelihood of a Nilotic People*. Oxford: Clarendon Press.
FERGUSON, D.
1979 *A Conceptual Framework for the Evaluation of Livestock Projects and Programs in Sub-Saharan West Africa*. Univ. of Michigan. Center for Research on Economic Development.
GALATY, John G.
1977 *In the Pastoral Image: The Dialectic of Maasai Identity*. Ph. D. Dissertation. University of Chicago.
1980 "The Maasai Group Ranch: Politics and Development in an African Pastoral Society". In: P. Salzman, ed., *When Nomads Settle*.
1981 "Organizations for Pastoral Development: Contexts of Causality, Change and Assessment". In: J. Galaty, et. al., eds., *The Future of Pastoral Peoples*.
1982 "Being Maasai, Being People-of-Cattle: Ethnic Shifters in East Africa". *American Ethnologist*. Vol. 9, No. 1 (February).
GALATY, J., D. ARONSON, P. SALZMAN, and A. CHOUINARD, eds.
1981 *The Future of Pastoral Peoples*. Ottawa: International Development Research Centre.
GOLDSCHMIDT, Walter
1979 "A General model for pastoral social systems". In: *Pastoral Production and Society*, L'Equipe écologie et anthropologie des sociétes pastorales. Cambridge University Press.
1981 "The Failure of Pastoral Economic Development Programs in Africa". In: J. Galaty, et. al., eds. *The Future of Pastoral Peoples*.
GORHAM, A. B.
1978 "The Design and Management of Pastoral Development: The Provision of Education in Pastoral Areas". *Pastoral Network Paper* 6b, London: Overseas Development Institute.
GULLIVER, Philip
1969 "The Conservative Commitment in Northern Tanzania: the Arusha and the Masai". In: *Tradition and Transition in East Africa*, P. Gulliver, ed., Berkeley: University of California Press.
HERSKOVITS, M.
1926 "The Cattle Complex in East Africa". *American Anthropologist* 28.

HOROWITZ, Michael
    1972   "Ethnic boundary maintenance among pastoralists and farmers in the Western Sudan". In: *Perspectives on Nomadism*, W. Irons & N. Dyson-Hudson, eds., Leiden: E. J. Brill.
    1979   "The Sociology of Pastoralism and African Livestock Projects". *A.I.D. Program Evaluation Discussion Paper No. 6.*
    1981   "Research Priorities in Pastoral Studies: An Agenda for the 1980s". In: J. Galaty, et. al., eds., *The Future of Pastoral Peoples.*

HYDEN, Goran
    1980   *Beyond Ujamaa in Tanzania: Underdevelopment and an Uncaptured Peasantry.* Berkeley and Los Angeles: University of California Press.

IRONS, W.
    1975   "The Yomut Turkmen: A Study of Social Organization among a Central Asian Turkic-Speaking Population". *Mus. Anthropol. Univ. Michigan, Anthropol. Pap. No. 58.* Ann Arbor: Univ. Michigan.

KJEKSHUS, H.
    1977   *Ecology Control and Economic Development in East African History: The Case of Tanganyika 1850-1950.* Berkeley: Univ. of California Press.

KONCZACKI, Z. A.
    1978   *The Economics of Pastoralism: A Case Study of Sub-Saharan Africa.* London: Frank Case.

LÉVI-STRAUSS, Claude
    1966   *The Savage Mind.* Univ. of Chicago Press.

RIGBY, Peter
    1979   "*Olpul* and *entoroj*: The economy of sharing among the pastoral Baraguyu of Tanzania". In: *Pastoral Production and Society.* L'Equipe écologie et anthropologie des sociétés pastorales. Cambridge University Press.

SAHLINS, Marshal
    1961   "The Segmentary Lineage: an organization of predatory expansion". *American Anthropologist* 63: 322-345.
    1972   *Stone-Age Economics.* Chicago: Aldine.
    1979   *Culture and Practical Reason.* Chicago: Univ. of Chicago Press.

SALZMAN, Philip
    1980   *When Nomads Settle: Processes of Sedentarization as Adaptation and Response.* N.Y.: Praeger.
    1980a   "Introduction: Processes of Sedentarization as Adaptation and Response". In: P. Salzman, ed., *When Nomads Settle.*
    1980b   "Is 'Nomadism' a Useful Concept?" *Nomadic Peoples* 6: 1-7.

SANDFORD, Stephen
    1976   Pastoralism under Pressure. *Pastoral Network Papers* 2. London: Overseas Development Institute.

SCHNEIDER, Harold K.
    1959   "The Subsistence Role of Cattle among the Pakot and in East Africa". *American Anthropologist* 59, 2: 278-300.
    1979   *Livestock and Equality in East Africa: The Economic Basis for Social Structure.* Bloomington and London: Indiana Univ. Press.

SOUTHALL, A.
    1976   "Nuer and Dinka are Peoples: ecology, ethnicity and logical possibility". *Man* (N.S.) 11: 463-491.

SPENCER, Paul
    1973   *Nomads in Alliance: Symbiosis and Growth among the Rendille and Samburu of Kenya.* London: Oxford Univ. Press.
    n.d.   "Pastoralists and the Ghost of Capitalism". Forthcoming in: *Nomadic Peoples in a Changing World*, P. Salzman & J. Galaty, eds., Philadelphia: ISHI Press.

SWIFT, J.
    1977   "Sahelian pastoralists: underdevelopment, desertification, and famine". *Ann. Rev. Anthropol.* 6: 457-78.

The Pastoralist Development Problem

H. K. SCHNEIDER

Indiana University, Bloomington, U.S.A.

ALTHOUGH the subject of this Symposium is nomadism, I want to make clear at the outset that I propose to talk about pastoralists, defined as people, whether nomadic or settled, who rely heavily on livestock production. That is to say, it seems clear to me that in the main the term nomad, as employed by the Commission on Nomadic Peoples, was meant to refer to a form of animal husbandry, while, on the other hand, it is my contention, as I will explain, that whether a pastoralist is nomadic or not is not of prime importance. For my purposes (Schneider 1979) I have defined pastoral people in East Africa as any among whom the ratio of cattle to people is one or more cows to one person, a fact which correlates importantly with egalitarian relations and statelessness, features often also associated with nomadism.

My thesis in this paper will be that current attempts to introduce development programs into pastoral areas face a problem which may be unsolvable in the sense of allowing pastoralists to continue pastoral livestock raising while at the same time contributing to national development. When the subject of how to proceed with pastoral development is broached the most common suggestion for a course of action, one shared both by developmentalists in general but also such anthropological specialists as Rigby (1968), is that ways be found to encourage pastoralists to increase the number of animals sold to meat processors. The report of Meyn (1970) on beef production in East Africa suggests to me that those societies in Kenya, such as Pokot, which have not become heavily development oriented, have low animal take-off rates—below about 13%, and in some cases, like Pokot, apparently as low as 7%. On the other hand people like the Meru, who seem to have become development oriented, have much higher take-off rates, perhaps as high as 35%. (How such a high rate can be achieved without decimating herds is a question of importance but irrelevant to the present discussion.)

The solution offered to the problem, then, is simply to raise the take-off rate, perhaps by offering incentives of one kind or another. And, in conjunction with this solution, there is the suggestion that pastoralism be further "rationalised" by introducing ranching schemes, which would provide for a more organized use of rangeland, bring about the production of lager animals, which would give a better beef output for grass input ratio, and help stop the erosion of land.

The problem with this solution, put very simply, is that it ignores the possibility, in fact the probability, that in East Africa, and without question in many other pastoral areas of the world, these animals to one degree or another play the role of what Einzig (1966) calls money: media of exchange, stores of value, standards of value, liquid reserves, standards of deferred payment and means of deferred payment. Einzig cuts his definition of money rather finely but each of these aspects of money can be importantly differentiated from the rest. For example, means of deferred payment: some monies, says Einzig, can serve as a means of deferred payment and some not. Those which cannot are monies which while useable for present exchanges, are so subject to inflation that noone wants to be paid back in them at some future date. A hard money, useful for deferred payments, can be the basis of a credit system, which, in turn, can stimulate production and the growth of wealth, with all the social and political consequences of this. Cattle in East Africa certainly do this, have done so in the past, and will apparently do so, at least in the near future.

In connection with this point I want to raise an issue which will serve to make my last point more plausible. There is a pervasive tendency among anthropologists, agricultural economists and, indeed, apparently, all developmentalists to look upon production of edible things in nonindustrial ("Third World") societies as for the purpose of satisfying hunger. The position seems unassailable. What else are yams, bananas, goats and chickens for but to satisfy hunger? Yet a moment's reflection will seriously challenge this conclusion. In America a maize farmer may plant 300 acres of maize and no one is surprised that he has no intention of eating it all himself. As a matter of fact, no one would be surprised if he and his family ate none of it but sent it all to the grain merchants. In economies where levels of production are much lower and opportunities for trade and exchange less, it is surely the case that farmers produce foodstuffs to feed the family, insuring its survival. Among the Kru, Massing (1977) notes that since colonial and nationalist policies have impeded trading, which used to be the basis for earning much wealth, many Kru have withdrawn to family farms, so to speak, biding their time and producing food for survival.

But not all nonindustrial people produce foodstuffs only on a small scale. As a matter of fact, the anthropological literature is full of accounts of people, like those in highland Melanesia, the Kwakiutl, or many Africans, who produce large amounts of foodstuffs, far in excess of family needs. To these farmers such "food" is not food but wealth, an asset to be manipulated in whatever way will bring the best return. Carrying this point farther, in some circumstances, unlike the Kru case mentioned, it does not make sense for the farmer to treat *any* of his "food" as food because at the harvest he has reason to believe that the amount he can get for selling it will exceed the cost to him of buying grain later in the year to feed his family. Thus, like the American, he sells all his corn to the grain merchant and buys his sweet corn at the supermarket.

My point, put another way, is that foodstuffs, like hardgoods or other types of goods, are probably not viewed by any people out of the context of the general system of supply and demand they face, but rather as an asset which can be eaten or traded, depending on which brings the best return.

The same is even more obviously true of our pastoralists. To a Turu pastoralist who has a cow, the cow has several values to him. For one thing, it can produce manure to keep his fields fertile. And it can produce milk. It can be killed and the meat eaten. It can be traded to another Turu as part payment for a wife who can produce grain and children. It can be loaned to another person for a period of time and the products of the cow, including some of its calves, given to that person in return for a hold on him which may be of some political value. And it can be traded for grain. In short, a Turu sees innumerable possibilities in a cow and he also calculates, as best he can, which of these uses will give him the best return. It is shortsighted, to say the least, to think that he will make primary considerations of the food value of the cow. In fact, among Turu the milk a cow produces is little valued and is given away to children. The manure has more value.

Which brings us back to the main point of this essay, the conflict between developmental and indigenous uses of livestock. Those people who are encouraging development see cattle as food (although if they owned cattle themselves they would also shortly see that they are more than food) and have convinced themselves that they are mainly food to the pastoralists as well. Hence the solution is simple: make it possible for the pastoralist to sell his cows for a price that will be high enough to compensate for their value to him as food and the pastoralist will sell. But, as I have just suggested, the pastoralist is, at best, thinking of cows as a food source only to some degree and, in some cases, to no degree at all. They are money—media of exchange and stores of value. The ability to sell cattle to the government is simply another option, one which sometimes is a good one, and so evokes good sales, but one which usually (to judge from the literature) is not, so no animals or few animals are sold.

The reason for this failure, in my judgement, is related to the implications of the fact that cattle (and other livestock as well as certain other goods in the past, like iron, cloth, cowry shells) are money, the significance of which is made more apparent if we think for a moment about how money functions in our own economy. Money is not just a means of exchange. Neither we nor pastoralist financiers desire money just to buy things. We see in money the possibility of investment to make more money and, if we can make enough money, the means to political freedom. To suggest that this obvious fact of our own economy applies as well to pastoralists might seem bizarre; in fact most people reject such an idea out of hand, depending on the notion questioned above, that nonindustrial people are subsistence oriented. Yet it is easy to demonstrate in some other parts of the world, in other types of production systems, that this is true. Melanesia is a good example. The evidence accumulating today (Strathern 1978, Sillitoe 1978) suggests strongly that among Melanesians the dynamic of their economy is one based on the production of surplus yams, which are fed to increasing pig populations, which are then given out live or as pieces of pork, which allows the producer to accumulate debts in other people through this credit, which ultimately is transformed into shell currencies, which are loaned out at interest, with the result that there is great opportunity in Melanesian society for individuals, capitalizing on this system, to increase wealth on an individualistic basis, to become big men. So volatile is the dynamic of this type of economy that chieftainship is not able to establish itself through monopoly of sources of wealth. The egalitarianism, or democracy, of Melanesia is thus a product of an economy combining the growth of wealth with the consequent growth of credit, which in turn, as in our own economy, stimulates production. The same seems to be true of the North-west Coast Indians, where production of goods on an individual basis, whose value was stored in blankets, led to the potlaches, which were a kind of credit extending process, leading to the rise of big men (Belshaw 1965) and the failure of chieftainship. Other examples of this process could be cited, including many among North and South American Indians, to judge from Clastres (1977).

In East Africa the process was different but the result the same. As far as I know loaning out cows on credit was not well developed although the various forms of stock associations described for Turkana by Gulliver (1955) and others (Schneider 1979) have some of the flavor of this, in the sense that the person receiving a cow could exploit that animal to one degree or another for the increase of his own wealth. The important fact about East Africa cattle is that the repository of value itself increases. So long as the demand for cattle is highly inelastic, any increase in a man's herd is a net increase in his wealth. As his wealth grows the opportunity for others to dominate him declines and so we find societies, where cattle-to-people ratios are at one or more to one, in which there are only big men and where, as in Melanesia and the Northwest Coast, wealth grows and declines volatilely, creating manifest opportunities for the poor to become rich.

Incidentally, it seems appropriate here to introduce a caution that has relevance for my point but also to the general question of the relation of pastoralists to land. It is almost conventional wisdom to assert that pastoralism requires open range. I think this is related to the confusion of pastoralism with nomadism. In those areas of East Africa where agriculture is possible in connection with pastoralism, range land is not necessarily open. The Turu, for example, everywhere have closed grazing, the grazing-lands being owned like crop-land. However, there are loosely organized herding groups, whose existence makes possible access to grazing for those who have no grazing land in return for herding services performed for the owner . The essential thing necessary to promote pastoralism is *any* condition that will allow regular growth of herds and widespread opportunity to gain access to wealth. Open range is necessary to this apparently only in the more arid areas.

The problem faced by the developmentalist, then, is not just to increase the amount of money a pastoralist can get for selling a cow, but to create the opportunity for growth of wealth (in this instance, one must conclude, through investments in banks) equivalent to the growth of cattle wealth in the sense that there is a stability to the monetary unit equal to the stability of demand for cattle, assured growth of real worth at the same rate as cattle (which some have suggested is at least 10% per annum) and consequent political freedom.

This is a tall order. Recently I heard a report of some new experiments in Kenya by pastoral developmentalists who had decided that the claim that pastoralists are capitalists is true and sought to use that decision to institute a new program that would take advantage of it. They created mobile banks that went to the pastoral areas and gave the pastoralists who would sell cattle the opportunity to put the money they earned into savings, thereby earning interest. But they were unsuccessful. The reason apparently is that the pastoralists either have no faith in Kenya currency, which has no value outside that country, or the interest rate was too low. In other words, the interest they would have earned would have given them little growth leverage and so little political leverage.

There are few developing countries in the world which have obtained a position of growth which brings with it political equity. It seems these days that all aim for this but few are fortunate enough to obtain it. In some cases, like Tanzania, the attempt is made to legislate equity by preventing anyone from becoming richer than anybody else. This, of course, defeats the basic fact that, as among pastoralists, the problem is not to keep everybody poor but to give more opportunity for all to become rich. Those countries, like Ivory Coast, and probably Kenya, which allow people to pursue wealth without interference, have too often found that polarization of wealth results, with a few becoming rich and the rest remaining poor or relatively poorer (e.g. in South Africa the level of income of blacks probably far exceeds that of any other blacks in Africa, but the lack of political freedom counteracts this). This approach defeats another basic fact, which is that it is not enough just to increase the level of wealth in a country but to get it spread more evenly.

It seems quite apparent to students of pastoral economies, like I. M. Lewis, speaking of the Somalis (1975), that having by their good fortune obtained the magic combination of increased opportunity for wealth and political freedom, there is not much sense to them in going along with development plans which promise only increased consumption. The pattern for the future for pastoralists could be that of the Kaputiei Maasai reported by Hedlund (1971). These people were badly damaged by the droughts of the early 60's, so much so it seems that some of them, for the first time, perceived the possibility that profit from cattle ranching for beef could allow them to recoup their loses quicker than by traditional methods. So a small portion of the richer of them banded together and obtained title (they thought) to a large part of the grazing area of the Kaputiei. Since this beef production system is radically different from the old one, requiring control of grazing lands in order to be able to plan for increased size of animals, and investment of proceeds of sales in banks, these new ranchers excluded other, nonparticipating Maasai from their ranges and along with this stopped participation in activities such as age-set organizations which would have run counter to their exclusiveness. The result is that the Maasai who were not included now found their grazing lands reduced, their opportunities for stock associateships diminished, and were faced with incipient proletarization. In other words, the process of polarization of wealth had begun for them.

I began this essay by suggesting that pastoral development, in the sense of retaining animal husbandry but transforming it to beef production, may be impossible. The shift to beef production is in fact a shift to agriculture from pastoralism and is no more meaningful to the pastoralist than a shift to crop production. Even the fact that the pastoralist has experience with livestock husbandry may not be relevant since he has learned to manage animals for other ends and may not be an expert on the process of managing them for slaughter.

But this should not suggest the abandonment of pastoralism. As I have noted, developing countries often strive for political equality combined with increased wealth, a condition which is being met by pastoralists. A decision will have to be made about how valuable this is in the context of national development goals.

REFERENCES

BELSHAW, C.
  1965 *Traditional Exchange and Modern Markets*. Prentice-Hall, Inc., Englewood Cliffs, N.J.
CLASTRES, H.
  1977 *Society Against the State*. Urizen Books, N.Y.
EINZIG, P.
  1966 *Primitive Money* (2nd ed.). Pergamon Press, N.Y.
GULLIVER, P.
  1955 *The Family Herds, A Study of Two Pastoral Tribes in East Africa, the Jie and Turkana*. Routledge and Kegan Paul, London.
HEDLUND, G. B.
  1971 *The Impact of Group Ranches on a Pastoral Society*. Institute for Development Studies, U. of Nairobi, Staff Paper 100, June.
LEWIS, I. M.
  1975 "The Dynamics of Nomadism; Prospects for Sedentarization and Society Change". In: T. Monod (ed.), *Pastoralism in Tropical Africa*. Oxford U. Press.
MASSING, A.
  1977 *Economic Developments in the Kru Culture Area*. Ph. D. dissertation, Indiana University, Bloomington, Indiana.
MEYN, K.
  1970 *Beef Production in East Africa*. Institut für Wirtschaftsforshung. Weltforum Verlag, Munich.
RIGBY, P.
  1968 "Pastoralism and Prejudice: Ideology and Rural Development in East Africa". *Nkanga*, 4, Makerere Institute of Social Research.
SCHNEIDER, H.
  1979 *Livestock and Equality in East Africa*. Indiana University Press, Bloomington, Indiana.
SILLITOE, G.
  1978 "Big Men and War in New Guinea". *Man*, 252.
STRATHERN, A.
  1978 "Finance and Production. Revisited: In Pursuit of a Comparison". In: G. Dalton (ed.), *Research in Economic Anthropology*, Vol. I. JAI Press Inc., Greenwich, Connecticut.

Ecological and Economic Factors in the Determination of Pastoral Specialisation

P. BONTE

Centre National de la Recherche Scientifique, Paris, France

SPECIALISATION in a pastoral form of production has played and continues to play an important role in the development of human societies. The present article seeks to identify some of the general factors which have, throughout history, had a direct bearing on pastoral specialisation. Particular attention shall be given to the influence of ecological factors which, in my opinion, have all too frequently been interpreted as playing an exclusive role.

By pastoral specialisation I refer to production where the labour invested in animal domestication is dominant, i.e., the labour involved in the transformation and reproduction of animals. This includes not only the immediate labour invested in animal production but also the labour accumulated in the herd. It is the domestic animal itself which, having been considerably changed, from the genetic point of view, in its behaviour and economic capacity (its output for human needs as processor of the vegetable ground-cover), represents this accumulation of human labour.

Archaeological and historical evidence enables us to distinguish between two situations in which animal domestication takes place. The first corresponds to the development of what has been called "proto-stock-raising" (A. Leroi-Gourhan, 1965, I, p. 244 *et. seq.*), i.e. the development of selective hunting practices and a certain degree of familiarity with the animal. This is to be observed in the first stages of many neolithic societies, especially in the Western Mediterranean (J. Guilaine, 1976, p. 47 *sq.*). J. Barrau has described the technological and ecological conditions surrounding the beginnings of stock-raising, with particular emphasis on the continuity between domestication and earlier practices of animal utilisation (1973).

There is another context where nomadic pastoralism may develop. This is the case of specialisation in pastoralism by human groups which previously had practised an agro-pastoral form of production. Far from constituting the first stage in the development of human society, the domestication and utilisation of animals is here preceded by a long process of change, particularly in social behaviour, brought about by the progressive incorporation of human labour into the structure of agro-pastoral society. The animal, separated from its natural habitat, partially fed on agricultural produce and having undergone modification in its herd behaviour and reproductive habits, becomes the basic element in a new technical system characterised by the utilisation of milk and transport animals in a context of widespread pastoralism. The most detailed analysis in this development is O. Lattimore's study of steppe nomads and Chinese who probably share a common origin. The use of the steppe-hoe in agriculture, a variation on an agro-pastoral technique belonging to the Ancient Chinese, slowly changed between 3000 and 500 B. C., as a result of the intensification of Chinese agriculture and the thrusting back into the hinterland of tribes considered to be barbarous and archaic. The extensive raising of horses previously domesticated under the agro-pastoral system, permitted the constitution of large nomadic pastoral societies, with the relationship of these groups to traditional Chinese society for the 4th and 3rd centuries B.C. being one of both complementarity and contradiction (O. Lattimore, 1967). This type of development took place in other parts of the world as well,—in India, for example (Leshnik, 1972), and in the Middle East (J. Moscati, 1959). And it is the type of development which I shall chiefly be considering here, inasmuch as it is typical of most of the nomadic pastoral societies actually in existence. When we come to investigate the conditions underlying pastoral specialisation in these societies, we realise that they involve complex historical processes.

There is clearly a correlation between this specialisation and a whole range of ecological factors limiting the efficiency of agricultural production in a given area. But it is not a direct correlation. For one thing, we see that, for the same area, there have been other forms of agro-pastoral production, prior to the specialisation. But the real point is that the constitution of the particular pattern of relationships between man, animal and vegetation known as nomadic pastoralism is a product of *history*. Thus it has been possible, by historical reconstruction, to study the formation of specialised pastoral societies in Europe during the second millenium B.C. Pastoral eco-systems made their appearance at a given stage in the clearing of forests by neolithic peoples who combined stock-raising with farming on burnt patches of land. The setting aside of areas reserved for pasture and the growing pastoral specialisation of many of the European peoples is to be explained by the decline of forest lands resulting from more intensive agricultural exploitation and a corresponding reduction in the area of unploughed land (A. Fleming, 1972). Similarly, in East Africa, the formation of a grassy steppe, rich in livestock and wild animals, is to be considered not so much the condition as the result of pastoral specialisation. Ecological research done on reserves such as the Serengetti illustrates this paradox: ''The particular short grassland regimes of these areas which today support vast herds of wild ungulates and their predators were not created by nature alone but rather by pastoralists and the intensive grazing of their domestic livestock and their judicious use of fire'' (Jacobs, 1975, p. 40).

Thus, if we wish to understand the manner in which ecological factors have influenced pastoral specialisation, we must look beyond the immediate effects of ecology on the selection of productive characteristics. Bearing this in mind, we shall deal first with environmental cases which are most immediately constrained by ecological factors—high mountain pastures.

Specialised eco-systems and pastoral specialisation: high mountain pastures

High mountain pastures provide us with an example of a very specialised eco-system which man can exploit only by the use of animals (llama, alpaca, yak and yak hybrids, etc.) which are exclusively adapted to this environment. In some parts of the world, these high pastures cover an area of sufficient size to support considerable numbers of men and animals. This is the case of the Andean *puna* (J. A. Flores Ochoa, 1977) which stretches from an altitude of 4,000 metres to the snowline. It is also the case of the Himalayan pastures, *bugyal*, or *payar*, stretching from the forest line up to roughly 3,000-5,000 metres (Paut, 1954), and above all of the vast pasture lands of Tibet, *abrog*, rising above the cultivated valleys to a height of from 4,500 to more than 5,000 metres in the South and from 2,500 to 3,500 metres in the North (Ekvall, 1968). All these pasture areas have features in common with the Arctic *tundra*. The chief characteristics are the cold and the great extremes of temperature, on the one hand, and the rarefication of oxygen on the other. Together, these conditions have the effect of generally slowing down the activity of photosynthesis (a low level of vegetable growth and energy production) and are responsible for the highly specialised character of the vegetable and animal species.

Another feature of these mountain eco-systems is the seasonal variability in the growth of vegetation. These variations are generally determined by the winter snowfall which prevents animals from having access to the grass and makes transhumance necessary, men and herds moving to lower pastures in order to exploit the totality of the eco-system. At the same time it is necessary to provide for winter feed for livestock, by using other ecological areas (forest) or laying in supplies of forage (Ekvall, 1968; Bonnemaire and Teissier, 1976). The equatorial *puna* does not have the problems of other mountain pasture lands arising out of variations in snow-level, but it has a dry season and a wet season, the latter occurring in winter, which is the season when the highest pastures can be utilised to best advantage. In order to increase the summer resources on which the animal population depends, Andean herdsmen create networks of irrigated pastures (*bofedales*), following the lines of depressions in the ground (Flores Ochoa, 1977).

In both cases, in order to exploit high pastures through the use of animals, ecological conditions make necessary an annual transhumant move from higher to lower pastures and back again. However, this in itself is no guarantee of pastoral specialisation. The ancient *aymara* communities of Peru, like the peoples of Tibet, have an agro-pastoral system of exploitation of pasture, founded on a division of labour within the community (Murra, 1965) or within the family, analogous to the forms of economic and social organisation found among the inhabitants of the Alps. (In this case the discontinuity between areas of pasture is a significant factor in that it limits the ways in which a society based on pastoral specialisation can be organised).

What precisely, then, are the conditions of pastoral specialisation among certain human groups inhabiting mountainous regions?

The history of nomadic pastoral societies in Tibet is a long and complex one and I am scarcely qualified to discuss it. There is, however, one point which is of particular interest. Throughout the course of this history, down to recent times, the conditions differentiating nomadic herdsmen, *abrog Pa*, "the men from the high pastures", from the agro-pastoralists of the valleys have been maintained. There is in fact also a third group, *Sa Ma a Brog*, the position of which provides a key to an understanding of the distinction between herdsmen and farmers. These semi-nomads, living in camps, move into the vicinity of the villages in winter, and in summer establish themselves on the high pasturelands, without ever breaking their ties with the village communities. They act as guards for the herds of the sedentary villagers during transhumance, often being members of a sedentary family, and having been given the duty of looking after the herds, subsequently establish themselves permanently outside the village, gradually separating themselves from the rest of the community. An essential moment in this rupture is their marriage to nomadic women who are more apt than the village women at filling the roles laid down for them under the sexual division of labour appropriate for pastoral production (Ekvall, 1968).

What are the factors underlying the differentiation and specialisation of the pastoral function in this case? One definite determining factor appears to be the domestication of the yak: "Numerous indications suggest that nomadic pastoralism, as distinguished from the case of livestock in various forms of transhumance in an agricultural community, developed only after domestication of the yak by farmers who already had common cattle and door herds of goats and sheep." (Ekvall, 1968, p. 12). There is, however, nothing to indicate that this domestication is of recent date. An additional technical factor which helps to explain the specialisation of the two groups, as well as the maintenance of relations between them, is the practice of interbreeding the yak with ordinary livestock. In view of the low fecundity of cross-breeding and the necessity of preserving a balanced rate of hybridization, there have to be constant exchanges of livestock between the two groups. It is often the case that sedentary groups raise livestock solely for the purposes of cross-breeding (Bonnemaire and Teissier, 1976; Bonnemaire, 1976). Hybrids generally have a higher output and they possess qualities of resilence which enable them to use both the higher pastures and the winter grazing grounds at the same time. The differentiation of pastoral and agro-pastoral societies thus favours higher pastoral productivity and at the same time guarantees the sedentary societies a supply of the transport animals which are indispensable in a country of steep and narrow valleys.

The situation in Andean societies is in many ways comparable to Tibet not only because they too have at their disposition vast pasture-lands exploited by the use of animals highly adapted to and domesticated in their habitat (there is a wild llama, the vicuna, just as, side by side with the domestic yak, there is a wild yak) but also because the exploitation of the different environments, corresponding to the different levels of altitude, makes a complex system of relations between the different zones of production even more necessary here than in Tibet. The llama as a transport animal, like the yak in Tibet, has played a determinant role in the social history of the region (Murra, 1965). However, pastoral specialisation appears to have been much more recent among the people of the Andes (since the Spanish conquest) and much less developed. In the large communities which formed the basis of Inca society, pastoral production was integrated into a whole series of productive activities corresponding to the different environments exploited: the coastal region (corn, vegetables), the valleys and low *puna* (potatoes), the *puna* (livestock). There were specialised herders in the community and the herd was communally tended, though owned at the level of the family. The most one can say is that a few communities, like the one near Lake Titicaca, were more pastoral than others; Murra (1965) sees in them a rough form of specialisation with differentiation between high mountain communities and lower settlements. Specialised stock-raising was above all a state responsibility among the Incas, whose vast herds (for transport and the delivery of military supplies) were periodically increased by the tribute levied on peasant and pastoral communities. The administration of these herds formed a special branch of Inca state organisation. Murra notes that, on conquest, the Inca State tended to seize partial control of stockraising as an essential aspect in the control and expropriation of peasant communities, an aspect that would result in the creation of a new social group of servile status. This course of development was interrupted by the Spanish conquest, which provoked a tendency towards the creation of specialised communities (whether or not linked to the institution of the great latifundiary properties). The essential features of the pastoral specialisation which thus developed seem to have been the growth of trade,—local trade (dried meat, known as *ch' arki*, in exchange for agricultural produce such as potatoes and corn)—and perhaps above all international trade, with a supply of alpaca wool entering the world market. Exports first took the form of finished products which were sent to Spain, but this activity declined sharply from the Seventeenth Century. Trade responded, and considerably increased, however, during the Nineteenth Century in the form of raw material for British spinning mills. This is also the period when the great pastoral *hacienda* begin to appear on the *puna* alongside the Indian communities.

What can we learn from these two examples? Without indulging in misleading comparisons, we can single out the important thing which they have in common: they both offer the same type of exclusive ecological determination of other pastoral production or hunting, that other utilisation of the animal which was formerly practised in these two societies. This is the reason for our choice. One of the first things we learn is that in those cases where pastoral specialisation seems to be most exclusively determined by environment, it does not necessarily result in the constitution of a pastoral society. Factors other than the environmental ones come into play and influence specialisation. Let us now identify them:

First, there are technical factors, such as the technique of hybridisation in Tibet which necessitates, because of high task specialisation and because of the fact that the two types of livestock live with two separate human groups, a strict division of labour. In Andean societies, pastoral and agricultural forms of production are more simply complementing at the same time partially equivalent. (In the *puna* food may be stored both in the form of livestock and of potatoes which are preserved by the cold temperatures).

A second important factor is the high productivity of pastoral labour which, because of the high degree of mobility necessary if optimum exploitation of the high pastures is to be obtained by the herds, tends to create a more and more clear-cut separation between the nomads and the sedentarists. This increase in the productivity of pastoral labour may have a variety of causes: in the Inca state, the growing monopoly of stock-raising by the dominating class favored the development of a system of exploitation of conquered communities; after the Spanish conquest, there was the development of the market value of one of the products of stockraising, namely wool; and in Tibet there has been the role of animals in trade (transport) and as a form of accumulation (The term *nor* is used to refer both to wealth and to livestock).

For all cases of pastoral specialisation there is also another aspect to be considered, the social value of pastoral production, itself the decisive factor when, unlike in the examples described above, ecological factors are not so exclusively determinant, i.e. in the majority of pastoral societies now in existence.

The division of labour, the value of livestock and pastoral specialisation in East Africa

The pastoral societies of East Africa (we are concerned here for the most part with the Nilotic societies which occupy the vast territory which stretches from the southern part of the Sudan and Ethiopia to Tanzania) have a much less constraining environment than the high mountain pasture-lands we have just considered. What is more, it is a diversified environment, with variations in climate, pedology, etc., and presents a less specialised character due in large part to this variability.

The climate is characterised by a dry season and a wet season varying in length and average rainfall (300 to 1200 mm and sometimes more). What is even more important than the total amount of rain is its distribution. Irregularity in precipitation can mean long periods of drought, even during the wet season. Thus there is a factor of unpredictability affecting the growth of vegetation and, more especially, agricultural production. According to the rainfall level, the landscape may be that of the steppes or wooded savannah. Important variations are also introduced by different types of soil (the presence or absence of rich, volcanic soil) as well as by water-drainage conditions (swamp areas, the accumulation of water in lakes which may be of sufficient size to modify local climatic conditions, the lack of water supply during the dry season in many areas, etc.) or by other elements in the eco-system (the existence of the tsé-tsé fly, for example, under certain conditions in the rainy season, or of a growth of vegetation, which renders pastoralism impossible). Finally, conditions in the mountain areas, which are often volcanic, with good irrigation and forest cover, make it possible to engage in other modes of exploitation.

With regard to the mode of human exploitation, i.e. the characteristics of the eco-system, there are two important points. First, there is no *direct* connection between ecological conditions and the mode of exploitation. Most Nilotic societies simultaneously practise agriculture and stock-raising. Second, there is no relationship between pastoral specialisation, where it exists, and the impossibility of practising agriculture, except in cases where agriculture is rendered absolutely impossible, i.e. where there is total uncertainty concerning the possibility of harvest. For example, Jie and the Karamojong peoples whose country receives from 500 to 600 mm annual rainfall practice agriculture, whereas the Maasai in a region which has almost twice as much rainfall, are entirely pastoral. The Turkana practice the maximum amount of agriculture possible in difficult conditions (300 to 400 mm), while their close neighbours, the Samburu, who have slightly better conditions, are specialists in stock-raising. I have already noted that, in this region as a whole, the constitution of eco-systems of specialised pasture has largely been the result of human activity—regular burning and selective pasturing led to the creation of a certain type of vegetation, helping, for example, to eliminate the tsé-tsé fly vectors.

The study of the pastoral societies of East Africa shows, then, that ecological conditions, far from being directly constraining are themselves largely determined by human intervention. Other characteristics of these pastoral societies are noteworthy. There are forms of stock-raising which use practically no transport animals; this limits the mobility of the society and prevents it from playing the role of intermediary between sedentary societies, as do many other nomadic pastoral groups. Again, pastoral production for trade is negligible or even non-existent in the pastoral and agro-pastoral societies of East Africa. The not inconsiderable exchanges between agricultural and pastoral communities, as well as with groups of craftsmen and hunters, are organized in strict accordance with networks of social relationships, extending to those which exist within the community.

What then are the factors determining pastoral specialisation in this region? A first reply—almost tautological—springs to mind immediately when we look at the facts: Pastoral specialisation is accompanied by a considerable development of the productivity of pastoral labour. If, for example, we take the number of head of livestock per person as our criterion, the difference between the agro-pastoral Jie and Karamojong (4 to 5 livestock units per person) and the Maasai (almost 20 livestock units per person) is clear (1 head of livestock = 5 heads of small stock = 1 cattle bovine = $^1/_2$ camel). But the relationship between increased productivity of pastoral labour and its *specialisation* undoubtedly remains a complex one. Increased productivity of pastoral labour implies greater mobility—giving the herd access to all the available resources and enabling it to make the best use of them. It also implies—or gradually helps evolve—social forms of the division of labour. The creation and reproduction of larger and larger herds require the institution of modes of cooperation between families (corresponding to the distribution among them of labour and livestock) and even within a single family (thus, among the Turkana, a family is often divided up into several production units organised around the wives, some occupied with small stock, others with camels, etc.). This development runs counter to the division of labour according to sex which is characteristic of agro-pastoral societies.

It is impossible to say which element in this whole process of change comes first. But it is obvious that the increased productivity of pastoral labour is characterised by growing mobility and the institution of new forms of the division of labour. It is accompanied as well by increased separation of rights over animals (which entails the development of a smaller, more mobile family unit, ready to enter into more flexible relations of cooperative labour with other families), and this means that when livestock are more abundant, one finds, paradoxically, increased competition between "fathers" and "sons" over control of animals and over marriage. (In these polygamous societies, it is often a question as to whether the livestock should be used to enable the father to take a second wife or to enable the son to marry and set up his own establishment with part of the family herd). The growth in productivity of pastoral labour thus appears to be a global process corresponding to the transformation of the material conditions of labour (pastoral specialisation and increased group mobility) and of the social conditions of production (i.e. the division of rights in animals, and forms of the social division of labour, etc.). No single one of these ecological, technical and social factors is the primary cause of this growth. Can it be maintained, then, that the increased productivity of social labour is self-engendered, originating, for example, in the aim of stock-raisers to maximally increase their herds? Many anthropological analyses are based on this hypothesis, interpreting this goal in terms of religion (the theory of the "cattle complex") or seeing in it a form of the capitalistic entrepreneurial mentality which pursues maximum profit (Goldschmidt, 1972). Since these theories were discussed at length elsewhere (Bonte, 1978c), they are mentioned here only in order to draw attention to the fact that they both constitute ways of interpreting pastoral production in terms of a rationality foreign to the herder, and in some ways may even go so far as to attribute irrationality to his behavior.

To gain understanding of the variations in the productivity of pastoral labour we must look once again at the place occupied by pastoral production in these societies (whether based on stock-raising) and more especially at the *value* put on pastoral labour and production. Except in recent times, there has never been, precisely speaking, an exchange value; and yet one can no more reduce the value of the animals' product to its alimentary use than to its value for the religious or sacrificial ends of production, which may appear dominant (Bonte, 1975a, 1978a and c). These different aspects of livestock value come together in what I have called "livestock fetishism", in an attempt to express the way in which livestock determines social relationships (and more specifically the relationships within a group of producers associated for the collective exploitation of natural resources, pastures and water) and the relation between man and God (the form of community thus restored being determined in the final analysis by religious organization and ideology). Thus interpreted, "livestock fetishism" refers to an aspect of ideological consciousness which not only "dissimulates" the real conditions of production, but also corresponds to a form of social labour necessary for the reproduction of the community. In order to ensure the surplus required for this reproduction of the community, there must be sufficient labour. But, in fact, labour not only goes to create a surplus, it also dominates and determines the whole production process, justifying in the eyes of the stock-raisers the primary condition of production, the relationship they maintain with their animals. The stock-raisers see it as a religious relationship, constituting part of the divine order of the world (myth of the origin of man and animal) which has to be constantly reproduced, notably by means of sacrifice. In themselves (ritual consumption of meat) or through their products (milk, blood), cattle assure the material base for the human groups which produce them.

Let us now look more closely at the fact that this labour, the production of a surplus, determines the whole process of production. I have also shown elsewhere (Bonte, 1974, 1978a) that the opposition between the domestic organisation of production (the family unit appropriating to itself a herd and providing pastoral labour, etc.) and community organization (appropriation of pastures at the collective level) result in a contradiction between the autonomous character of domestic production and the necessity for each unit of production to have equal access to collectively exploited resources. This contradiction manifests itself, particularly, in the fact that inequalities of livestock accumulation between domestic groups (arising out of their autonomy) have to be constantly reduced in order to restore their equivalence within the pastoral community. This is rendered possible by the fact that the labour invested for the production of a surplus (reproduction of the community) determines the whole process of production, i.e., each producer increases production as a member of the community, reproducing both his relationship with other producers and the relationship of the group with God, the latter being seen as the ultimate condition of social reproduction.

On the other hand, the difficulties of reproducing the community (i.e. the equivalence between domestic groups) arising out of unequal accumulation within it are the cause of an increase in the amount of labour necessary for reproduction, i.e., an increase in the surplus. It seems likely that herein lies the law governing the growth of the productivity of pastoral labour—a law which could also be expressed as the process of perpetual transformation of unequal accumulation between domestic units of production into an increased accumulation for the community as a whole. This seems to be a characteristic feature of development, common not only to pastoral (or agro-pastoral) societies but to all societies having this form of communal organisation (Bonte, 1978b). From all of this we can derive a general and appropriate idea—which still requires elaboration through concrete analyses—of the processes which can lead to pastoral specialisation in certain Nilotic agro-pastoral communities in East Africa. The first condition resides in the nature of pastoral labour itself and in the value of livestock, the two factors functioning in this type of communal society which inevitably cause growth in the productivity of pastoral labour.

Unequal accumulation (in the form of livestock) among producers leads to an increase in the surplus (always in the form of livestock) necessary for the reproduction of the community as a whole. This increase in pastoral production has as its consequence a transformation in the nature of the labour process (social forms of the division of labour) and the units of production (nature and extent of the family unit) with a corresponding increase in mobility, a factor which taken alone is sufficient to promote growth in the productivity of pastoral labour. It thus appears that pastoral specialisation is the result of these processes while at the same time constituting in itself a factor in the growth of the productivity of pastoral labour.

The conclusion to be drawn from this analysis is the following one: Ecological factors are *not* a primary cause of ecological equilibrium (or rather, disequilibrium) as we might have been content to verify empirically, and even the equilibrium notion itself as a determining factor in economic and social change seems to be called into question. There can be no doubt that the growth in the productivity of pastoral labour encounters a limit in the productivity of the pastoral eco-system as a whole and can thus lead to over-exploitation and degradation of the environment. It seems however, that the limit has as a rule been much more quickly reached since colonialisation, for multiple reasons related to the introduction of new factors favourable to the growth of pastoral production (taxes, a commercial value for livestock and a monetary economy), as well as to the colonial expropriation of many tribal pasture-lands (particularly in Kenya) and, perhaps most significantly, the registration (and hence stabilisation) of communal territories. This last point seems to be of particular importance and makes it necessary to introduce an additional one into our analysis, the matter of relationships between communities. The development of contradictions resulting from the communal form of organisation is the cause not only of the growth of surplus but also of territorial expansion, in response to the need for new pastures. This is followed by an increasingly rapid separation of livestock rights within the unit of domestic production and the development of neolocal modes of residence (among the Turkana, for example, who underwent a noteworthy expansion at the end of the 19th Century, the age class of the ''sons'' established themselves at the periphery of the territory occupied by the ''fathers'' (Gulliver, 1958)). This type of expansion does not take the form of organised conquest but consists rather in movements of population into the community and the absorption of groups from without (often by intermarriage). Turton gives a remarkable description of this process in his study of the Mursi, a Nilotic population living in Southern Ethiopia and, as it happens, untouched by colonisation (1978). However, it is not the purpose of this essay to introduce the notion of a pre-colonial, pastoral Golden Age. On the contrary, these movements of population have frequently been the occasion of murderous wars, as the history of the Maasai shows (Jacobs, 1975). And it must be added that other more specifically ecological factors, such as droughts and epidemics, have always acted to reduce the effects of growth in the productivity of pastoral labour. (The re-introduction of agriculture has had the same effect.) But these ecological factors never play a decisive role (in the sense of a first cause) because they can never be isolated from the context of the entire system of production and its material and social conditions.

Before discussing this point, we might take another look at the problem of the respective positions of agriculture and stock-raising in agro-pastoral societies. The foregoing analyses enable us to understand the close relationship which exists between these two types of activity and they place in new light the historical and cultural differences which have always isolated the study of these societies in exclusive fields. Rigby has shown, for example, that, in Bantu-speaking Gogo communities, livestock play a role identical to the one we have discussed here (1969). In this type of agro-pastoral society, not only is livestock the characteristic form of accumulation, but the movement of livestock—and consequently pastoral labour itself—dominates and determines the whole process of production, the formation of production units, cooperation in labour, etc. Hence, it would seem to be fair to ask why the processes which produced pastoral specialisation do not act in as efficacious a manner in this case? This complex question cannot be resolved in the course of a brief discussion, but it would seem that the solution is to be sought in a more general analysis of the articulation of agricultural and pastoral production in this entire region. A brief description will serve as an introduction to this inquiry.

The dominance of pastoral labour and production in an agro-pastoral society is clearly visible in the division of labour according to sex: male herders/female farmers, in a context of male supremacy. This dominance is equally clear in the symbolic representations and practices characteristic of relations between specialised pastoral communities and those practising agriculture as well as stock-raising. J. Galaty gives a convincing demonstration of this in his study of the Maasai (1977) where he notes, for example, that Maasai exchanges (which are not negligible, although they do not take a commercial form) with the agricultural *Il Meek* (a pejorative term used by the Maasai) are effected for the most part through the intermediation of the Maasai women. In all likelihood, this global context of inequality and sexual specialisation in social and economic relations (and exchanges) is the reason why certain groups have had difficulty in developing pastoral specialisation.

The importance of the sexual division of labour as the form of social relationship between agriculture and stock-raising also appears when we examine the organisation of these two activities in neighbouring state societies where an aristocracy of specialised stock-raisers dominates a group of dependent farmers who are largely excluded from the herding of cattle, as in Ankole (Y. Elam, 1973, 1974). It is not just in this case that the women of the pastoral Hima are excluded from pastoral labour and from exercising rights over livestock, being thus symbolically assimilated to the Iru farmers. In addition the practices and representations appropriate to "livestock fetishism", that is, those concerned with the reproduction of the communal form of production, are transformed, founding the hierarchical class structure upon the introduction of the hierarchical representation of sexual dysmorphism within the domain of symbolic categories centered on cattle (Bonte, 1978c). Pastoral specialisation here takes on another aspect, for a class-based society permits, simultaneously, a higher level of productivity from herding practised in better pastures with exceptionally good climates (more than 10000 mm of rain per year), and a hierarchical circulation of agricultural products.

Ecological and Economic Determination

In the absence of the development of exchange value and the imposition of complex systems of relations (i.e., the international division of labor, in which pastoral nomadic societies—as well as societies having other material bases—are involved, through taking on, for example, the functions of transport), the fundamentals of pastoral specialisation reside in the same conditions of pastoral production, that is, in the value of labor and livestock.

If livestock in all pastoral societies does not have this value in the full sense, still such value is always somewhat assumed. It is true that we do not have many examples, other than those of East Africa, of pastoral and agro-pastoral communities without exchange values and the function of animal transport. So one cannot appropriately postulate the generality of the specialisation process in pastoral production here described. However, it is possible to draw from it certain conclusions concerning the role of ecological factors in the formation of nomadic pastoral societies.

Up to this point, I have placed particular emphasis on the fact that ecological factors, are not the "determinants" or the "first causes" of pastoral specialisation, for they may, in complete reinterpretation, appear as functions of production. But that is not to say that they have no influence at all, and I wish to conclude by attempting to show how they contribute to the specialisation of pastoral production. The problem was stated in a particularly pertinent manner, for our purposes, by the debate in *Man*, on the origin of the Nuer and the Dinka. I shall simply restate the main points of the argument I have developed in full elsewhere (Bonte, 1977, 1979). Using an idea introduced by Sahlins (1961) to describe the specific social function (territorial conquest) of the segmentary lineage system, Newcomer (1972), the initiator of the debate, attempted to show that the development of such a system among the ancestors of the Nuer was the result of a "social mutation" deriving from their settlement in a difficult environment—the flood area between the branches of the Nile.

Newcomer's analyses have been much disputed, in particular because of their "evolutionist" tendencies (the assumption of the superiority of the segmentary lineage system), tendencies which are highly questionable. It seems, however, that the more fundamental mistake of Newcomer and of other contributors to *Man* is their failure to see existing patterns of relationships between the various aspects of Nuer society, which testify to the over-all unity of economic and social transformational processes, the end result of which may have indeed been the separation of the Nuer from the Dinka and from a common origin. The segmentary lineage system and the territorial expansion character of the Nuer can be understood as a function of their tendency towards differentiation, both economic (the position of the *big-men* or "bulls") and social (aristocratic families, lineages and the others), a differentiation which appears as the consequence of increasingly unequal accumulation and the growth of pastoral production. Here we find all those characteristics of the process of pastoral specialisation previously described.

Another aspect of this debate deserves our attention. It has been noted that the environment in which Nuer society was developed, while harsh from the point of view of living conditions, is also particularly favourable to pastoral production. Moreover, the expansion of the Nuer, following their initial impulsion, was carried out in a quite different milieu than the one which the less "pastoral" Dinka inhabited. Not only does the flood area, which is the centre of Nuer expansion, provide exceptionally good pasture-land, but in addition the annual variations in flood-level (and therefore in available pasture-land) cause a drastic reduction in the herd, requiring, a rapid increase in the productivity of pastoral labour when the herd has been thus reduced. Herein lies the main cause of the movements of rapid expansion characteristic of the Nuer. An initial "impulse" provokes, so to speak, a series of "waves", which accumulate in the development of pastoral production. The development of the productivity of pastoral labour at the "centre" reverberates and is increasingly amplified at the "periphery". This explains why the segmentary lineage system, which constitutes, as it were, the social form which carries out the expansion, is characteristic of the Eastern Nuer who have recently migrated, but not of the Western Nuer, established in the flood zone. What conclusions can be drawn from this brief analysis of Nuer expansion? Environmental factors intervene in favour of the process of pastoral specialisation, but this does *not* imply that the environment dictates from without any type of selection of these productive characteristics.

In the vast area of East Africa under pastoral or agro-pastoral exploitation, the regions which are the most intractable and marginal from the point of view of human life paradoxically constitute the centres of expansion of pastoral societies. This is true of the Nuer country and of the swamplands of the Nile. It is also true of the arid region around Lake Rudolph. It is not simply that these regions which are difficult to utilise for agriculture provide good pasture-land, nor is it sufficient to say that in these regions the extremely delicate balance of the eco-system is the cause of regular demographic movements to the periphery. These factors are important, to be sure, but they do not give us a key enabling us to explain why these pastoral regions function literally as the geographical matrix of expansion and political change. It has often been observed that demographic growth does not precede expansion but accompanies or follows it (Bonte, 1978b). And, in my view, the decisive factor is the one which is specific to this type of environment, namely, the extreme variability in the productivity of pastoral labour with the possibilities it affords for the rapid accumulation of livestock. Similar observations might be made for other pastoral regions of the world. The dry region of the Tiris-Zemmour in the Western Sahara, for example, where there is a very irregular supply of rich pasture-land, constitutes the veritable matrix of the population movements and political movements which make up the history of Mauritania.

In this latter case, however, we find ourselves confronted with pastoral societies part of whose production is determined by trade and whose history cannot be studied without taking into consideration the relations which have been established, by their mediation, among non-pastoral societies. The formation of pastoral communities in the Western Sahara cannot be understood without reference to the trade route, the ancient *triq lemtouna* which, as it happens, crosses the Tiris-Zemmour. Here there are other factors at work which may be the cause of pastoral specialisation. I shall limit myself to a few suggestions.

The introduction of animals of transport often contributes to a more specialised development of stock-raising. They encourage greater mobility of the pastoral group and hence improved productivity of pastoral labour. They also make possible the development of a new form of activity linked to stock raising: transportation. One of the most striking examples is the "bedouinisation" or "mongolisation" of former agro-pastoral populations living in the mountains regions of the Mediterranean and the Middle East as a result of the introduction, in the twelfth and thirteenth centuries, of the camel (the dromedary or half-breed dromedary and the Bactrian camel) and the horse into communities pursuing a combination of transhumant stock-raising, arboriculture and agriculture with some irrigation (X. de Planhol, 1962). In the case of a tribe in the Iranian Zagros, the Baxtyari, J. P. Digard shows that this specialisation—which is only to a relative degree, for each period of transmigration sees the cultivation of summer or winter crops—corresponds to a considerable increase in the productive force of labour (1973).

The Iranian example draws our attention to another factor of pastoral specialisation—the development of commercial and monetary production. Stock-raisers participate in an overall system of interethnic and international economic relations within the framework of which they must develop a unique form of production in order to derive the best advantage from trade. This necessity may indeed be the cause of the movements in favour of "pastoralisation" which have been recurrent features of life in the Mediterranean and Balkan areas every since the Sixteenth Century. Similarly, the development of pastoral societies in Afghanistan has been interpreted in terms of the importance of trade. Pastoral specialisation in these cases is not governed by the same factors as in East Africa. Nevertheless, it corresponds to a similar need to produce an increase in the productivity of pastoral labour. With the increased importance of exchange values and the growing commercial unification of the world—a world where pastoral nomadic communities were to continue to play a major role down to the Fourteenth Century owing to their control of continental trade routes, a control which sometimes led to the creation of veritable nomadic "empires", such as the Mongolian and Almoravidian Empires, for example—these factors became decisive in determining pastoral specialisation. They brought about a new expansion of the pastoral eco-systems, either as a result of increased specialisation of formerly agro-pastoral regions (Iran, Afghanistan) or by the introduction of pastoralism into relatively marginal and little exploited regions.

Along with the rapid development and integration of commercial relations, the pursuit of increasing productivity by pastoral labour leads to the development of new social relations of production different from those which persist among nomadic stock-raisers. The Andean *hacienda* which raises *llama* for their wool is only one example of the feudal (latifundiary) and later capitalist forms of pastoral exploitation which developed on a grand scale in Latin America. To a lesser degree, similar phenomena can be observed in Italy and Spain at the end of the Middle Ages. In vast regions, emptied of their original inhabitants (who were often hunters) as happened in Australia, South Africa and elsewhere, there has developed a purely capitalist ranch-type form of stock-raising.

It is obvious that I have not attempted in this paper to retrace the whole history of stock-raising and pastoralism. The purpose has been to provide historical and ethnographic reminders which serve to draw attention to the relativity of ecological factors—too frequently considered to be exclusively decisive—in determining the pastoral specialisation of a whole series of human societies. This issue is not without importance for those concerned with present developments in these societies. Projects which aim to increase productivity in regions occupied by these societies by creating vast areas of ranchlands and, if necessary, by introducing different modes of exploitation, are—quite apart from the way one may feel about them politically—in danger of destroying the pattern of relationships which man has already established with his environment and even of destroying the environment itself. The disastrous effects on both stock-raisers and their environment brought about by the drought of the 1970's in the Sahel is an eloquent example of what can happen as a result of the uncontrolled development of commercial production and of the ensuing destruction of part of the economic and social framework.

REFERENCES

BARRAU, J.
    1972   "Domestication, Ecologie et conditions d'apparition du pastoralisme nomade". In: *Cahiers du CERM*, 109, Paris, p. 51-66.

BONNEMAIRE, J.
    1976   "Le Yak domestique et son hybridation", in: *Le yak, son rôle dans la vie matérielle et culturelle des éleveurs d'Asie Centrale*, Ethnozootechnie, No. 15, Paris.
BONNEMAIRE, J. et J. M. TEISSIER
    1976   "Quelques aspects de l'élevage en haute altitude dans l'Himalaya Central: yaks, bovins, hybrides et métis dans la vallée du Langtang (Nepeal)", in: *Le Yak, son rôle dans la vie matérielle et culturelle des éleveurs d'Asie Centrale*, Ethnozootechnie, No. 15.
BONTE, P.
    1974   "Etudes sur les sociétés de pasteurs nomades. Organisation économique et sociale des pasteurs d'Afrique de l'Est", *Cahiers du CERM*, 110.
    1975a   "Cattle for god, an attempt at a marxist analysis of the religion of East African herdsmen", *Social Compass* XXII.
    1975b   "Pasteurs et Nomades: l'exemple de la Mauritanie". In: *Secheresses et Famines au Sahel*, ed. par J. Copans, F. Maspero, tome II, Paris.
    1977   "Les Nuer sont-ils des Dinka?" *Bulletin Production Pastorale et Société*, No. 1 hiver 77-78. Paris Maison des Sciences de l'Homme.
    1978a   "Non stratified social formations among pastoral nomads". In: *The Evolution of Social Systems* ed. by J. Friedman and N. Rowlands, Duckworth, London.
    1978b   "Organisation de la production et lois de population dans les sociétés de pasteurs nomades", Colloque *Mode de production et démographie*, Mexico, (à paraitre, en espagnol).
    1978c   "L'approche marxiste des sociétés d'éleveurs dans les pays occidentaux". In: *Nomadic Peoples in a Changing World*, conférence, Londres. Forthcoming in P. Salzman & J. Galaty, eds., Philadelphia: ISHI press.
    1979   "Pastoral production, territorial organisation and kinship in segmentary lineage systems". In *Social and Ecological Systems*, ed. by P. Burnham and Roy F. Ellen, ASA 18, N.Y.: Academic Press.
DIGARD, J. P.
    1973   "Histoire et Anthropologie des sociétés nomades: le cas d'une tribu d'Iran", *Annales E.S.C.* 6.
ELAM, Y.
    1973   *The social and sexual roles of Hima women*. Manchester University Press.
    1974   "The relationship between Hima and Iru in Ankole", *African Studies* 33-3.
EKVALL, R. B.
    1968   *Fields on the Hoof. Nexus of Tibetan Nomadic pastoralism*. Case Studies in Cultural Anthropology, Holt Rinehart and Winston.
FLEMING, A.
    1972   "The genesis of pastoralism in prehistoric Europe", *World Archaeology*, 4, 2.
FLORES OCHOA, J. A.
    1977   *Pastores de puna, uywamichiq punarunakuna*. Instituto de Estudios Peruanos, Lima.
GALATY, J. G.
    1977   *In the Pastoral Image: the Dialectic of Maasai Identity*: Ph.D. dissertation, University of Chicago.
GOLDSCHMIDT, W.
    1972   "The opération of a Sebei capitalist: a contribution to economic anthropology", *Ethnology*, XI, 3.
GUILAINE, J.
    1976   *Premiers bergers et paysans de l'Occident méditerraneen*. Mouton, Paris, La Haye.
GULLIVER, P. H.
    1958   "The Turkana age organisation", *American Anthropologist*, 60.
JACOBS, A. H.
    1965   *The Traditional Political Organisation of the Pastoral Maasai*. Unpublished Ph.D., Oxford.
    1975   "Maasai pastoralism in historical perspective". In: *Pastoralism in Tropical Africa*, ed. by T. Monod, for IAI by OUP.

LATTIMORE, O.
    1967   *Inner Asian Frontier of China*. Boston.
LEROI-GOURHAN, A.
    1965   *Le geste et la parole*. Albin Michel, Paris, 2 vols.
LESHNIK, A.
    1972   "Pastoral nomadism in the archeology of India and Pakistan", *World Archeology*, 4, 2.
MOSCATI, J.
    1959   *The Semites in Ancient History*. Cardiff, University of Wales Press.
MURRA, J.
    1965   "Herds and Herders in the Inca State". In: *Man, Culture and Animals, the Role of Animals in Human Ecological Adjustment*, A. Leeds and Vayda, American Association for the Advancement of Science, 78, Washington.
NEWCOMER, P. J.
    1972   "The Nuer are Dinka: an essay on origins and environmental determinism", *Man* (ns) 7.
PANT, S. D.
    1954   *The Social Economy of the Himalayans*. G. Allen and Unwin, London.
DE PLANHOL, X.
    1962   "Caractères généraux de la vie montagnarde dans le Proche Orient et dans l'Afrique du Nord", *Annales de Geographie*, 384.
RIGBY, P.
    1969   *Cattle and Kinship among the Gogo. A Semi-Pastoral Society of Central Tanzania*. Cornell University Press, Ithaca.
SAHLINS, M.
    1961   "The segmentary lineage: an organisation of predatory expansion", *American Anthropologist*, 63.
TURTON, D.
    1978   "Territorial Organisation and Age among the Mursi". In: *Age, Generation and Time. Studies in East African Age Organisation*, ed. by P. Baxter and U. Almagor, (Hurst), London.

Ethnic Transformation, Dependency and Change

The Ilgira Samburu of Northern Kenya[1]

ANDERS HJORT

University of Stockholm, Stockholm, Sweden

THIS ARTICLE is primarily concerned with the issue of ethnic ascription and ethnicity in a situation of change. Focussing on the Ilgira Samburu in the Isiolo area in northern Kenya, I intend to demonstrate how ethnic ascription and ethnicity (I shall return to a brief definition of these terms shortly) become assets in a situation of an expanding capitalist economy and an increasingly centralized political system. The general problem concerns what is sometimes called acculturation, which has a contemporary dimension added to the historical. Contacts between farmers and pastoralists in East Africa seem to be long established. To these have fairly recently been added new types of movements and new forms of sedentarization undertaken in response to a growing reliance on the capitalist economy. Hence, even if the article is largely concerned with a particular case, the implications are of more general interest. What may be the forms for interaction and, indeed, bargaining across ethnic boundaries in unstable situations created by a rapid development process? What bargaining power remains when established principles for social control cease to exist?

The category of Ilgira is made up of former Turkana or Turkana descendants. They form a "rather endogamous" group within the Samburu society and identify with a particular territory to the north of Isiolo town, where they claim grazing rights within Samburuland. This opportunity has made Ilgira status attractive for Turkana wage earners and poor pastoralists.

There are many cases throughout East Africa to show how groups merge, dominate each other and find forms for symbiosis, changes that occur continuously. Some have been studied from an economic point of view while other studies have dealt with identity and ascription problems. My concern here is not primarily with the issue of the identity of members of such groups but rather with how an ethnic ascription can be utilized and possibly manipulated for obtaining material goals.

Pastoralism and the development process in northern Kenya

The history of the pastoral peoples in northern Kenya is marked by a pattern of expansion and contraction of various groups' control over grazing grounds, water points and natural salt licks. A situation of continuous change has been induced by the ecological uncertainty of the area. This uncertainty is exacerbated by the integration of the area in the market economy. New factors that condition the present pastoral economic systems in northern Kenya are: (1) political centralization; (2) land pressure from farming areas with an expanding population; (3) a capitalistic economic expansion; and (4) competition from alternative land use practices such as wildlife, tourism, commercial ranching and irrigation farming.[2]

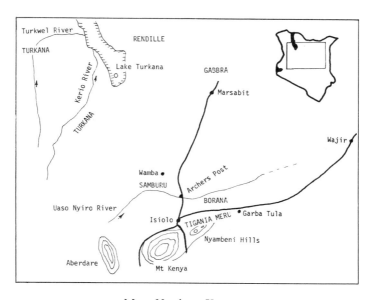

Map: Northern Kenya

The expansion of commercial agriculture has increased the necessity for poor farmers to move out into drier zones in spite of the low productivity there. As a result many pastoralists have experienced a loss, particularly of dry-season pasture, and their already uncertain economic situation has become even more vulnerable. This process has, in turn, brought about an increased wear on remaining, more arid, regions, a condition which has been accentuated by the increased political centralization and capitalist expansion in the fields of tourism and food production. The overall effect is one of a peasantization process in a general sense, where pastoral households become dependent on both their own food production and their limited monetary income for their survival (Hjort, 1979b).

The long-established forms for taking precaution against loss focus on a safety-first principle and economic diversification in order to improve ''recuperative power'' rather than on maximizing productivity (Dahl and

Hjort 1979: 18ff). Traditional insurance strategies may be summarized as follows: (1) to maintain more than one species of livestock; (2) to divide one's livestock holdings into spatially separate units (both for production reasons and in order to achieve a geographical dispersal); (3) to establish various social systems involving stock associates instrumental for systems of borrowing and lending; and (4) to maintain large herds. These insurance techniques may prove insufficient either when the ratio of manpower to domestic animals becomes too low for efficient herd management, or when the number of stock becomes too low to support all household members. This means that there are specific man-animal ratios which are more or less prohibitive (*ibid*: 26ff). In order to maintain household viability individual members may migrate to seek wage employment both in order to relieve their pastoral household of a member and to contribute to the overall household income. If absolute losses are too great, entire households are forced to migrate, leaving their few animals with a relative.

Such out-migration from pastoral areas easily creates a vicious circle with a lack of manpower in many areas leading to further losses of livestock and pasture. The richer pastoral households are able to take advantage of this situation. Through a greater real or potential access to livestock they remain secure within the pastoral economic sphere whereas others are forced out of it, temporarily or permanently, leaving their nonviable herds in the hands of those remaining. The social, political and economic differentiation gains additional impetus from the present political system which i.a. implies a differentiated access to the information flow from the political centre, to the benefit of the richer household heads who control the political offices. Hence, there is an emergence of a new ''elite'' (if by this term we refer to economic resource control, political power and prestige without implying any other superiority). At first glance the process seems to imply an emerging class society due to changing control over the means of production. The new elite's control is, however, only conditional on relations with the political centre (Dahl and Hjort 1979: 32ff).

In sum, the development process today in northern Kenya causes an increased stratification. Large households with access to much manpower and to many domestic animals can diversify their activities into various economic fields, thereby increasing their safety and profit. Small households become increasingly vulnerable since they have less access to manpower and, accordingly, have fewer opportunities to spread risks, while at the same time they are increasingly pressed to produce cash for various purposes. Those who are not successful enough in countering the threats of their ''marginal'' situation are forced to seek new forms for making a living, at least temporarily in order to rebuild a family herd. The recent irrigation projects and small towns are products of increased integration into the national framework and, in many instances, of exploitative relations between centre and periphery (Hjort 1979a). These projects offer new sources of subsistence or cash for former pastoralists.

There are, however, numerous alternatives which might be tried before settling in a town or on an irrigation scheme. Various forms of adoption are common, sometimes involving individuals, sometimes whole households who are adopted into families and clans other than their own, and sometimes whole contingents of people are affiliated with other ethnic groups. People with few animals seek economic support from those who are better off but who could do with greater access to manpower. These adoptions take various cultural forms. On the individual level they may represent anything from slave status to economic integration, depending among other things on the ethnic ascription of the partners to the relationship and on the ethnic "distances" between them[3] if they belong to different groups. On the collective level, too, there is a wide span of protective relations, from an assimilation of defeated groups into those of their conquerors' to institutionalized host-tenant relationships such as those "tenant" hunters/gatherers normally establish with pastoral or agricultural neighbours. The latter case illustrates the symbiotic economic relationship common in East Africa, significant also for the discussion of the Ilgira category.

Production, symbiosis and ecological complementarity

There is a wide range of examples of collective host-tenant relations between (seemingly) ethnic groups in East Africa. A typical example, which in many ways resembles that of a caste system, involves the relationship of Wata hunters with the dominant Borana pastoralists (cf. Dahl 1979: 38). Although Wata social organisation reflects that of the Borana, they are treated as having an inferior status by their Borana "hosts" since they are associated with both polluted and ritual activities.

Another kind of relationship exists between the Wandorobo hunters/ gatherers of neighbouring forests and the Tigania farmers to the southeast of Isiolo town. Recruitment to the Wandorobo category, as indeed to most of the scattered small groups associated with the term Wandorobo in Kenya, is multiplex and to a considerable extent draws from impoverished households, both of farmers and pastoralists, members of which have been forced to seek new livelihoods (cf. Spencer 1973: 200).[4] In the process of adoption they have assumed both the age-class system and the clan system of the Tigania and become linked to them through an institutionalized blood-brotherhood relationship. A third principle for collective adoption is illustrated locally by various Somali *shegat* client groups (groups that have become too small for military protection and therefore seek a collective adoption with a larger kinship group) and by those Maasai of Laikipia who have been assimilated into the Tigania community (Hjort 1979a: 20f). In the latter case there is clear evidence that Maasai were adopted in large numbers into the Tigania society through an assimilation process founded on intermarrying, in the beginning of this century, when their domestic herds were reduced due to epizootics, and they experienced great losses in manpower through epidemics and warfare (also even with the Tigania), and when the majority of the Maasai were forced by the colonial government to move to southern Kenya.

By means of briefly sketched examples I have tried to indicate that various forms of collective adaptation to change have existed in the area before the occurrence of the more recent factors so decisive for today's development process—factors that were mentioned in the introduction. The economic assets available have stemmed from the three major subsistence niches of farming, hunting/gathering and pastoralism. To the three should be added a limited number of specialist occupations; i.e. those of ritual leaders, blacksmiths, and artisans. These categories are not to be underrated since they hold functionally important positions even though their number may be small.

Before I embark on the effects of the development process as outlined in the previous section I wish to provide some illustration of how local ethnic groups can continue to exist as such and yet be interrelated, exploiting complementary subsistence niches. One example is that of the Rendille proper, the Samburu and the intermediate Ariaal Rendille, analyzed in Spencer (1973). Here I wish to point to a few aspects relevant for comparative purposes.

The Ariaal Rendille are situated between the Rendille proper and the Samburu, whether considered from an economical, geographical or social point of view. Economically, the camel herding Rendille and the cattle herding Samburu complement each other. Due to the slow growth rate in Rendille camel herds,[5] Rendille society has stagnated, with the camel herd as a rather constant resource. Samburu society is in comparison economically expansive. The Ariaal Rendille who live in an area suitable for keeping small stock attract impoverished Rendille proper who feel the need to build up family herds through exploiting new sets of opportunities. Samburu households also live in this Ariaal area, which allows for frequent contacts between members of these two groups. Ariaal tend not to herd cattle themselves but leave them to Samburu stock associates. The Rendille system of inheritance selects the oldest son as the sole heir in order to keep the family herd of camels intact. The scene is set for an outmigration of "population surplus" to the Samburu or the intermediate Ariaal from the Rendille society. Those who migrate are then primarily men who are younger brothers and women who do not find marriage partners among the Rendille proper. The migration alternatives open to one who is "pushed out" of the Rendille society are either to join the familiar Ariaal (speaking the same language, dressing in the same manner and also herding some camels) or to join the Samburu cattle herders who display a different culture and speak another language.

When an Ariaal man has been married to an Ariaal wife in his first marriage and Samburu wives in the others, which is a typical state of affairs, the inheritance of his estate follows a particular pattern, described by Spencer (1973: 132-133):

"The eldest son inherits the bulk, if not the whole, of his father's camel herd and builds up a herd of cattle from his mother's allotted herd (as any Samburu son). Thus, he is in a position to follow his father in being *both* Ariaal *and* Samburu. The younger sons may try to build up herds of camels and cattle; but unlike their Rendille proper counterparts, they are well placed to turn to cattle if they find the camel economy less rewarding. In doing so they implicitly and even imperceptibly are emigrating from the Ariaal to the Samburu. The choice is an easy one and an obvious one.''

From an economic and herd management perspective both sufficient man-power and food production are required. This means that continuous manipulation in household composition is necessary. In the case of the neighbouring Borana it is typical for the head of the household to attach his son-in-law as a client as a means of providing the household with sufficient manpower (see Dahl 1979: 107ff). For the Gabbra, neighbours of the Borana and primarily camel herders, the need for manpower varies greatly over the year, and they attach temporarily impoverished Borana Gutu (primarily cattle herders) and also other entire households in order to obtain sufficient man-power for herding purposes (Torry 1977: 16). Since the Gabbra area like the Ariaal allows for both cattle and camel herding, there is no need for an intermediate category for social reasons; daily interaction is already there. The relations between Samburu and Turkana in the Isiolo area, on the other hand, are marked less by differences in economic systems than in ethnic ascription. The Ilgira status, rather like that of Ariaal, acts as a means for a possible gradual assimilation of people with one ethnic ascription to another.

The emergence of Ilgira

The case in focus for the present discussion—Ilgira in the surroundings of Isiolo town—relates to a settlement originally of Turkana wage labourers and animal husbandrymen who settled within an area which is dominated by Sam-buru pastoralists. Before the arrival of the Europeans, the Isiolo area had been inhabited by cattle-keeping nomads, predominantly Maasai, Maa-speaking Samburu[6] and some Somali groups. After the Maasai and the Samburu had been weakened by serious epidemic and epizootic diseases in the beginning of the 1890s, they were pushed southwards by expanding Turkana groups. (The Maasai were further weakened by local wars and by an internal schism between sections.) Later, growing demands from white settlers for access to the so-called White Highlands resulted in a 1911 agreement between the British and the famous Maasai leader Lenana, that all Maasai-proper living in nor-thern Kenya since the 1904 Maasai Move should be moved to the southern part of the country. This transfer was carried out in 1913. That some Maasai managed to hide is evident from the fact that the dialect spoken today in some of the Samburu settlements close to Isiolo town more closely resembles Maasai-proper than Samburu.

I have already indicated that many Maasai were absorbed into the Tigania Meru. Others preferred to be assimilated into the Samburu rather than being forced to move. The Samburu groups in the Isiolo area are thus to some extent the result of relatively recent merging processes.

The transfer of the Maasai corresponded with the British policy of demar-cating administrative areas along ethnic lines, a policy that even today influences the ethnic situation in parts of Kenya. Even though the present national policy is to deny the existence of ethnic rights to territory, the district boundaries are still to some extent accepted by the local populations as limits to the expansion of ethnic groups. Isiolo District was intended as a Borana district to prevent further expansion by Somali groups coming from the northeast. The area north and west of Isiolo town was reserved for Samburu. Despite the fact that the site of the town was once predominantly a Samburu grazing area, the Samburu today play an insignificant role in the life of the township. Only a handful of the townsmen are Samburu, although they are one of the major pastoral groups in Isiolo's rural surroundings. During the dry season, they might migrate to the town to find pasture and water and a market for cattle when they need to purchase foodstuffs. Some Samburu live permanently on the fringes of the town. The total number of Samburu in Kenya is 55,000 according to a census carried out in 1969 (Kenya 1970), and almost all of them live in the present-day Samburu District.

The Turkana, who are related to people of the Karamojong cluster in Uganda, number 203,000 (1969 census) and inhabit the area to the west of Lake Turkana and southwards in the lowlands along the Rift Valley into the Kerio Valley.[7] They practise nomadic pastoralism for subsistence, tending both camels, cattle and small stock and where possible supplementing pastoralism with farming, by growing millet or maize especially along the Turkwell and Kerio Rivers.

In the first years of colonization, the Turkana expanded their grazing lands to the south. During the severe rinderpest epizooty in the 1890s, an epidemic that struck most stock in northern Kenya, the cattle belonging to the Turkana survived to a greater extent than those of their neighbours. Subsequently they made use of lands vacated by other less fortunate groups. Lamphear (1976b: 229) mentions severe droughts in Kerio and Turkwell Valleys around the end of the 19th Century as a major cause for the Turkana expansion in a southeasterly direction into the Samburu area.[8] Local oral history, as told by old Turkana men, says that the Turkana moved in a southerly direction under the leadership of Loparala, mainly in search for grass, causing chaos among their neighbours, since they had to fight their way through other peoples' territory. They found Samburu living around Uaso Nyiro River and in the area of what is now Isiolo town, then called *Akop na Akiyar*, "the land of survival", by the Turkana. The presence of Samburu at Isiolo is also confirmed by the stories of Samburu elders.

Throughout this century, Turkana, looking for pasture and employment, have immigrated to the Isiolo area, often after being forced to leave the pastoral economy because of local droughts, epizootics or other disastrous events. A steady trickle of Turkana kept coming as Isiolo town grew and the labour demands of administrators and traders increased. Many of the men were employed either locally in Isiolo town as manual labourers or recruited there for work further south as farm hands on white farms. Such recruitment increased during the Mau-Mau emergency, when the white farmers did not want to employ Kikuyu or Meru.

Before the British left domestic politics in Kenya, three attempts had been made to force those Isiolo Turkana who were not employed in town to move back to their area of origin.[9] Only once, in 1952, did the administration succeed in transporting a considerable number of people, but many soon returned again. This is not surprising, since the fundamental reason for their migration to Isiolo was shortage of livestock, grazing land and water, and there was little future for them in returning to their original areas. After Kenya's independence they were able to settle permanently in and around Isiolo town. Many of them married into Samburu families.

It has been noted that in other areas where they live in close proximity, Samburu men often marry Turkana women. For example, Gulliver (1955: 260) and before him Emley (1927: 161) have written that intermarriages of Samburu into Turkana seem to have taken place in large numbers in areas where Turkana dominate. In contrast, Spencer (1973: 160) maintains that the case of Turkana men marrying into Samburu society, which is my concern here, is unusual. One should keep in mind, however, that the area discussed presently lies on the outskirts of established Samburu territory. The Isiolo area provides an exception both in the amount of interaction between the Samburu and the Turkana, and in the degree of integration of Turkana into the Samburu society. This process has created an intermediate "semi-endogamic" category called Ilgira by the Samburu (Ilgira means "people who keep quiet" from *agira*, to be quiet). The category Ilgira is a local phenomenon, and members strongly emphasize that their appropriate home area is around Archers Post to the north of Isiolo town, an area traditionally inhabited by Samburu.[10]

The emphasis on Archers Post as the home area of Ilgira has a historical explanation. During the colonial period, an abattoir for cattle, and later for camels, was constructed there. The workers were predominantly Turkana who were preferred as wage labourers since Turkana had by then established a reputation with the administration of being "hard working". Most of the employees therefore were people who had migrated to Archers Post from Turkana District. These labour migrants eventually brought their families and livestock when they considered the situation around Archers Post sufficiently secure. Raids from Somali and Borana across the Uaso Nyiro were a threat which faced Samburu and Turkana alike.[11] Hence, Samburu and Turkana had common enemies, which served to unite them, even though they had conflicting interests between themselves. With Turkana immigration there was increased pressure on grazing and water resources. But there was also a risk that Turkana would become victims of raids by the Samburu in the area who were carrying out an almost sedentary pastoralism on the banks of the Uaso Nyiro River.

The first Turkana immigrants found themselves weak and isolated as compared with the dominant Samburu. In order to gain some immunity from Samburu raids, Turkana began to offer their help to Samburu neighbours, first with little things and later by exchanging small stock or even cattle. In many cases it was found advantageous to settle next to each other for purposes of defence against cattle raiders from other groups and against predators, and for the pooling of herding labour. When the situation proved to be feasible, whole Turkana households began to migrate gradually to the Archers Post area in search of a livelihood.

Another step towards establishing friendly relations was adoption, either collectively through whole Turkana households being adopted by Samburu households and thereby assuming the latter's clan (and lineage) names, or individually in various ways. For example, if the Samburu household lacked young boys for herding purposes they might be allowed to adopt a boy from the friendly Turkana household. Another less amicable kind of adoption had sometimes occurred in precolonial time when youngsters were captured in inter-ethnic clashes and forced to work within the Samburu houshold. These youngsters were treated harshly according to Samburu norms in order to make them more "sensitive to what cattle mean to a Samburu".

The people who were adopted in either of these ways, their off-spring, as well as the children of inter-ethnic marriages between Samburu and Turkana (that is Turkana marrying into Samburu society), are all referred to as Ilgira by the Samburu. They treat Ilgira as a separate entity and are of the opinion that members of Ilgira will never be accepted as Samburu. Ilgira is regarded as an endogamous unit and referred to as a separate "tribe" by many Samburu who claim to be extremely sensitive to any of their lineages having even the slightest blood mixture from Ilgira. This would be a stigma and they feel that they would then be treated by other Samburu as if they were Turkana.

The Samburu not only ascribe generally to the Turkana an inferior status, but also hold them to be less competent in herding and husbandry. The Turkana are considered polluted in terms of food practices, not least since they eat wild animals other than the ones which are, according to the Samburu point of view, "wild relatives" to domestic stock (buffaloes to cattle and antelopes to small stock).[12] This issue of polluted food was explained to me by a Samburu informant in the following words:

> "The Turkana are known by the Samburu to eat any live mammal and birds on earth. How far true it is may be questioned. The animals eaten by them include dogs, zebras, donkeys, tortoises, etc., etc. All these animals are unclean from the Samburu point of view in the sense that they are unfit for human consumption. However, in my own opinion the Turkana may have had all the right to eat all these unclean animals for diet compensation to combat malnutrition. I believe the scarcity of cattle meat led them to exploit and make a thorough use of the environment. To the Samburu the only animals which can be eaten are the buffalo and the gazelles which are included in the list of domestic animals. For example, a buffalo is the same as a cow, and the meat of the gazelle tastes like sheep or goats' meat. Eggs of any bird, even a hen, and fish are all discarded. This therefore creates a feeling of contempt vis-à-vis the Turkana as humans of a more degraded species. To get married to a Turkana is believed to lead to adherence to such a diet, an issue which they have been conditioned to see as highly distasteful."

The allegations of different food habits are not entirely denied by Turkana informants. The hint of the Samburu informant that Turkana food practices are linked with their harsher environment can probably also be expanded to the fields of herding and husbandry: they sometimes milk domestic animals that are not milked by the Samburu; they slaughter family herds in a fashion that may be detrimental to their continued reproduction when forced to for immediate consumption; their domestic herds are less productive than those of the Samburu, etc.

The process of ethnic transformation

The more recent settlements around Isiolo town, both to the north of it and to the south, provide ample demonstration of contacts between Samburu and Turkana. The settlements consist of households that have been struck by the "shifta war" (a secessionist war fought in northern Kenya by some groups in the 1960s, after independence; cf. Hjort 1979a: 31ff) or by other misfortunes. On both sides of town the right to pasture is questioned by other groups, a fact which encourages the Turkana and Samburu to settle in fairly large camps or clusters of camps. These can also be inhabited by non-Ilgira depending on whether the settlement is recent or occurs in areas where Samburu claims for land rights are less obvious.

The presence of both Samburu and Turkana pastoralists in the Isiolo area actually creates a situation of increased vulnerability. For example, few of the Samburu settlements to the south of town contain households that can manage to make a living solely off their animals. Their limited farming activities are both of low productivity and subject to high risks (Hjort 1979a: 144ff). They are tied to the vicinity of the town by the need to trade milk and some farm products in order to buy cheap maize flour which forms their staple food. Adjacent to these Samburu settlements lie Turkana settlements, in many cases containing poor households similarly tied to the township as commodity producers.

A survey of sedentary pastoralists engaged in the irrigation projects within Isiolo town showed that 45% of the Turkana inhabitants spoke the Samburu language, while in a neighbouring Turkana settlement comprising wage labourers (and jobless) 30% spoke the Samburu language. The reasons given for such a high degree of fluency in the Samburu language was invariably the fact that it was or had been needed for daily communication.

These indications of interaction between the Samburu and Turkana, coupled with the process of Turkana integration into the Samburu society, within the Archers Post area, seem to demonstrate how new bases for some form of cooperation emerge in a situation of change through new circumstances. The form may be either a neighbourhood solidarity based on mutual interests or, as in the Ilgira case, a matter of involvement in another culture. Whatever form, one fundamental aspect is the fact that both groups rely on new, and similar, subsistence niches: apart from livestock rearing perhaps with some farming, a little market trade, charcoal production, the gathering and sale of firewood or trade in tourist items.

The completely negative ideal view on intermarriage with Turkana obviously does not prevent some Samburu from marrying Turkana "immigrants". The reason for this kind of marriage is invariably claimed to be economic. The Turkana men have traditionally higher normative amounts of bridewealth than the Samburu. When they marry Samburu girls they are still required to pay according to the Turkana standard. The Turkana man who marries and becomes Ilgira adopts Samburu customs in that he dresses and behaves like a Samburu, speaks their language and, if not too old, eventually goes through circumcision. This issue of circumcision is important since the Turkana do not circumcise and regard this as a particular mark of cultural distinction.

Ilgira members are bilingual and, at least in some cases, speak the Samburu language even among themselves, using the Turkana language solely in interaction with a Turkana.[13] To outside observers, then, they have really "become" Samburu. It is also quite possible for an Ilgira youth to migrate and live with other Samburu in the same way as a Samburu youth would do, but which would be impossible for a "proper" Turkana. It may be interesting to note that an identical phenomenon was observed by Jacobs (1968: 15) for an assimilated group of Maasai warriors in southern Kenya. As an Ilgira however, the youth would still have the stigma of an inferior status among Samburu outside the Isiolo area.

The Ilgira are continuously reminded of their status since the area is inhabited by both Samburu and Turkana. Their ambivalent status can sometimes even be seen in small details of their dress where an occasional Turkana item may appear.[14] The Samburu informants emphasize that they are continuously conscious of the Turkana blood flowing in the veins of their Ilgira neighbours. Hence, the Samburu view of Turkana as being polluted is held for the Ilgira as well. One expression of this attitude is the fact that the Ilgira circumcision takes place outside the fence of the Samburu camp for the sake of ritual purity. In company with the Samburu association of Ilgira with Turkana goes the opinion that they are less efficient husbandrymen. The higher payment of bridewealth when a Turkana or Ilgira man marries a Samburu woman confirms the Samburu opinion of the Turkana or Ilgira as having an inferior status.

From the Turkana point of view, the Ilgira are considered to be "lost people", being just like Samburu. The Turkana term for this category is Ng'igirae, which is simply a transformation of the Samburu word. The step for a Turkana to take in order to become Ng'igirae is very definite: he or she sides actively with the Samburu society against the Turkana with the result that their relations to most Turkana (other than close kinsmen) become very tense.

Turkana see the Ng'igirae as a phenomenon typical of and limited to the Isiolo area and linked with the migration to the abattoir in Archers Post. This migration provided an opportunity for impoverished Turkana to seek a possible livelihood within that area, and many once drought-stricken households later joined Samburu households as a result.

Both Turkana and Ilgira male informants claim that it is possible for the latter to marry Turkana women, granted that they have not yet been circumcised. But this must not overshadow the basic reason for intermarriage which is the desire of some Turkana migrants to gain rights to pasture and security against raids from Samburu inhabitants of the area. This makes such marriages less likely, or at least of lesser interest for the present discussion.

The common interest in (or, indeed, need for) exploiting new resources when pastoral nomadism has failed, is strikingly similar to the position of the Ilturia within the Ariaal Rendille as discussed by Spencer (1973: 132):

> "Gradually, a tradition developed that inside the Ilturia, it was possible to build up herds of camels primarily by trading small stock with the Somali at Arbah Jahan or elsewhere. Rendille proper from many clans were tempted to join this clan: Ilturia, in fact, means literally a collection of people from all over the place (a-turit = to mix and grow—Samburu). Along with the other Ariaal, they live in country which is better for small stock (even if worse for camels) than the areas to the north inhabited by the Rendille proper."

My Ilgira informants actually referred to Ilturia as the equivalent to Ilgira, formed by Samburu households who had become impoverished by one of the most severe droughts in history, who therefore sought refuge in the Rendille settlements and became absorbed into the Rendille society.[15] They claimed that in contrast to the tense relationship between Ilgira and both Samburu and Turkana, the Ilturia had far better relations with both groups (Rendille and Samburu) due to a "stronger similarity". Ilturia are similar to both groups since they maintain contacts in both directions.

Of great significance for the existence of the Ilgira category is the substantial difference in bridewealth between the Samburu and the Turkana. A high but realistic figure for a Turkana man marrying into the Samburu society would be 80 head of cattle, which can be compared with 50 for a Turkana marriage in the area and 5-10 for a Samburu marriage. The higher level of bridewealth for a Turkana man marrying a Samburu woman is coupled with a "need for compensation" for the Samburu household for accepting an inferior status by associating with Turkana. This pattern is common for interethnic marriages in the area (Hjort 1979a: 202ff). The otherwise common aspect of a lower degree of social control for "the bridegiver" over "the bridetaker" is not so relevant in the Ilgira case since marriages are often uxorilocal, given the fact that the Turkana men need access to pastures.

Due to the high level of bridewealth many marriages are arranged "on credit". This represents another reason why they become uxorilocal, for the wife's father gains access to the labour of his son-in-law if the latter is also tied up by "the credit" of unpaid bridewealth. Furthermore, the difference between the Ilgira and Turkana bridewealth amounts can be even greater than it may seem at a first glance. Among the Turkana the bridewealth is high but on the whole involving few further redistributive demands on the "wife-taker". Among the Samburu, in contrast, bridewealth is fairly low but the "wife-taker" has an inferior position and may be urged to contribute more animals if economic circumstances become difficult for the "wife-givers"

(Spencer 1973: 75). The Turkana man marrying a Samburu woman then has to endure both an initial bridewealth of Turkana magnitude and the Samburu's prospects of further demands upon him, whether of livestock or labour. For the poor Samburu it is advantageous to marry away their daughters to Turkana. This enables them to get a share in the wealth acquired by Turkana labourers.

The fact that Ilgira tends to be endogamous and Samburu clans are exogamous presents no problem as long as there are Ilgira members in several clans. If there is a shortage of suitable Ilgira marriage candidates for a male Ilgira, however, this could serve as further incitement to marriages between Ilgira and Samburu proper. The cases that I know of consist of Ilgira men who have married Samburu women from poor households. In all such cases the bridewealth has still been considerably higher than what is normal for Samburu in the area. This second (or more) generation marriage seems to be the definite step for an Ilgira man to take so as to get rid of the family's stigma; the off-spring from such a marriage are no longer considered Ilgira. One necessary prerequisite is that the Ilgira cannot then have any close Turkana relatives still alive.[16]

The required period of time for a complete assimilation of Turkana into Samburu then seems to be at least two generations (this is not unlike, for example, the assimilation process of immigrants into Swedish society). Why, then, does Ilgira represent a one-way flow whereas the Ariaal Rendille (between Rendille proper and Samburu), including the more particular Ilturia, represent a two-way symbiotic flow?

The situation of the Ilgira may at first seem rather similar to that of younger Rendille sons who also become assimilated into the Samburu society (Spencer 1973: 132-133; quoted above). However, there is a fundamental difference in that in the Rendille case the migrant has a possibility either to return to the Rendille proper after having rebuilt a camel herd through trade in small stock, for example, or to move on into the Samburu society. This choice does not exist for the Ilgira; his sole alternative is to get as heavily involved with the Samburu society as possible. A strategy of diversification of the family's sources of income is always a problem of labour allocation. Only by absorption into Samburu can the Turkana labourer get access to nearby pastures and maintain both an engagement in his job and, at the same time, take an active part in the critical first phases of the development of a family herd. The existence of Ilgira supports the traditional structure of the Samburu but gives no feedback to Turkana society, whereas the Ariaal are essential for the continuity of both Rendille and Samburu.

Ethnic ascription as a means to resource control

The discussion so far has concentrated on how members of two distinct ethnic groups adapt to new circumstances which have been generated largely outside their control. I have mentioned how economic and political change have brought about an increased dependency on monetary resources, how situations of inequality thereby tend to increase and remain more permanent than before and, more particularly, how the redistribution of monetary wealth may occur from rich Turkana households to poor Samburu households through an assimilation process involving secure access to grazing. The fact that Samburu and Turkana do cooperate may seem surprising since they are traditionally enemies. In this last section I want to dwell a little upon how cultural assets, as they are expressed in terms of ethnic ascription and ethnicity, can become economic assets in a development process which generates a multiethnic situation within a geographically limited area.

First a few words of definition. By ethnic ascription I refer to an individual's status as it is formulated in ethnic terms, whether ascribed by outsiders or insiders to a particular group. Ethnicity represents the apparently deliberate display of this status by the individual, i.e. in multiethnic situations when he/she demonstrates membership in a particular group. It may be noted that other solidarity principles than those based on a common ethnic identity may be perceived by outsiders as based on ethnicity due to differences in perspective.[17]

When studying today's development process there are, ideally, two possible perspectives. One is to concentrate on the ethnic ascription as such, analyze the relevant cultural features and identify the impact of change within a particular cultural system as expressed in ethnic transformation. The focus is then on internal factors prohibiting or inhibiting change. The other perspective is to concentrate on economic systems and treat ethnic ascription as one asset among several to get access to needed or attractive resources, be they subsistence niches in a multiethnic context, land rights in a predominantly monoethnic area or some other economic significance. In the latter case the focus is on factors partially external to the ethnic group. In this article I have treated ethnic ascription and ethnicity as dependent variables, in this particular case relating to the need for groups of people to exploit new resources. My position is similar to that of Knutsson (1969: 99):

> "It seems first of all to be quite clear that any concept of ethnic group defined on the basis of 'cultural content'...will not suffice as a tool for the analysis of ethnicity in its various interactional contexts. Only when ethnic distinction, stratification, or dichotomization are part of the individual's or group's strategies for preserving or increasing control of resources, social status or other values is a meaningful interpretation feasible."

One focus of study would then be to concentrate primarily on processes of identity change in response to the development process outlined above. This implies, also, the need to touch upon more general ethnic processes: "the emergence, continuation, and change of interethnic relations" (*loc. cit.*). I hope that I have brought home the argument that there is an economic factor in the case of Samburu and Turkana interaction. The Rendille-Samburu case referred to above demonstrates how ethnic ascription can be associated with particular economic systems, a camel and a cattle pastoral economy, respectively.[18]

Jacobs (1968) provides another case of ethnic assimilation. This study concerns a Maasai village in southern Kenya where most inhabitants are immigrant Sonjo of first or second generation. Jacobs suggests i.a. that this is a process which presents a survival opportunity for people who cannot be supported within a static farming economy (*ibid.*: 17). They have then nothing to lose by denying their Sonjo origin and everything to gain from becoming Maasai as quickly as possible. In this respect the Maasai assimilation of Sonjo migrants seems identical to the Samburu assimilation of Turkana.

Yet another case, from Sudan, is Haaland's (1969) account of how the Fur turn into Baggara nomadic pastoralists when they reach a practical limit of accumulating wealth in their farming economic system. Having settled for a nomadic life-style these Fur are "categorized as if they were Baggara and their performance is judged by the standards of Baggara culture" (*ibid.*: 69). However, in contrast to the Ilgira, it seems, the pastoral Fur are not stigmatized. Haaland does not see them as a transitional category but instead emphasizes the interactional aspect whereby "the nomadized Fur will be classified as Fur, Baggara or a separate category depending on how their participation in social situations is defined" (*loc. cit.*).

If one disregards for the moment such interactional aspects associated with ethnicity, and instead concentrates on the quality of ethnic ascription, I think one sees more clearly some benefits of displaying it. In rural areas of northern Kenya, ethnic ascription and membership in an ethnic group are usually associated with a territory. Ethnicity is not immediately relevant within such areas since a display of one's ethnic ascription simply implies membership in the total community. In the inter-ethnic context both in Isiolo town and its surroundings, however, this display is important for gaining access to economic resources. Ethnic ascription has, in this kind of context, a different quality since it communicates a differentiated access to such assets. The Ilgira need to emphasize their Samburu identity in order to maintain grazing rights and membership in one local community for protection against outsiders. Hence, one's ethnic ascription not only implies an association with a particular set of cultural values but by displaying it one constantly reminds people in the surroundings, many of them strangers, about one's rightful claims to essential economic assets. This means from an economic point of view that a particular ethnic ascription may be either desirable (or, indeed, necessary) or not desirable. There may accordingly be situations of a pressing need to change ascription such as the Ilgira case illustrates. Hence, I think that such ethnic processes rather than the ethnic groups *per se* deserve attention in a study of today's development process. It is not necessarily the ethnic boundaries that may be of interest nor the issue of an individual's experienced identity (even though the identity as perceived by others is crucial). Of immediate interest would be instead an analysis of basic cultural traits and of the larger framework of interaction that may, apart from economic circumstances, condition a change. By this I mean that the many dimensions of intraethnic ties are also conditional, especially in degree of involvement with particular social groups, in efficiency of social control and sanctions, and in forms for devolution of property and inheritance. If one were to concentrate solely on economic factors and ecological conditions one might be led to expect an emerging class consciousness among the Isiolo poor. Keeping the relevant cultural factors in mind it seems obvious that one effect of the development process in the Isiolo town area, apart from increased vulnerability and dependency, is one of increased emphasis on ethnicity. Hence, rather than a class formation, the cultural systems give rise to efforts to mobilize ethnic ascription as a means to secure a particular mode of survival. Such a mobilization may well be of a short duration. In the Ilgira case the situation might change drastically if the Samburu households could no longer make efficient claims on land rights. It seems to be an open question as to when such a system breaks down to be replaced by one formed by class consciousness.

REFERENCES

ADAMSON, G.
   1971   *Bwana Game.* London & Glasgow; Collins. First published in 1968.
BARBER, J. P.
   1968   *Imperial Frontier.* Nairobi: East African Publishing House.
DAHL, G.
   1979   *Suffering Grass: Subsistence and Society of the Isiolo Borana.* Stockholm: Stockholm Studies in Social Anthropology, University of Stockholm.
DAHL, G. and HJORT, A.
   1976   *Having Herds: Pastoral Herd Growth and Household Economy.* Stockholm: Stockholm Studies in Social Anthropology, University of Stockholm.
   1979   *Pastoral Change and the Role of Drought.* SAREC Report R2.
EMLEY
   1927   "The Turkana of Kolosia District", *JRAI* LVII: 157-201.
GALATY, J.
   1977   *In the Pastoral Image: the Dialectic of Maasai Identity.* PhD Thesis, University of Chicago, Department of Anthropology.
GULLIVER, P. H.
   1955   *The Family Herds: A Study of Two Pastoral Tribes in East Africa: The Jie and Turkana.* London: Routledge and Kegan Paul Ltd. Reprinted in 1966.
GULLIVER, P. and GULLIVER, P. H.
   1953   *The Central Nilo-Hamites.* Ethnographic Survey of Africa, East Central Africa, Part VII; London: International African Institute. Reprinted 1968.
HAALAND, G.
   1969   "Economic Determinants in Ethnic Processes", in: F. Barth (ed.), *Ethnic Groups and Boundaries: The Social Organization of Culture Difference*, Bergen, Oslo: Universitetsforlaget; pp. 58-73.
HENRIKSEN, G.
   1974   *Economic Growth and Ecological Balance: Problems of Development in Turkana*, Occasional Paper No. 11, Institutt for sosialantropologi, Universitetet i Bergen.
HJORT, A.
   1979a *Savanna Town: Rural Ties and Urban Opportunities in Northern Kenya.* Stockholm: Stockholm Studies in Social Anthropology, University of Stockholm.
   1979b "Sedentary pastoralists and peasants: the inhabitants of a small town", in A. Southall (ed.), *Small Urban Centers in Rural Development in Africa*, African Studies Program, University of Wisconsin-Madison.

JACOBS, A.
    1968   *The Irrigation Agricultural Maasai of Pagasi: A Case of Maasai-Sonjo Acculturation.* Paper
           read to the Social Science Conference, Dar es Salaam, University of East Africa;
           January 2-5.
KENYA, REPUBLIC OF
    1970   *Kenya Population Census, 1969.* Statistics Division, Ministry of Finance and Economic
           Planning, Vol. I-III.
KNUTSSON, K. E.
    1969   "Dichotomization and Integration: Aspect of inter-ethnic relations in Southern
           Ethiopia", in: F. Barth (ed.), *Ethnic Groups and Boundaries: The Social Organization of
           Culture Difference.* Bergen, Oslo: Universiteitsforlaget; pp. 86-100.
LAMPHEAR, J.
    1976a *The Traditional History of the Jie of Uganda.* Oxford: Clarendon Press.
    1976b "Aspects of Turkana Leadership During the Era of Primary Resistance", *J. of Afr.
           Hist.* XVII, 2: 225-243.
MITCHELL, J. C.
    1970   "Tribe and Social Change in South Central Africa: A Situational Approach", *J. of
           Afr. & As. Stud.* 5: 83-101.
SPENCER, P.
    1959   "Samburu Notions of Health and Disease and Their Relationship to Inner
           Cleanliness", *One-day Symposium on Health and Disease among some East African Tribes.*
           MISR 1973. December.
    1965   *The Samburu: A Study of Gerontocracy in a Nomadic Tribe.* Berkeley and Los Angeles:
           University of California Press.
    1973   *Nomads in Alliance: Symbiosis and Growth among the Rendille and Samburu of Kenya.*
           London: Oxford University Press.
TORRY, W. I.
    1977   *Labor Requirements among the Gabra.* Paper presented at the ILCA Conference on
           Pastoralism in Kenya, Nairobi, August 22-26.

NOTES

1   This article is based on a paper presented at the symposium on Change and Development in
    Nomadic Societies at the Xth ICAES held in New Delhi in December 1978. I am par-
    ticularly grateful for comments by G. Dahl, J. Galaty and W. Östberg, as well as those
    made by the collective research seminar at my department. My attendance at the con-
    ference was financed by the Smithsonian Institute and I wish to express my gratitude for
    this. The material was collected in the process of carrying out a social anthropological
    fieldwork in the Isiolo area in northern Kenya 1973 and 1974. It is included in a research
    project, "Pastoralism, Society and Ecology" sponsored by the Swedish Agency for
    Research Cooperation with Developing Countries (SAREC).

2   These factors are identified in Dahl and Hjort (1979) where we also elaborate some of the
    points made in the present section.

3   Cf. Mitchell (1970: 89ff). He suggests that ethnic distance varies essentially with cultural
    similarity, geographical distance and social status.

4   A detailed account of ecological adaptations to farming, hunting/gathering and pastoral
    economic systems with reference to the issue of a Maasai identity is given in Galaty (1977).

5   The Rendille camels are of a different breed from most other camels in northern Kenya.
    They do not compare favourably, being smaller, reproducing slower, and producing less
    milk.

6   For a presentation of the Samburu see Spencer (1965 and 1973).

7   For details on the Turkana see for example Gulliver (1955), Gulliver and Gulliver (1953:
    53-86) and Henriksen (1974).

8   For further historical details see Barber (1968) and Lamphear (1976a and 1976b).

9   An account of the attempts that failed is given in Adamson (1971: 170-175). On that occasion the move had to be stopped in the last minute when an outbreak of foot-and-mouth disease was discovered among the gathered goats.

10 The number of inhabitants in Archers Post Location in 1969 was 3,017 (Kenya 1970). I have no way to estimate the number of Ilgira in the Archers Post-Isiolo town area.

11 Security problems became severe as late as in the 1960s when both the Somali and many Borana supported the secessionist guerrillas of the so-called "Shifta war".

12 The issue of purity and pollution is briefly discussed by Spencer (1959) who lists unclean food and reasons for it not to be clean according to the Samburu notion of purity.

13 I regret that I do not have detailed quantitative information about the degree to which respective languages are spoken at home, first and second language learning, etc. Such data were not possible for me to gather at the time of my fieldwork. This means that I do not feel confident in elaborating the issue of Ilgira identity beyond stating that individuals identify with the Samburu clan that they belong to or have been adopted by, and with a particular territory. This territorial association in turn implies an inferior status due to the Turkana association. Daily interaction occurs with Samburu (including Ilgira). In occasional interaction with Turkana, the Ilgira have the asset of knowing that language.

14 I cannot tell whether this represents a conscious emphasis on ties to both Samburu and Turkana culture.

15 One significance of keeping only small stock is to try to rebuild a viable family herd as quickly as possible (cf. Dahl and Hjort 1976: 233f).

16 It may be significant in this context that Turkana lineages (in Isiolo) are shallow and that deceased persons are only mentioned on the particular occasion of name-giving. They are otherwise treated with a collective term signifying "the dead" for the fear of spirits.

17 I have discussed these issues for the case of Isiolo town in Hjort (1979a: 176ff).

18 The Borana Gabbra and Gutu, mentioned briefly earlier in the text, provide the third possible "combination", i.e. similar ethnic ascription and differing economic systems (a fourth combination, which is trivial, is both similar economic systems and ethnic ascription).

Land and Livestock among Kenyan Maasai

Symbolic Perspectives on Pastoral Exchange, Social Change and Inequality[1]

JOHN G. GALATY

McGill University, Montréal, Canada

In RECENT YEARS, the economic and social geography of African pastoral societies has been drastically influenced by forces of change—forces such as the increased power and influence of the state, the growing monetization and market penetration of local economies, the spread of education, and the privitization or nationalization of land tenure. In this paper, I propose to investigate the implications of some of these forces for the system of inequality found in Kenyan Maasai society,[2] with special attention given to the changing relationship between Maasai and their land, due to comprehensive adjudication and registration of the two districts of Maasailand as free-holdings during the 1970s.[3] My major thesis will be that Maasai relations of inequality have undergone qualitative change along with the change in the essential means of production which forms the basis for these relations, i.e., from the exchange of 'cattle' and the use of 'pasture', to the sale of 'livestock' and the ownership of 'land'.[4]

Relevant to the inquiry is a more general theoretical issue regarding the relationship between culture and class. Class has been depicted as a fundamental reality inadequately represented by the cultural categories of society, but taken in this sense it appears marginal to social action carried out within an ethno-sociological framework. It would be my view that, from a semiotic perspective on culture, the dialectical tension between the apparent and immediate categories of social classification and their underlying symbolic predicates can be maintained and that the problem of class can be represented at both levels. A semiotic account of class would be related to indigenous categories of such key economic domains as resources, production, consumption, ownership and exchange, and would aim to uncover the underlying features which both generate and make possible the transformation of this ethno-economic system. My thesis will be that this symbolic system mediates, defines and modulates exogenous forces of change, and insofar as it is itself transformed, follows the predicates of its own logic, generating novel class categories out of the symbols of the old.

Exchange in Pastoral Economics

The forces of pastoral production involve resources of pastoral labor, water, pasture and livestock. In Maasai society, pastoral resources are transformed into pastoral products through domestic production carried out in a political context: young boys (*ilAyiok*) and client herdsmen tend flocks and herds; young men (*ilMurran*) perform community functions of communication and defense and assist in the more arduous aspects of herd movement; women (*inKituaak*) are concerned with primary food production, preparation and distribution (primarily associated with milk); and male elders (*ilPayiani*) involve themselves primarily in administration, and in overall management and policy decision, at both domestic and community levels. Since a certain amount of labor is required for the management of a given herd, the size of that herd is roughly limited by the labor available in the specific domestic group which manages it; conversely, given a relatively high degree of pastoral specialization—as is found in Maasai society—the size of a group and the labor it can supply is itself limited by the size and structure of its herd, on which it must largely subsist. The extent to which animal and human populations represent functions of one another is, it should be emphasized, influenced by the degree of pastoral specialization of the group, as measured by its degree of dependence upon animal products for subsistence and the amount of available labor actually used in animal husbandry and related activities (i.e. social and political), as opposed to other economic pursuits (i.e. agriculture or wage labor).

The relationships between Maasai and their means of pastoral production are mediated by three social institutions: the territorial political system and the primary unit of the section (*olOsho*); the descent system and the primary unit of the clan or lineage (*olGilata*); and the age-group system and the primary unit of the age-set (*olPorror*). Sectional affiliation determines *general* rights of access to "pasture", or to be more specific, the right of "pasturing" (*Shoo*) in a given area. Only for the circle of grass (*olOkeri*) immediately outside the cattle gate of a family are there *exclusive* rights for the use of calves or sick animals, but these exclusive privileges are temporary and endure only until the semi-nomadic household shifts its residence. Specific control of cattle is associated with the male head of a polygynous family, while general association of the herd is with his descent group. Males agnatically related to a man may inherit his livestock, but his primary heirs should be his sons, with special emphasis on the first and the last. If descent group determines *who* may inherit, the age-set system is the determinant of *when* they may inherit, for sons become eligible heirs only after initiation by circumcision and affiliation with a specific age-set. In effect, the primary units of productive organization—the polygynous family and the multi-family homestead, within a territorial system—are constituted through these three institutions, in a political interplay of descent and age-set principles (cf. Galaty 1979a, 1980a).

It has been necessary to avoid the conventional term 'own' to describe the relationship between the section and its pastures, or between men and their cattle, since individual exclusive proprietary rights associated with 'ownership' do not strictly obtain. Indeed, the notion of 'ownership' often does violence to relations of production in pastoral societies and fails to provide an adequate account of the agency involved in the link between persons and material objects.[5]

Two dimensions of reciprocity—'generalized' and 'balanced'—may be added in order to better depict the Maasai relationship to their livestock (cf. Sahlins 1965: 147). First, a form of generalized reciprocity exists in several senses. In a general sense, a patriline shares rights in the herds of its members, but in actual practice those rights must be carefully calculated before being acted upon, as for example in claiming animals gained through bridewealth or bloodwealth or "begging" an animal when in need. While on the one hand, agnates have general rights over whole animals, wives may have specific rights over portions of animals. For instance, a man allocates certain animals from his herd to his new wife at marriage, for her to care for and transmit to her sons; in return for her service, she gains rights over their renewable products (i.e. milk, urine, dung, blood), and claims upon their skin, internal organs and other portions, if they are slaughtered. These animals, and others added to her herd, represent the fraction of the total herd to be inherited by her sons, who exercise certain rights over the animals which will compose their future herds. Thus we find generalized reciprocity between and rights claimed by those persons related through two temporal agnatic poles: members of the same descent group are signified as having shared the same herd in the mythical past; and sons (via the link of matri-filiation) are signified as sharing the same herd in the actual present and will divide the herd in the projected future.

A second form of reciprocity may be found in the balance between those who exchange cattle, either as in-laws or as stock-partners. Marriage between families and lineages require the exchange of a wife for bridewealth, the key component of which is a number of cattle (approximately 4-6). The marriage does not end the process of exchange, for exchange is not strictly related to giving and receiving, but to enduring ties which are created by these passing acts. Indeed, the Maasai notion of an exchange does not entail the definitive alienation of the giver from his prestation, or the acquisition by the receiver of exclusive rights over the gift. In some cases, enduring claims exist, as when the giver may claim the offspring of the animal which has been given, or its skin if it is slaughtered or has died. In other cases, rights are more general and involve only the expectation of a gift of one of the cow's offspring, or another cow, in return. Clearly, however, an enduring symbolic link exists which defines the prestation as a metonymical sign of its giver, who because of this bond exercises certain supernatural power over it.[6] This enduring and mystical bond established through gift exchange may be seen in the relation between families of wife-givers and wife-receivers (*inkAaputi*, reciprocal term). In particular, this bond is manifested in the cross-generational relation between the mother's brother and the sister's son (*olApu*, reciprocal term), in which, despite their familiarity, the former commands a most powerful curse over the latter, following from the familial transfer in marriage of the means of *re*production: a wife who is at once a sister and a mother of the two.

It should be evident from the above that no account of the individual '*ownership*' of the means of pastoral production is possible in Maasai society, in a strict sense, for the various rights in productive resources are social and are invariably constituted through exchange. Since pasture is internally indivisible, it cannot serve as a factor of intra-group class discrimination or inequality. Cattle, on the other hand, are divisible not only by unit but also by origin and function and readily serve as the basis for social differentiation of various classes, including those distinguished by wealth. The properties of livestock which make them desirable forms of investment beyond their subsistence functions have been admirably described by Harold Schneider (1979, n.d., and in this volume). However, as a result of constraints on the size of a herd managed by any given household, the absence of other material items esteemed by Maasai as objects of consumption or investment, and the lack of banking facilities *per se*, there are definite limits on the capacity of a head of household to actually 'possess' livestock. Thus, the exchange of livestock is basic to the process of capital accumulation, but the social relations so established act as a continuous check on and leveller of inequities in livestock holdings. Further, since numbers of livestock generate marriages, and marriages generate children who eventually provide increased labor for the herd, the variable ratio of cattle to people is maintained within certain limits. Wealth, in the author's view, cannot be assessed simply in terms of immediate control of livestock and size of herds, but is related to a temporal process of exchange during which livestock are transformed into social relations and social relations into prestige and power. This process is not extrinsic to but an intrinsic part of any assessment of the relations between Maasai and their means of production and of the resulting social inequality.

To sum up, the purpose of the foregoing discussion has been to establish the groundwork for an analysis of the categories of Maasai culture associated with economic roles. Such pastoral notions of economic 'class' must, it would appear, focus on relations of 'exchange' between men, rather than relations of 'ownership' between men and resources. The ensuing discussion will aim to relate Maasai concepts regarding exchange, production, consumption and wealth to a more abstract transactional typology utilized by Marriott for the analysis of caste strategies in India (1976). Each Maasai 'class' category will identify distinct strategies of pastoral pursuit, which are indigenously signified as social types; but this ethno-sociology will be seen to identify, as well, distinctions *between* pastoralism and other productive classes within Maasai society. Thus the symbolic features of exchange will be seen to define categories discriminated at several levels, two of which will be developed here: one, within the pastoral sector, and the other between the pastoral sector and other productive sectors.

Exchange Strategies and a Pastoral Ethnosociology

The ideal pastoralist is one involved in multiple relations of exchange, through multiple marriages and stock-partners. As a result of a high number of such exchange relations, this pastoralist establishes his own security (through the accumulation of obligations to reciprocate on the part of others), disperses his herds to various parts of the country to minimize risk to the whole through regional drought or disease, and, in effect, diversifies his holdings. At the same time, this network involves an increase in his personal influence, for the qualities of a good stock partner are likely to be the same as those of a leader. The essential strategy of this ideal pastoralist is not the local accumulation of wealth, which is the social counterpart of hoarding, but the increase of his personal solidarity with others, and thus his influence. This ideal pastoralist may be seen as following a 'maximalist' strategy. The maximalist diversifies his involvements by creating an extensive network of complex relationships, appropriately balances lineage and age-set solidarities, and, while gaining influence and prestige, inculcates a culturally necessary attitude of reciprocity and equality with other men. If he succeeds in building a large herd, this maximalist may well appear as a prototypical "big man" (*olKitok*), and will invariably act as a patron to poorer clients. However, such relationships need not solidify, both because of the possibility that clients may build up their own herds and regain independence, and because non-economic ties with strong egalitarian norms also regulate patron-client interaction.

If the economic image of the ideal pastoralist is that of a "big man", his political image may well be that of an age-set "spokesman" or "chief" (*olAiguenani*), an office of political leadership. The spokesman leads primarily by discussion, persuasion and example, rather than by coercion or threats of force. His office depends primarily upon his personal qualities of oratory, cajolery and influence, and the last depends primarily on relationships outside of the immediate political domain. The spokesman occupies the center of collective decision-making as much by character as by office, and this character is identical with the maximalist strategy of establishing ties and influence rather than accumulating wealth in a manner which the Maasai may consider antisocial.

Insofar as a Maasai pastoralist may aim to accumulate wealth, without exchanging, or to gain a commanding edge through exchange, he follows an 'optimal' strategy. A maximalist can redirect himself towards an optimal strategy by narrowing his range of partnerships, by beginning to cut ties which demand balanced exchange or generalized reciprocity, and by aiming to benefit absolutely from most interactions. The pastoralist known as a "rich man" (*olKarsis*) often makes himself inaccessible to ordinary pastoralists, for in fully reciprocal exchange he cannot ultimately benefit. Since he has more than others, he would inevitably enter into more relationships through giving than by receiving. Insofar as the number and range of his exchanges are diminished, the optimalist gains a reputation for exclusivity and selectivity; if he does not freely give, neither does he freely receive. Intertwined with a certain refinement of transaction goes a more elusive spirit of honor and purity, contrasted to forms of pollution associated with those who enter more freely and indiscriminately into the melée of social intercourse. The optimalist may well exemplify pastoral values despite a certain asocial stance, by consuming only the products of his own herd and maintaining an optimal diet based only on milk and meat.

The economic persona of the pastoral optimalist is without doubt the "rich man" with many cattle, but the optimalist type is best exemplified by the class of ritual specialists or "diviners" (*ilOibonok*, pl.), whose powers allow them to mediate between man and God. These unusual powers allow *ilOibonok* to exercise clairvoyance (*enAibon*) through dreams and intoxication, to divine (*a-idong'*) through the use of pebbles shaken from a horn, and to prepare special ritual medicines (*inTasimi*) for protection. The diviners are consulted by individuals, corporate groups, and age-sets at times of affliction or transition, and they are invariably the recipients of livestock payments or gifts. At each major age-set ceremony, age-set leaders bring the leading diviner forty-nine cows in exchange for his help in revealing through divination the most auspicious time and place and the officiants for the ceremony, and providing participants with ritual protection. He is, as well, given wives by the section which he serves, the obligations of affinity being waived and the bridewealth being paid by the age-set concerned rather than by himself. Many of these same attributes of sacred power (though not clairvoyance or divination), the elevation, the ritual purity and the gift of wives from an entire group, are shared by the ritual officers chosen to officiate at age-set ceremonies (e.g. the *olOtuno* of the eUnoto ceremony).

If the maximalist is involved in a high level of ultimately symmetrical exchanges, from which he gains influence, the optimalist is involved in a lower level of ultimately asymmetrical exchanges, from which he gains honor and prestige. The aim of the former is to transform wealth into influence via exchange, with solidarity being the means; the aim of the latter is to transform supernatural power into honor and prestige, with wealth being the means. The first strategy integrates men with respect to influence, while the second strategy discriminates between men with respect to honor. The forms of inequality born out of each strategy may be seen by contrasting the big man, who gains influence through density of exchange, with the rich man, who gains honor through the direction of exchange. In the political domain, the age-set "spokesman", who leads through influence, forms a contrast with the "diviner" and "ritual officers", who lead through an honor born out of supernatural power and prestige. The source of power in the former case lies securely within the domain of Maasai society, for maximalists simply play the pastoral game well. The source of power in the latter case lies decisively outside the perceived domain of Maasai society, for optimalists ultimately are graced and in their elevation represent the amazing and sacred rather than the ideal.

Opposed to those who maximally exchange are those in Maasai society who minimally exchange, those who withdraw from social interaction and represent economic and social isolates. The 'minimalist' strategy may be predicated on political or economic timidity, born out of insecurity and fear of losing what little has been achieved. The minimalist may be known as anti-social and may be shunned, bringing into play a self-fulfilling prophecy that in exchange others would not reciprocate. Such individuals may be known as stingy if they maintain exchange only at the formal level, if they fail to freely reciprocate, and if they downplay affinal relationships and begrudge age-set solidarity. The minimalist may be represented by the individual who, although initiated, never joins in the corporate activities of an age-set and thus exerts little or no influence on the activities of others. In relation to the maximalist big man, the optimalist rich man operates according to a relatively more minimalist strategy by cutting down on the density of social ties. Indeed, the son of a rich family may forego age-set activities in order to pursue domestic responsibilities. However, the true minimalists are loners in a sociable society and have no other sources of esteem or influence. They are seen as polluted through their isolation.

In Maasai society, the minimalist extreme is manifested by the class of blacksmiths (*ilKunono*), who are considered to be a virtual caste of specialists by ordinary pastoralists. Their interaction with our Maasai is strictly limited to the instrumental functions of exchanging the products of iron-craft, such as knives, swords, spears, arrow-heads and ornaments, for livestock and, nowadays, money. Their isolation is doubly enforced. They are considered to be instrinsically polluted by other Maasai, expressed in terms of their "bitter blood" (*Kedua Sarge*), and thus are avoided, especially with respect to marriage or sexual relations. It is said that the curse on the blacksmiths will contaminate anyone who closely associates with them. From their own perspective, the myth of "bitter blood" is considered to be a ploy by the Maasai to avoid exchanging their women. However, blacksmiths represent a specialist group of craftsmen and tradesmen in a society of generalists, whose abilities to generate and accumulate wealth thus extend beyond the strictly pastoral economy. It is, in effect, commensurate with their commercial status that they would minimize their involvements with those who patronize them, since in relationships of generalized reciprocity, their specialized advantage in technically balanced reciprocity of trade would be lost. Essentially, they are involved in low levels of symmetrical exchange of a balanced order, limited to the channels appropriate to their specialization. Their autonomy is dependent on the productive skills which lend them a unique and marketable role in pastoral society, while isolating them from it. The costs are those of inequality, for they are deemed polluted and hence shunned, and are considered to be ones who receive livestock in despised instrumental commercial transactions, and who asocially do not reciprocate in kind. They form the polar opposite of the "spokesman", who enjoys maximum social relations and influence, and socializes even instrumental exchanges.

Opposed to those who optimally exchange are those in Maasai society who pessimally exchange, who retain social engagement with other Maasai at the cost of balanced reciprocity and their own prestige. It is clear that to maintain a stance as a pastoralist, one must have an initial stake with which to commence exchanges and must be able to minimally subsist. Those trying to enter the pastoral system, or who are slipping out of it, may manifest 'pessimal' strategies by engaging in asymmetrical exchanges with pastoralists for slight benefit. The obvious pessimal case is that of the client, who accepts the obligations of herding (a boy's job) in a richer man's homestead in exchange for subsistence and a few livestock, in the hope of eventually building up his own subsidiary herd at the same time, enabling him to return to independent pastoralism. The pessimalist may have to accept responsibility for despised tasks, such as herding and slaughter, and will have to endure association with extrinsic pollution attached to such activities. Both the economic and attitudinal aspects of the pessimalists' inequality may be temporary, however, because of the nature of pastoral culture. Livestock represents a volatile form of capital which may indeed reproduce at a rate which allows future independence for clients. Ideologically, even the rich realize that one day they may be poor, and this, combined with Maasai ideals of age-set and pastoralist equality, mitigates the tendency of wealth differentials to solidify into a fixed hierarchy of persons and groups.

In Maasai culture, the prototype of the "poor man" is the "hunter", the man without cattle, for the term *ilTorrobo* refers both to "poor men" and to "hunters". Without livestock, the hunter is obliged to pursue production and consumption activities deemed of categorically lower honor than those of pastoralists. If slaughter of domestic animals be found repulsive, the killing of game on a regular basis is more so from the pastoralist perspective. Maasai pastoralists may carry on limited relations with hunters from the forest based on the simple exchange of certain commodities prized by one and possessed by the other, for instance, honey from the forest exchanged for fat from domestic animals. But hunters often associate with pastoral homesteads in the status of clients and carry out despised functions in exchange for small-stock or other commodities. Still, the exchanges are considered asymmetrical because they are never in kind, but represent the receiving by Maasai of prized commodities in exchange for the giving of—to them—less prized commodities. No better example may be found than the asserted tradition by which Maasai pastoralists may take *ilTorrobo* women as wives, in exchange for bridewealth of a relatively low value, while the reciprocal exchange of Maasai women is denied. Since the hunting ethic and commodity values are different from those of Maasai pastoralism, an overall assessment of the relationship requires an account of both sides of the transaction (cf. Galaty 1982, 1979b, 1980c). However, in Maasai terms, pastoralists benefit and hunters do not, and the former are exploiters and the latter exploited. Thus, the costs of economic engagement may be not only the loss of prestige and honor, but also the inequality manifested in loss of economic resources without apparent just return. Just as clients form the necessary antithesis to patrons, so poor men form the antithesis to rich men, and in the Maasai case, hunters the antithesis of diviners. In each case, exchange is transacted through a system of negative reciprocity (cf. Sahlins 1965: 148), to the benefit of rich men and diviners and to the detriment of poor men and hunters. The forms of exchange underpin a system of attitudes which are similarly polarized, with the rich men and diviners achieving honor through gain and the poor men and hunters reaping dishonor and shame through loss.

Up to this point I have reviewed four strategies of exchange found in Maasai pastoral society, each of which is defined in opposition to another, with the maximal-minimal pole opposed to the optimal-pessimal pole (see Table 1). Each strategy represents a culturally defined relationship of exchange, based on reciprocal ties to cattle and women, which are, respectively, the means of pastoral production and social reproduction. Access to these key resources is best understood in terms of systems and strategies of 'exchange', rather than 'ownership', since in Maasai society the latter is a product of the former, where 'ownership' implies effective control. In each case, I have identified an exemplary category within the larger Maasai domain of productive classes opposed but linked to pastoralism. Within the domain of pastoralism, the pastoral "big man", "rich man", "poor man", and "loner"; within the categories of the Maasai culture of production as a whole, the ideal pastoralist or "chief" ("spokesman"), the "diviner", the "hunter", and the "blacksmith" (see Table 2). In effect, the symbolic nature of each Maasai

Table 1

Exchange Strategies

OPTIMAL

—*positive*—

		Balance			
MAXIMAL	—*high*— Degree	of	Exchange	—*low*—	MINIMAL
		Exchange			

—*negative*—

PESSIMAL

Table 2

Ethno-economic Classes: Subsistence Sector

Strategies	Within Pastoralism	Between Sectors
MAXIMAL	Big Men	Pastoralists/"Chiefs"
OPTIMAL	Rich Men	Diviners
MINIMAL	Loner	Blacksmiths
PESSIMAL	Poor Man	Hunters

category with respect to pastoralism is illustrated in a more extreme form by the productive classes defined in opposition to pastoralism. While I have elsewhere described the pollution concepts associated with each class of pastoral ''anti-praxis'' (Galaty 1979b), and the verbal labels used to discriminate betweeen the ''Maasai'' 'ethnicity' of ideal pastoralists and that of non-ordinary classes (Galaty 1982), in the present study, I aim to investigate the nature of the resources, exchange strategies, social attributes and attitudes, and forms of economic inequality associated with each pastoral 'class'.

These relations are schematically summarized in Tables 3 and 4. In Table 3, the four categories are aligned according to their involvement in either sym-

Table 3

Relations Between Ethno-economic Classes: Exchange

Balance of Exchange

	Symmetrical	Asymmetrical

High
 	
Prestige
(Level)
	MAXIMAL
	1. generalized
	    reciprocity
	2. central position
	3. influence
		OPTIMAL
		1. exploitative
		    reciprocity
		2. elevated position
		3. honor

Low	MINIMAL
	1. balanced
	    reciprocity
	2. peripheral position
	3. isolation
		PESSIMAL
		1. exploited
		    reciprocity
		2. submerged position
		3. degradation

** Types of Relations: 1. form of reciprocity; 2. social position; 3. attributes.

Table 4

Relations between Ethno-economic Classes: Production

Productive Talents (Origin/Type)

	Internal/Producers	External/Specialists
High Prestige (Level)	MAXIMAL 1. management 2. social (pastures) 3. respect	OPTIMAL 1. mediation 2. heaven 3. awe
Low	PESSIMAL 1. service 2. non-social (forest) 3. contempt	MINIMAL 1. technical 2. underworld 3. fear

** Types of Relations: 1. talents or occupational type; 2. locus of origin of productive talents; 3. attitudes attributed.

metrical or asymmetrical exchange, and their association with either high or low prestige. Three dimensions of comparison are noted, within each of which a system of relations between the four categories can be seen. These dimensions are: (1) form of reciprocity, (2) social position, and (3) attributes. Table 4 represents a rotation of Table 3, and expresses the diagonal relation of Table 3 in vertical and horizontal form, for simplicity of illustration. This table again contrasts prestige, but this time with the internal or external sources of productive talents commanded within each of the four categories. Tables 3 and 4 could be collapsed in order to express in a condensed form the over-determined relations between the four categories, within a three dimensional paradigm of prestige, exchange and productive talents.

The maximal/minimal dimension of exchange is one of symmetry, and is thus basically non-exploitative. If the maximal strategy involves high intensity and generalized reciprocity, through virtually all channels of social life, the minimal strategy involves low intensity and balanced reciprocity, through only the commercial channel of economic life. While the maximalist is situated in the central and pivotal point in the pastoral society, the minimalist occupies the distant periphery. But while the resources or skills of the former are derived from pastoral society (for which he represents a quintessential image), the single skill of the latter is acquired outside of the society (through some supernatural intervention) and excludes him from it. This dimension, then, is based on perceptions of social power, which in the maximal form of the pastoralist becomes influence and in the minimal form of the blacksmith becomes the antithesis of influence, a curse born of repugnance and isolation. But, at the same time, the minimalist has his compensation in self-sufficiency and in the opportunity of accumulating wealth by restricting social demands upon his resources through withdrawal from an extensive network of reciprocal exchanges. The optimal/pessimal dimension of exchange is one of asymmetry, and represents the Maasai manifestation of human exploitation. The optimal strategy involves the exchange of a unique capacity (grace) for wealth, and as a result limits the channels of exchange to those in which this special skill is pertinent. The diviner is said to hold the key not only to auspicious ceremonies but to the success of cattle raids, and from every successful cattle raid he recommends, he receives a portion. The optimalist is not engaged in cycles of cattle-exchange, but prototypically in one-way flows of cattle to him and away from others; conversely, the pessimalist is also not engaged in cycles of cattle exchange, but primarily in one-way flows of whatever resources he may have (primarily labor) away from him toward patrons, in exchange for subsistence. The resources or skills of the pessimalist hunter are derived from the hard realities of pastoral production, while the resources of the optimalist are derived from God. This pole, then, is based on honor and grace, which are present in the optimalist diviner and absent in the pessimalist hunter, who is despised and rejected. If the former is elevated, the latter is submerged.

The optimalist and the minimalist appear as similar because their capacities stem from outside the pastoral system; they are the pastoral specialists, in the form of the diviner and blacksmith, who make ordinary production possible. Each claims supernatural skill, but that of the former is transformed into divine charisma and grace, that of the latter into a chthonian curse. The maximalist and pessimalist appear as similar because their capacities stem from within the pastoral system: they are producers, in the form of the ideal pastoralist and the hunter-client. But the social skills of the former are transformed into influence, while those of the latter result in contempt. This contrast of supernatural versus social affinities may account for the origin of talents, but not for the nature of inequality, which rests on forms of exchange.

The maximalist and optimalist share positively valued sources of esteem, though of a qualitatively different nature. While the optimalist withdraws from maximal involvement in society, yet accumulates wealth in a fashion which may stimulate resentment, he represents a generalized sign of divine grace

Table 5

Two Modalities of Evaluation

		Modality 1	Modality 2
System 1	*Attributional:* (See Table 3)	Influence vs. Isolation	Honor vs. Degradation
System 2	*Attitudinal:* (See Table 4)	Respect vs. Contempt	Awe vs. Fear

which may illuminate the entire society. Indeed, the diviner is considered by many to be an arch-exploiter, yet one who makes an indispensable contribution to the specific and general well-being of the society. The minimalist and pessimalist share negatively valued sources of esteem, though also of differing nature. The trajectory of the minimalist is away from the society which he selectively serves, while the trajectory of the pessimalist is towards the society which he indiscriminately serves; the minimalist blacksmith reaps fear and rejection, while the pessimalist hunter attracts familiarity and contempt.

It would appear that within the framework of these two poles of relationship between men, based on the exchange of cattle and women, two modalities of esteem and discrimination emerge, each of which manifests an attributional facet and an attitudinal facet, the first system depicted in Table 3, the second system in Table 4 (see Table 5). It should be pointed out that the attribute of Influence and the attitude of Respect converge in the maximal category, which exemplifies the first modality of prestige; similarly, the attribute of Honor and the attitude of Awe converge in the optimal category, which thus exemplifies the second modality of prestige. However, the reciprocal attributional and attitudinal forms opposed to each of the prestigious forms do not converge in specific categories of exchange, for Isolation and Fear from each of the two modalities depict the minimal category, while Degradation and Contempt, also from both modalities, depict the pessimal category. In effect, disparaging traits doubly accrue to these latter cases, through their internally negative relations with both of the high prestige modalities.

The pastoral system, however, is combined with a high sense of human dignity and equalitarianism, which has been appropriately described in the ethnographic literature on pastoral societies. By investigating the forms of inequality and hierarchy in such a society, it is not being suggested that there are no differences between such pastoral societies and truly stratified and hierarchically-organized societies. I have not discussed aspects of inequality founded on the division of authority and control of wealth within the age-set system, partly because the temporal turnover of personnel in such systems prevents a rigid system of stratification from emerging. If young boys are indeed technically exploited, they do grow up, inherit, and become technical exploiters in turn.[7] The system I have described is not as fluid as that of the age-set system, since classes of hunters, blacksmiths and diviners are conceived as hereditary, while the choice of age-set spokesmen and ritual officers tends to run along family lines. However, for most Maasai pastoralists, wealth and influence are considered to be achieved attributes, and given the nature of animal husbandry and the relative independence of homesteads, fortune is largely considered to be dependent on God rather than on the will—or spite—of other men. This attitude in part reflects those properties of livestock previously mentioned, the foremost of which is the high rate of increase—a poor man really can recover his herds and rejoin the pastoral process. Further, the dominant process of exchange does involve livestock redistribution for the good of a community rather than for the conspicuous consumption of a few. A cow "in milk" is never wasted, but quickly loaned if her products are not needed. And, as part of this dominant process, the accumulation of livestock is continually checked by cattle exchange, so the social influence and prestige of the fortunate are purchased with the increased economic security and potentially increased wealth of others. If, as has been argued, the process of exchange and, thus, redistribution is basic to the pastoral relations of production, then economic growth in the traditional pastoral sector will be primarily transformed into more general economic security, with a modicum of social inequality.

The Ethnoeconomics of Change

Although the processes just described continue today in Maasailand, they are carried out within the larger context of an increasingly more active central government and an increasingly more resilient market system. Maasai subsistence now includes substantial inputs from the market in the form of grains, cereals, sugar and tea, etc., and the occupational and employment possibilities are no longer circumscribed by the productive classes described in the previous section. The education rate has been increasing, and the general pursuits of those inhabiting the two Maasai districts have been diversifying. While the pastoral pursuit and the growing livestock industry still dominate the Maasai districts (and perhaps will continue to do so), they are combined with other industrial sectors which must be taken into account, including the growing tourist industry centered on the national parks. In short, any account of class and inequality in Maasailand must deal not just with the pastoral sector but with the forces of change as well.

An important influence on the traditional exchange of cattle has been the spread of monetization and increased access to centers of livestock marketing. For every opportunity for the social exchange of cattle, the option of sale exists, within the limits of shared rights in animals, transportation, disease restrictions and price. As cattle assume a monetary value, the generalized social value of their exchange is altered, as can be seen in the frequent augmentation of brideprice in the form of livestock combined with cash. Cattle marketing has been kept within limits, however, due to several factors. During colonial rule, the incorporation of Maasai livestock into the marketing system was legally inhibited in order to protect the developing European beef industry. Today it is inhibited through central control of prices, which are maintained at an artificially low level (cf. Heyer 1976).

The change of greatest consequence in Maasailand since the imposition of colonial rule has been the program of land adjudication. During colonial rule and into the independent period, the two Maasai districts were constituted as a ''reserve'', held by the government for the Maasai people. This system has now been altered following the general policy of the Kenyan government that citizens be allowed to own their own land. During the 1960s, various progressive Maasai were allocated individual sections of land within their respective sections—land on which they could pursue the form of individualized improved ranching deemed desirable, to the end of increasing livestock marketing and influencing the pastoral practices of neighboring Maasai as well. The individuals who were allocated ''individual ranches'' in this way had usually been exposed to education, served in various agencies of the government, as teachers, medical assistants, or government chiefs, and often were closely associated with various missions which had been formed in Maasailand. After certain allocations had been made in Kajiado district, it became clear that this plan did not represent a general solution to the collective plight of Maasai pastoralists emerging from the 1960-61 drought and faced with the pressures of change; there was simply not enough land to create individual ranches for all. A timetable for the creation of ''Group Ranches'' was set up, and the process of their adjudication, the registration of their members and the legitimation of titles as collectively-held free-holds was begun. The Groups in some cases did not correspond to traditional locational or sub-locational boundaries, but in other cases (those created later) appear to do so. (The logic behind the formation of Groups, and some of the possible outcomes have been described elsewhere (Galaty 1980a, 1981).)

In a legal sense, then, Maasai now ''own'' their land as they never did their pastures, either as individuals or as collective units called ''Groups''. Only with individual ranches does this "ownership" entail individualization and exclusivity of title, or the possibility of unilateral alienation of the land through sale. One of the governmental objectives in clearly demarcating land was the prevention of livestock movement across boundaries, a form of mobility which is a prerequisite for the exchanges which have been so socially and economically important for the Maasai. The cessation of stock movement had, as its end, the specification of responsibility for the welfare of land and the eventual reduction in overall herd sizes to serve that conservation goal. As a result of these changes there is an increasing tendency for some of the generalized aspects of rights in cattle to be eliminated in favor of stricter individualization of cattle ownership.

Without underemphasizing the continuing importance of the pastoral economy in the subsistence of the Maasai, it is necessary to point out that the dominant resource in defining Maasai social relations is becoming "land" rather than "livestock", in a way that "pasture" never was. But while "cattle" represent in the pastoral economy a virtually universal medium of symbolic exchange and value, "land" in the wider economy of Maasailand today is apparently only one commodity among many given value through the market system. I say "apparently", because I am suggesting that the relationship to land will in the future prove crucial in defining relationships between men and key resources within the context of Maasai society, and the differences between "land" and "livestock" will represent the basis for a more radical transformation of Maasai culture.[8] With respect to the wider context of change, I propose to use the four relational strategies (i.e. Maximal/Minimal-Optimal/Pessimal) previously discussed as a device to depict class differences in Maasailand today (cf. Table 1).

Individual ranchers represent the maximal strategy of today, relating as they do in diffuse and multi-lateral ways to the body of pastoralists in the Group Ranches surrounding them. They represent centers of leadership and influence, and often are seen as spokesmen for their local areas, more so than the official leaders of the Group Ranches. Indeed, individual ranchers often are, as well, members of Groups, though perhaps not elected leaders. These ranchers represent the centers of economic and political energy in the district, both with respect to their ranches and beyond. The Government "Chief" represents the most local level of government, and the office which complements the traditional position of "spokesman", as well as at times conflicting with it. Government Chiefs, who invariably hold individual ranches, operate according to a maximalist strategy which encompasses both the traditional pastoral sector and the sector of town-based trade and government bureaucracy. These individual ranchers thus exemplify the diffuse relations of "big men" in the modernizing sector, being mediators, authoritarians, opportunists and counselors. Such men, who straddle sectors, exercise great influence and gain prestige in each.

If the "Chief" exemplifies the maximalist possibilities of the individual rancher, an optimalist option also exists. An individual rancher has an intrinsically assymmetrical relationship to the Groups which surround him. Through his influence and often his joint membership, he may gain access to the Group ranch for his own cattle in times of drought, thus making viable an environmentally difficult circumscription of an exclusive pastoral territory in a land which has evolved *semi-nomadic* pastoralism for good reason. On the other hand, the very limited nature of his ranch precludes his reciprocating by allowing Group Ranch members to use his resources. In effect, the individual ranches diminish the viability of nearby Groups, through which they gain their own viability. Insofar as an individual rancher utilizes this asymmetry of attracting benefits to himself while narrowing the channels of exchange by which he interacts with neighboring pastoralists, he pursues an optimal strategy.

The optimal strategy is best exemplified, however, by politicians, who are, of course, also holders of individual ranches. They are the most visible representation of the national government in the local area, by their position as much as by their actual presence. The relationships between politicians and pastoralists are invariably few; the politician requires generalized support during general elections, while the local Maasai see the politician as an individual with benefits to dispense. Indeed, government resources, such as health services, programs of development, inputs such as cattle dips, water sources, and veterinary services, come from a source outside that of the local system, and are considered to depend on the abilities of the politician. If the Government Chief and the average individual rancher have influence over ordinary Maasai, the politician rarely needs to exercise influence as such; rather, he is a man elevated above the normal because of his charisma and governmental power, who can at little personal expense make benefits available to the people.

If governmental resources anchor the powers of the politician, they also embody the specialized purview of the bureaucrat. The minimalist strategy is represented in Maasailand by two rather different classes: (1) civil servants who administer offices and agencies rather than dispense largesse, and (2) the petty traders, who interact with the public over a narrow range of goods for which cash is exchanged. In both cases, the powers of the minimalists are narrow and specialized and are derived from outside of Maasailand, either from the government or the market system.

Given the commercial nature of trade, it is appropriate for the trader to limit his social relations to that domain and minimize the strain which generalized reciprocity would put upon his business. Indeed, the large number of outsiders engaged in trade in Maasailand may be partially explained by the difficulty experienced by Maasai traders in limiting their social relations to the commercial channel in a locale where relations have been traditionally diffuse, if not maximized. Civil servants, teachers included, have other reasons to narrow their social purview, being exemplars of salaried individuals upon whom social demands easily fall because of the reliability and liquidity of their periodic resource. The majority of individuals emerging from Maasai educational institutions aspire to the security of a position in the civil service and invariably partially detach themselves from the diffuse ties which integrate them with the network of Maasai social relations. Traders in Maasailand from other ethnic groups may well be kept at some social distance, or even rejected, thereby representing in the modern sector a modified counterpart to the blacksmith. But just as a certain grudging admiration was accorded to the blacksmith for his skills, so the civil servant is the recipient of a certain prestige based on the services he performs and the educational level he has attained. It is a rude shock, however, for many young, educated persons to return to Maasailand with or without a secure position in the civil service to find that their local influence has not increased along with their education and does not increase as they, of necessity, loosen the ties with their kinsmen. Despite Group Ranch membership, their involvement in groups may be slight.

The pessimal strategy, along with the minimalist strategy, is likely to predominate within the emerging class system of Maasailand. The pastoral sector, in general, is largely composed of members of Group Ranches, which are already and will increasingly be plagued by problems of resource limitation, social and political schisms, political and economic pressures, higher taxation, and increasing population. Without joining doomsayers in projections which ignore pastoral resiliency and environmental plasticity, I can suggest that the average pastoralist in the Group Ranch relates to the classes of individual ranchers and other political factions from a pessimal perspective, as best illustrated by the asymmetrical exchange of pastoral resources between Individual and Group Ranches. With increasing government intervention and extension into the pastoral sector, the resources needed for the pastoral pursuit (innoculations, dips, boreholes, fencing, sprays, etc.) will lie outside the ability of the pastoralist to produce, just as the decisions regarding livestock management, marketing and pricing will be beyond him and will be taken by others. As a result of the increased population of ranches, combined with the limits on their growth implied by the nature of ''land'', many individuals will be marginalized; those without education may become agricultural laborers, while those with the educational capacity to function in the wider economy will become wage laborers or the urban poor, such as those who increasingly inhabit the small rural towns of Maasailand. In both cases of marginal pastoralism and marginal wage-labor, the occupational token will be dependency on those whose independence has been secured in one of the other emerging classes of Maasailand. Those who increasingly lack power but whose abilities are derived from their experience in pastoralism or from primary education, radically contrast with the Politicians, whose power is derived from outside, along with the honor and prestige which the marginal pastoralist will increasingly lack.

Relevant to the impact of social change on Maasai-land, this discussion has identified classes characterized by the four exchange strategies which relate to a transformed pastoral sector and the urban-based nationally-oriented sector (see Table 6). The maximal/minimal pole contrasts two groups: those who are most intensely involved with a wide range of persons and classes, including the continuing pastoral sector; and those who are minimally involved with others through restricted channels of a commercial or bureaucratic nature.

The private ownership of land by individuals is a mark of influence and becomes a factor in generating further influence as the Individual Rancher increasingly becomes an ideal social image for the pastoral sector. While the skills and capacities of the Government Chief and the Individual Ranchers lie within the scope of the society at large, the skills of the minimalist trader or civil servant are derived from outside pastoral society and as such are specialized and of limited influence. The dimension of social involvement and influence is apparently based on the premise of symmetrical exchange, though of two types: generalized with multiple channels versus balanced with limited channels.

Table 6

Ethno-economic Classes: Social Change

Strategies	National Sector	Ranching Sector
MAXIMAL	Government Chiefs	Individual Ranchers/Big Men
OPTIMAL	Politicians	Individual Ranchers/Rich Men
MINIMAL	Civil Servants/Traders	Group Ranchers/Isolated
PESSIMAL	Urban poor/Wage laborers	Group Ranchers/Poor pastoralists

The optimal/pessimal dimension contrasts the pole of the Politicians, whose unique capacities represent the resources of government, with the pole of the Group Rancher, whose pastoral resources are diluted by collective yet increasingly non-viable modes of ownership. In the optimal strategy, the channels of exchange are minimized primarily because the holding of privileged access to government makes general exchange less beneficial; in the pessimal strategy, the lack of resources makes maximization desirable but unobtainable, since the pessimalist has little to offer. This asymmetrical dimension involves exploitation, as optimalists can demand more and pessimalists must give more. With wealth and prerogatives come honor and prestige.

The combination of the maximalist and optimalist appears dominant and monopolizes prestige in the emergent class system. Each controls key resources, within and without the pastoral sector, though this control and prestige are transformed into distinct characteristics, i.e., influence vs. honor. The combination of the minimalist and pessimalist represents the nondominant classes of low control over resources: the tradesmen and civil servants marginalized (though recipients of their own store of esteem) and the Group Ranchers submerged. Lack of influence and lack of honor are not equivalent, however, for if generalized pollution is to be attributed to the pastoralists of the future who lack honor (in an urban-oriented class system), no comparable pollution will hold with respect to the minimalists, whose influence, however, is limited to their specialization.

This contrast of inequalities may appear to identify the dominant axis of future relations. But it seems likely that the issue of governmental resources will not serve to define a permanent class apart from that of civil servants and bureaucrats, for politicians are transient and government services affecting the pastoral sector are often fickle. It might be tentatively suggested that in the future the dominant pole will be defined not by a coalition of the maximalist and optimalist, but as a result of the coalescing of the maximalist and pessimalist groups into categories of individual vs. collective land-holders, as opposed to the temporary politicians of irrelevant honor, and the permanent petit bourgeois sector of marginal pastoral influence. If the governmental and state forces from without have the appearance of dominance, the relationships to the land will have enduring consequences for class-based relations in Maasailand, supplanting cattle as the major medium of symbolic exchange, value and quality.

By identifying two relatively distinct systems of class, I do not imply that the classes of the first have been or are being neatly transformed into the classes of the second. In actuality the opposite is true, as the paths between systems traced by social and spatial migrations of individuals and families are complex and varied. What I have suggested is that the *terms* by which categories of inequality were defined in the first system have been transformed into the *terms* of definition in the second (cf. Tables 3 & 4). From a cultural perspective, one can analyze the nature of class by scrutinizing—as we have—the symbolic features by which class categories are distinguished and discriminated. In effect, a cultural account of Maasai class may be possible.

Between optimal and pessimal strategies, one can detect the contrast of honor and degradation, refinement and lack of discrimination, underpinned by net gain and loss in the exchanges of life. Between maximal and minimal, one can find the contrast of influence and marginality, and general activity with narrow passivity, defined by the difference in density of exchanges and concommitant degrees of sociability. Between maximal-optimal and minimal-pessimal strategies we find a contrast of general prestige and control with lack of prestige and control—a general hierarchy. But between the maximal-pessimal and optimal-minimal poles, the contrast becomes the feature of pastorally-bound with externally-derived resources.

While, in the first system, *cattle* represented the means of expression of all strategies, in the second system *land* represented a narrower emphasis, combined with government resources and influence. But I would maintain that as land relations become more rigid, the strategies of maximalist Individual Ranchers will become optimalist, and the symmetrical features of influence and sociability will be subserved to the asymmetrical features of honor, accumulation, hierarchy and the emergence of class based on the control of land, in a society which once knew only the process of ''pasturing''.

REFERENCES

DUPRÉ, Georges, and Pierre REY
   1978   "Reflections on the Relevance of a Theory of the History of Exchange". In: D. Seddon, ed., *Relations of Production, Marxist Approaches to Economic Anthropology*. London: Frank Cass.
EVANS-PRITCHARD, E. E.
   1940   *The Nuer*. Oxford University Press.
GALATY, John
   1977   *In the Pastoral Image: The Dialectic of Maasai Identity*. Ph.D. Dissertation. University of Chicago.
   1979a *Ritual Performatives and Performative Rituals: The Ceremonial Cycle of the Maasai Age-Group System. The "Great Feast Cycle" Seminar.* Michigan State University, May 1979.
   1979b "Pollution and Pastoral Antipraxis: The Issue of Maasai Inequality". *American Ethnologist*, 6,4: 803-816.
   1980a "The Maasai Group-Ranch: Politics and Development in an African Pastoral Society". In: P. Salzman, ed., *When Nomads Settle*. New York: Praeger.
   1980b "Models and Metaphors: On the Semiotic Explanation of Segmentary Systems." In: L. Holy & M. Stuchlik, eds., *The Structure of Folk Models*. ASA 20. New York: Academic Press.
   1980c *East African Hunters in a Regional Perspective: An 'Ethnoanthropological' Approach*. 2nd International Conference on Hunting and Gathering Societies. Québec, Canada.
   1981   "Organizations for Pastoral Development: Contexts of Causality, Change and Assessment". In: J. Galaty, D. Aronson & P. Salzman, eds., *The Future of Pastoral Peoples*. Ottawa: International Development Research Centre.
   1982   "Being 'Maasai', Being 'People-of-Cattle': Ethic Shifters in East Africa". *American Ethnologist*, Vol. 9, No. 1 (February).
HEYER, J., Maitha, J. K., and Senga, W., ed.
   1976   *Agricultural Development in Kenya: an economic assessment.* Nairobi: Oxford University Press.
LLEWELYN-DAVIES, Melissa
   n.d.   *Women, Warriors and Patriarchs.*
MARRIOTT, McKim
   1976   "Hindu Transactions: Diversity without Dualism". In: B. Kapferer, ed., *Transaction and Meaning: Directions in the Anthropology of Exchange and Symbolic Behavior*. Philadelphia: ISHI Press.
OKOTH-OGENDO
   1976   "African Land Tenure Reform". In: Heyer, et al.
RIGBY, Peter
   n.d.   "Pastoralist Production and Socialist Transformation in Tanzania". Forthcoming in: P. Salzman and J. Galaty, eds., *Nomads in a Changing World*. Philadelphia: ISHI Press.
SAHLINS, Marshal
   1965   "On the Sociology of Primitive Exchange". In: M. Banton, ed., *The Relevance of Models for Social Anthropology*. ASAI. London: Tavistock Publications.
SCHNEIDER, H. K.
   n.d.   "Development and the Pastoralists of East Africa". Forthcoming in: P. Salzman and J. Galaty, eds., *Nomads in a Changing World*. Philadelphia: ISHI Press.
   1979   *Livestock and Equality in East Africa: The Economic Basis for Social Structure*. Bloomington and London: Indiana University Press.
SMITH, L. D.
   1976   "An Overview of Agricultural Development Policy". In: Heyer, et al.
SWYNNERTON, R. J. M.
   1954   *A Plan to Intensify the Development of African Agriculture in Kenya*. Nairobi: Government Printer.

NOTES

1 The present paper is an outgrowth of the essay, "The Maasai Group Ranch: Politics and Development in an African Pastoral Society" (Galaty 1980a), which was presented to the Symposium on Change and Development in Nomadic Societies at the Xth International Congress of Anthropological and Ethnological Sciences in Delhi, December 1978. I wish to acknowledge a travel grant from the Smithsonian Institute, arranged through the Commission on Nomadic Peoples, which made my attendance in Delhi possible. This paper was first presented at the 1980 Meetings of the Canadian Ethnological Society held in Montreal. Comments on the initial draft made by Dan Aronson and Philip Salzman were greatly appreciated.

2 The paper is based, in part, on material gathered during study among the Kenyan Maasai in 1974-5. For support and facilitation of that study, acknowledgement is due to NSF Doctoral Dissertation Grant (Number 74-24627), the Bureau of Educational Research of the University of Nairobi, and the Department of Anthropology of the University of Chicago (Galaty 1977).

3 This transformation of pastoral systems of land tenure was provided for in the section on the development of Kenyan rangelands in the Swynnerton Plan (1954) and has been described in recent publications (Okoth-Ogendo 1976; Smith 1976).

4 This dual relationship is also discussed in Bonte's paper in this volume.

5 This important question of the applicability of Western notions such as 'ownership' and 'property' to pastoral societies such as the Maasai has been the object of recent discussion. Llewelyn-Davies (n.d.) maintains that the power of 'ownership' of 'property' lies with Maasai males and is expressed through the notion *a-itore*, or "rule over", entailing rights of alienation and authority over livestock and people; in contrast, female rights involve the use of livestock which are only "allocated" (*a-itodol*) to them. Rigby (n.d.), on the other hand, has denied that Western notions of property are properly applied to the relations of humans to objects in which rights are diffuse. While generally supporting Rigby's position, I recognize the need to salvage the comparative enterprise through the judicious use of general notions, where their partial and tentative nature as translation devices is understood. Such is the case in Llewelyn-Davies' analysis, where the focus is put on Maasai concepts and not on Western glosses.

6 I have elsewhere developed the nature and significance of this 'metonymical' part-whole or causal sign relationship in Maasai culture (Galaty 1979a, 1979b).

7 I would disagree with Dupré and Rey (1978) that age grades in Africa may represent a form of exploitative or 'class' relations, because of this processual dimension.

8 A perceptive discussion of the different social, political and economic significances of land and livestock as forms of capital holding may be found in Schneider (1979).

Fulbe Continuity and Change under Five Flags Atop West Africa

Territoriality, Ethnicity, Stratification, and National Integration

CHARLES FRANTZ

State University of New York, Buffalo, U.S.A.

COMMUNITIES known as Fulbe over the last millenium have spread from their putative homeland in Senegambia across the sudanic ecozone as far as Ethiopia. They have ranged from full-time nomads to full-time sedentaries; have been rural or urban; have developed systems of production that depended differentially upon a variety of animal and vegetable species; have filled a range of occupations; have participated in or developed stratification systems varying from egalitarian to distinctly inegalitarian; have varied from being peaceful and pacifistic to being aggressive and militaristic; have been politically dominant or subordinate to other ethnic/national groups; have followed several forms of mating and marriage with both other Fulbe and with non-Fulbe; have come, in various locations, to possess biogenetic characteristics quite dissimilar from those of their ancestors; have differentially accepted a variety of Muslim beliefs and practices; have retained, spread, modified, or given up primary dependence upon their language, Fulfulde; and have borrowed or developed a significant number of other customs or practices that vary in time and space.

This striking and seemingly paradoxical diversification in the social and cultural systems of people labelled 'Fulbe' attests to their successful and innovative adaptation to opportunities and challenges found in multiple biophysical and socio-cultural environments. This paper will focus on one segment of the pastoral Fulbe (Mbororo'en) who have moved into West Africa's most unusual ecozone, the montane grasslands along the south central border of Nigeria and Cameroun. The study[1] of Mbororo life in this area has several attractive features not found in most other locales. First, it has West Africa's highest elevation, its coolest weather, and some of its heaviest rainfall and best grassland. (It is also the southernmost latitude at which Fulbe are living.) Second, Fulbe immigration has been recent enough that both oral and written records are quite good and lend themselves to validity checks with comparative ease. Third, since the area was, prior to Fulbe penetration, generally unaffected by political, economic, and religious events in either the coastal or sudanic zones, there was almost no presence of Islam or of Hausa language, culture, and trade to confound the study of Fulbe adaptive changes. Finally, the area has been under the influence or hegemony of five regimes: Fombina (Adamawa), Germany, Great Britain, and then divided between independent Nigeria and Cameroun. (The immediately adjoining Banyo-Ngaoundéré area to the east was under French hegemony prior to Camerounian independence and is not considered in this paper.)

The sequence of shifting hegemonies will be used to periodize the data. However, the main temporal concern in this paper will be after 1915, when Great Britain replaced German overrule, and more particularly the period since Nigeria and Cameroun attained independence in 1960. Substantively, the focus will be on continuities and changes in settlement and land use, production and distribution, political organisation, religion, ethnicity, stratification, and integration into larger (regional, national, and international) networks or systems. These topics will be examined in the context of physio-biotic and demographic factors, the latter including both human and livestock populations. Comparing the situations on both sides of the present international boundary will enable some projections to be made about the future prospects for continuing Fulbe identity and ethnicity in the montane grasslands. Lastly, from this study some more general thoughts can be formulated about the retention or loss of ethnicity among other Fulbe and non-Fulbe pastoral communities in sub-Saharan Africa.

It is worth noting that Fulbe, like members of other ethnic and national identities, have been contingent upon the historical interaction of what analytically are distinguished as separate factors, such as biotic, climatic, edaphic, demographic, economic, political, military, religious, and intellectual. Many African ethnic groups—subnational, and even international—are the result of such factors, and their territorial boundaries have varied over time. Both ethnic groups and labels are notoriously imprecise and unstable, even when identifications and classifications exclude genetic, morphological, and linguistic criteria. Yet similar conceptual difficulties, it seems, exist with respect to other central concepts, such as peasant, pastoral, urban, subsistence, surplus, carrying capacity, nomadism, capitalism, social class, and integration. These problematics, however, need not terminate the search for better data about the past and present, and the need for subjecting such data to more critical and complementary analyses and interpretations.

Fulbe in the Montane Grasslands

The area under study, located between 5°30'-7°30' N. latitude and 10°20'-12°00' E. longitude, is divided between two nations, with portions in the Mambila District of Sardauna Division, Gongola State, Nigeria, and the Donga-Mantung Division of the North-West Province, United Republic of Cameroun. Before these two nations attained independence, the former portion was included in the Northern Cameroons, and the latter in the Southern Cameroons, both being administered by Great Britain under a mandate from the United Nations.

Mambila contains approximately 100,000 people (in 1975) and over 400,000 cattle (in 1977) living in an area of 3575 km² (1375 mi²). Rainfall varies from 1650 to 2100 mm (65 to 83 "), the mean annual temperatures around the district range from 20° to 30° C (70° to 83° F), and the elevation varies from 800 to 2100 m. In Donga-Mantung some 184,516 inhabitants (in 1976) and 240,000 cattle (in 1976) live in an area of 4340 km² (1740 mi²). Rainfall varies from 1835 to 3922 mm (72 to 154 "), but the elevation and temperature ranges are similar to those in Mambila. In general, as one goes from north to south, the amounts of rainfall and vegetation both increase, although the latter also varies considerably according to altitude. Human population density increases in the same fashion. Grazing activity during the rainy season generally occurs between 1500 and 2100 m, whereas valleys as low as 800 m are utilized by cattle during the dry season. Topographically, the grasslands extend northeastward into the somewhat lower and drier central (Adamawa) plateau of ex-French Cameroun and the Central African Empire.

Most pastoral Fulbe have migrated into the area during the past 60 years. Immigration of pastoralists into Mambila, however, was proscribed almost three decades ago, whereas new Mbororo'en (from central Nigeria) continue to arrive in Cameroun every year. The modes of movement have involved both migratory drift and direct or intentional migration (cf. Stenning 1957). Although agnatic ties have been important in choosing where to reside or move, they have not been fully deterministic criteria; hence, today, the descendants of over 50 lineages or clan-segments are found living in almost every section of the grasslands.

Mbororo'en generally live on the tops of ridges and hills, and are interspersed among several horticultural groups, the principal ones being Mambila, Yamba, and Wimbum (War, Wiya, and Tang 'clans'). At least portions of these peoples entered the montane area during the 19th century. During the last four decades, several thousand Camerounian grasslanders have moved northward into Mambila, and a smaller number from many ethnic groups have migrated from other parts of Cameroun and Nigeria to live on either side of the border. Mbororo'en—in distinction to the very small group of Town Fulbe, most of whom have been/are members of the administrative elite, merchant traders, or religious officials—now number slightly more than 10% of the total population in Mambila, and about 5% in Donga-Mantung. The *lingua franca* in Mambila is Fulfulde, whereas south of the border it is Pidgin English.

The Fombina Period[2]

According to Brackenbury (1924: 209), a few Mbororo'en may have reached the northeastern edge of the montane grasslands early in the 19th century. However, the first Fulbe whose presence is certain were probably horseborn raiders from the subcapitals of the Fombina lamidate, headquartered in Yola, before the middle of the century. Their forays, like earlier ones by

Chamba (and probably Jukun) groups, were designed to procure ivory, food, slaves and other laborers, and sexual mates, and to establish a system of paying tributes to the *lamibe* (rulers). None of the ethnic groups in the Mambila and Donga-Mantung areas were conquered and administered by the lamidates, however, although captives and tributes were periodically extracted from some villages. Unlike elsewhere in Nigeria and Cameroun, no sedentary villages (*rumde*) of non-Fulbe captives were established in the grasslands to produce crops for the town-based Fulbe.

Due to the disturbed situation, many of the horticultural communities moved to more inaccessible sites and/or fortified their villages. Despite repetitive conflict between the sub-lamidates in Fombina, and between some of them and Yola, Fulbe military success seems to have established a relatively secure and expanding zone in which a few Mbororo'en, at least seasonally, could pasture their herds. The resources needed by their cattle were generally those not utilized by the resident horticulturalists, hence an open ecological niche allowed for the introduction of a new source of food and type of productive activity in the area. From about 1875, a small but growing number of Mbororo'en occupied some of the area to the west of Banyo, Tibati and Tignère that is now included within Nigeria. Except for a few disputes over the use or control of newly discovered sites containing salt or natron, the pastoral Fulbe displayed little concern with territorial identity or the defence of particular grazing areas. In common with many pastoral Fulbe elsewhere, those in the grasslands were more interested in rights of access to pastures, water, and salt for their cattle than they were in the ownership of land. None of the Mbororo'en in the area seem to have engaged in the production of either crops or craft items.

The pastoral Fulbe, providing all the essential laborers themselves, raised cattle almost entirely for subsistence consumption; yet in making tributes and helping the *lamibe* to raid, the former made a small contribution to the lamidates' broader systems of production and exchange. Although good evidence is lacking, it seems probable that the Mbororo'en engaged modestly in voluntary and non-monetary food exchanges with horticulturalists. As the sub-lamidates' military successes brought an expansion of their territories, and as the number of pastoral Fulbe increased, a growing number of Hausa and Kanuri traders frequented the area. Most of these were itinerants and served the sedentary Fulbe, along with the dependents and captives; they mainly bartered salt, natron, phosphate and cloth for cattle, kola nuts, ivory, and slaves. Mbororo'en rarely participated in the periodic markets (which were more social, recreational, and religious than economic) of the farming communities within which they were dispersed. Numbering but a few dozen families from various lineages or clan-segments, the pastoral Fulbe were peripheral to the economic life of the grasslanders, and only slightly less so to the centers of the Fombina lamidates.

Politically, the Mbororo herding groups were essentially as autonomous and non-hierarchical as most horticultural communities in the Mambila area.

Authority was exercised in a limited fashion by the heads (*ardo'en*) of such trans-humant groups, although the senior men (*maube*) gave advice and participated in making decisions. Ties between the Mbororo'en and the town-based Fulbe were nominal and weak, and seemed to necessitate only that the former make regular gifts and payments of cattle to the latter. The pastoralists were linked only tenuously with the beliefs and rituals of Islam, the major component of the religion of various segments of the sedentary Fulbe communities.

In sum, the small number of pastoral Fulbe who entered the montane grasslands during the Fombina era were basically autonomous in their economic, political, religious, and social life. They were, however, minimally involved in exchanges which politically and economically linked them with Adamawa, and very indirectly with both trans-sudanic and trans-Saharan spheres of activity.

The German Period[3]

German control over the montane grasslands was of limited duration and significance. The sub-lamidates based at Tibati and Banyo were conquered in 1889 and 1902, respectively. In the latter year a German military station was constructed at the southern edge of the grasslands, at Mankon (Bamenda), replacing the first one built in 1889 at Bali. The grasslands thus were ad-ministratively divided by the Germans into two districts, Banyo and Mankon, but Mbororo'en lived only in Banyo.

During the period of German rule a modest number of pastoral Fulbe con-tinued to drift southward from Yola, but most of them took up residence in localities which, after 1916, were under French rather than British control. The German presence in the Mambila area helped to diminish the scale of slave-raiding and sale by town-based Fulbe, Hausa traders, and others. Many captives from montane farming communities returned to their homes, having converted to Islam and undergone other social and cultural changes. Several indigenous villages relocated themselves again in more open sites. At the same time, the slowly increasing Mbororo'en seem to have had little difficulty in grazing their herds over an increasing amount of rangeland. Virtually no efforts were made to settle them or to recruit them as workers for German plantations, businesses, or administrative-military stations.

The Mbororo'en seem to have continued with their primarily subsistence-oriented productive activities, not growing crops, becoming permanently settl-ed, or developing claims of ownership over resources utilized seasonally by their cattle. Although the Germans inaugurated the poll or head tax in 1909, it apparently was not levied on the pastoralists. Herding labor continued to be carried out by family or lineage members, and modest annual gifts or tributes were transmitted to the town-based Fulbe *lamibe*. With the southward expan-sion of the Fulbe, the number of Hausa and Kanuri traders also increased, bartering natron or salt and a few consumer goods for cattle and kola nuts.

The Mambila area was visited by itinerant cattle traders at the beginning of the 20th century and by 1910 the first of them had become permanent settlers. These traders moved well beyond the montane grasslands and their growing numbers and success led the Germans to limit their activities in order to strengthen the profitability of newly-established German firms. When World War I hostilities broke out, these savannah traders were all expelled, at least from the Bamenda region. Prior to that, however, the Mbororo'en were gradually being encouraged to sell more cattle, in order to meet an increasing demand for beef among European settlers and a rising number of African workers in the more coastal areas of Kamerun and adjoining Nigeria. Hence the autonomy of Mbororo livestock production and distribution began to be modified slightly with the intrusion of a wider market. Also, the locus of market exchange, involving not only livestock but other local and foreign commodities as well, began to shift geographically from the Fulbe lamidates and trans-Sahara on the north to the coastal southern areas and to Europe.

The authority of pastoral Fulbe *ardo'en* seems not have changed, although competition for headship probably increased with the arrival of segments of several lineages and clans to graze their cattle within the same area. The Germans seem to have made no efforts to articulate the Mbororo political system with their own, and no reforms were introduced to change or develop local government among the pastoralists. Although both livestock and human populations increased modestly, little conflict occurred during the German period between Mbororo'en and sedentary horticulturalists, probably because there was little or no scarcity of natural resources and no problem of access to them. With the spread of traders from the sudanic zone, it seems likely that the pastoral Fulbe became more familiar with Muslim beliefs and practices, even though there is little evidence that they modified their traditional religious system in any major way.

The British Mandate Period[4]

In 1915-16, German control over Kamerun passed to the British and French, the latter receiving the major portion of the colony, and the sections where the vast majority of both sedentary and migratory Fulbe lived. British administration began immediately in the southern part of the montane grasslands; one of the first measures (1916) was to invite the expelled Hausa traders to return, and a quarter was laid out for them in Mankon (Bamenda). The Mambila area was first visited by a British officer in 1917, but direct administration did not get underway there until 1926. The poll tax was reintroduced in 1917, and a tax (*jangali*) on cattle was introduced in 1921, but collections were irregular during the first years.

The League of Nations, in 1922, granted mandates to Great Britain and France to administer the former Kamerum, and similar arrangements continued under a United Nations' trusteeship until independence was granted. Instead of establishing a separate government in its mandated area, Great Britain administered the southern portion as part of Southern Nigeria (later the Eastern Region of Nigeria) and the northern portion as an integral part of

Northern Nigeria (later the Northern Region of Nigeria). The 'Southern Cameroons' under British administration voted to unite with the Republic of Cameroun in 1961, while the 'Northern Cameroons' under British administration elected to join the Republic of Nigeria the same year. The boundary between these two, located in the montane grasslands, later became the international border between Cameroun and Nigeria.[5] The dissimilar policies and practices of the British in these two areas had differential consequences in subsequent years upon Mbororo life, their interaction with non-Fulbe, and their integration into regional, national and international economic, political, and religious systems.

Significant numbers of pastoral Fulbe migrated into the grasslands after 1916, including the first ones in the southern (Bamenda) section. The verdant pastures and absence of the tsetse fly allowed for a virtual bovine explosion to occur; this, along with a rise in the horticultural populations and a growth of villages and towns, had brought, by 1940, considerable deforestation and shortages of firewood, a striking reduction in the number of wild predators of livestock, and some overgrazing and erosion. Individuals and families of many horticultural ethnic groups, both from on and off the grasslands, also began to move into new farming areas or to seek wage employment.

The Mbororo'en, particularly in Mambila, began, with British encouragement, to settle permanently and to construct homes in wet season grazing locations. Several horticultural villages, where kola nuts and cattle were traded, expanded significantly during the 1910-30 period; also, new ones were founded, often because of forced relocation, a practice first started by the Germans (Chilver 1963: 93). A few pastoral Fulbe settled near the emerging administrative or market centers in order to sell dairy products to traders, wage-earners, and others.

Mbororo production changed little before the Second World War, however, as few efforts were made by the British to improve either the quantity or quality of cattle. Market demands for beef and milk continued to rise slowly, but they by no means kept pace with the phenomenal increase in the number of cattle. Since Fulbe herds increased at a significantly higher rate than the pastoral population, it became necessary to employ *gainako* ('cowboys') to assist in herding tasks. This new pattern of an inter-ethnic division of labor subsequently expanded, as Mbororo'en became sedentary and needed workers to build houses and to cultivate newly-established gardens. Some of the non-Fulbe herders and household helpers entered easily into Mbororo employment, since the Mbororo had adopted or fostered them when they were quite young.

Along with Fulbe and their cattle, the horticulturalists were expanding in population, and, as well, beginning to diversify and intensify their food production by embarking upon the cultivation of cash crops. Interestingly, a few non-Fulbe—including both those employed as *gainako*, who were paid in livestock rather than money, and town-based administrators, traders, merchants, and religious officials—started to own a modest but growing number of cows. Serious competition for access to and control of natural resources thus began in the 1930s, and it was to become increasingly important in subsequent decades.

During and after World War II, the British implemented a number of regulations that brought significant changes in both the production and distribution of livestock products. One measure proscribed the further immigration of cattle into the Mambila area; and other measures, affecting Mambila and Bamenda areas, introduced a program of demarcating the land into grazing and farming zones, placed limitations on the size of herds and the minimum number of herdsmen required to care for them, inaugurated innoculation, stock improvement, and milk and butter production programs, and provided for the creation and stimulation of regular cattle markets.

Before 1940, Mbororo'en were engaging in market exchanges through the medium of money, although bartering still was more common. Much of this inter-ethnic trade was dyadic between Mbororo and non-Mbororo women, especially for firewood and foodstuffs. The horticulturalists neither drank milk nor used cattle for plowing; and, unlike the situation in much of the savannah ecozone, cattle dung had little exchange value. The circumstance was due to the fact that the farmers generally practiced crop rotation, contouring, intercropping and fallowing, and during these activities they often grew *yom* (*Tepharosia vogeli*), a nitrogenous legume of considerable value as fertilizer.

Pastoral Fulbe participated only minimally in the markets held every eight (Bamenda), ten (Mambila), or seven days (where villages had concentrations of Muslims). Cattle were sold both at pastoralists' residences and, increasingly, at established cattle markets, which were not necessarily held on the same days as those of the farming communities. Most sale livestock were not eaten locally, but rather were for urban consumption and might be driven by foot up to 800 km away. During the Second World War, there was a striking increase in the external demand for beef, not only to supply soldiers in both Nigeria and Cameroun, but also for the growing populations of Africans and Europeans. Later, mainly after the War had ended, a demand for cowhides began to arise.

Motor roads did not reach the Donga-Mantung area until 1946 and the Mambila area until 1963, following Nigeria's independence. Even though until very recently most goods—other than cattle—were transported on donkeys, or more commonly on the heads or shoulders of humans, the grassland peoples increasingly became involved in progressively-widening spheres of exchange. The sedentarization of the Mbororo'en, combined with increased commercial sales of cattle, generated more demand for manufactured clothing, kerosene, utensils, and other consumer goods. A few Mbororo'en in Southern Cameroons began to sell stock without their fathers' permission, and to purchase commercial beer, tobacco, expensive jewelry and clothing, and the services of prostitutes.

Throughout the period of British administration, most pastoral Fulbe continued to distribute cattle to kinsmen and friends at traditional ceremonial occasions. Similarly, customary tributes or gifts to political leaders among the

Town Fulbe continued, although other cattle were transferred to the *lamibe* and his subordinates through extortion and bribery. This pattern was more common in Mambila and accompanied the 'indirect' system of administration practised in the Northern Region of Nigeria. Through this practise, officials of Fombina Lamidate, based at Yola, actually strengthened their influence over both Fulbe and non-Fulbe, whether they were pastoralists, horticulturalists, or urban-dwellers.

Possibly of greater importance than the serving of consumption and social needs, however, was the sale of cattle in order to pay the annual *jangali* tax, and to a lesser extent, the head tax on adult males and various fees for innoculation, slaughter, or the sale or transit of livestock. Although Mbororo'en generally sought to evade, deceive, bargain, or bribe persons doing the censuses, the open terrain of the montane grasslands probably contributed to more accurate population assessment than did the savannah locations. In any case, *jangali* was, throughout the British colonial period, the major source of revenue for differing levels of government—local authorities, districts, divisions, and provinces. The need to generate sufficient income to pay for colonial administrative costs paradoxically, therefore, worked in contradiction to the efforts to limit the total cattle population and to encourage sales outside the grasslands.

The political role of the pastoral Fulbe in Mambila and Donga-Mantung were quite dissimilar during the British period. In both areas, though, many *ardo'en* were made responsible for the collection of *jangali* from all the Mbororo'en who lived within a specific territory (ardoate), irrespective of lineage affiliation. Since the administration allowed them to retain 5-15% of the tax collected, the *ardo'en* usually sought to increase both their followings and the number of cattle being grazed; this, in turn, led to the growth of illegal migration, bribery, and extortion. In addition, the practice generated so much competition and fission among lineages and clan-segments that the administration was forced to establish several new ardoates.

In Mambila, the British created a dual administrative structure, one involving non-Fulbe village headmen (*arnabe*) and the other embracing Mbororo *ardo'en*.[6] The District Headship, a new and appointive office, has been filled by a Pullo ever since German control ended. The *ardo'en*, encouraged by the combined British-Adamawa system of 'indirect rule', exercised considerably more authority over both their fellow pastoralists and horticulturalists than was true in the Southern Cameroons. Although the pastoral Fulbe comprised only about 10% of Mambila's population, they were predominant in the major positions of power and authority. For example, one crucial area was membership in the Cattle Control (or Land Use) Committees which had been established to demarcate land for the exclusive use of farmers or graziers. Other positions included those in local administration offices, the veterinary department, local councils, and *ad hoc* commissions to investigate disputes between farmers and graziers. Generally speaking, the interests of the Mbororo'en were more frequently upheld or strengthened than were those of

horticulturalists in Mambila, while the reverse was true in the Southern
Cameroons.

In the Northern Cameroons, Great Britain directly encouraged the spread
of Islam through its overt support of *shari'a* courts, Koranic education, construction of mosques, and the assignment of religious teachers. The teachers,
along with Muslim merchants from the Northern Region of Nigeria, helped to
spread Islam, many elements of urban Hausa (and/or Town Fulbe) culture,
and the Hausa language among both Mbororo'en and other ethnic groups
(Frantz 1972b). Such efforts received only minimal support in the Southern
Cameroons, however, since European (or Afro-European) culture, Christianity, and Pidgin English were spreading rapidly.

Overall, the pastoral Fulbe in the Southern Cameroons were at a greater
disadvantage under British rule than were those north of the border. Since they
had arrived in the Bamenda area only after the British had taken over from the
Germans, both the officials and the farming population considered them to be
strangers, transients, and non-citizens; and, as such, they were not entitled to
permanent ownership or usufruct rights to natural resources. Constituting a
smaller percentage of the total population, the Mbororo'en had come into an
area of higher population density and more intensive farming. They were not
encouraged by the administration to construct permanent homes and were
prohibited from establishing gardens. Due to greater pressures on the land,
measures such as the demarcation of farming and grazing zones were introduced earlier than in Mambila. Conflicts between horticulturalists and
pastoralists soon became more frequent and intense, especially after cash cropping (mainly of coffee) became widely practised from the 1940s onward.

Nevertheless, officials allowed Mbororo immigration into Southern
Cameroons to continue, as some of the less fertile sections were not being
utilized for either crop or animal production. In addition, several horticulturalists began to convert some of their profits into purchasing cattle. Over
much of this period, the British prohibited the export of market cattle from the
Southern to the Northern Cameroons. Instead, it stimulated a transient trade
in Northern Cameroonian cattle that were destined for markets near the Atlantic coast. Cattle traders no longer were entirely Hausa or Kanuri, as newer
ones came from southern Nigerian or Cameroonian ethnic backgrounds. Consumer goods also were imported into the Bamenda area largely from coastal
Nigeria and Cameroon, rather than from Northern Nigeria, particularly after
motor transportation became possible.

Ardo'en in the Southern Cameroons were not allowed to exercise as much
authority as those in the Northern Cameroons. In addition, although a large
proportion of local revenues frequently came from *jangali* collections, virtually
no Fulbe served on local, district, or divisional councils. At least three attempts
were made to establish Fulbe councils in Bamenda, but these failed, in part
because the British could not find sufficient justification for their existence. In
the provincial context, the Mbororo'en were quite unimportant in the
Southern Cameroons. Their most likely allies were the Islamicized Bamum,

and both the pastoral and sedentary Fulbe, who lived across the border with Francophone Cameroun.

Since the Southern Cameroons was administratively linked to the more Christianized and Europeanized Eastern Region of Nigeria, the Mbororo'en living there were less subject to the informal processes of Islamicization and Hausafication. The preservation of the pastoralists' moral code (*pulaaku*), rituals, and control over the behavior of family members was more difficult. Also, the greater exposure to town life and secular schools generated more acculturation to European norms than occurred among the pastoral Fulbe in Mambila. Ethnic cohesion, if not ethnic identity, among the Mbororo'en in the Southern Cameroons was weakening somewhat by the end of the British epoch. While some pastoral Fulbe had become quite wealthy, possessing capital well above the mean among the horticulturalists, as an ethnic group or category their status was perceptibly lower than that of the numerically preponderant horticultural societies among whom they lived—particularly in terms of prestige and in having access to, or control over, crucial natural resources.

Independent Nigeria[7]

The inhabitants of the Northern Cameroons under British administration voted to join independent (1960) Nigeria in 1961. Since then, the population of Mbororo'en in Mambila has continued to grow, although less than that of non-Fulbe, especially since many of the latter have immigrated from both Cameroun and other parts of Nigeria. More new villages have formed as the result of building motor roads and of the government's efforts to resettle them. Other villages have expanded, with the result that several settlements now number from one to five thousand inhabitants each. All pastoral Fulbe now have permanent homes situated in rainy season grazing areas, and most have surrounded them with gardens of vegetables and grains. A small percentage have also erected homes in villages or towns.

The livestock population has also risen since 1961, but due entirely to natural increase rather than immigration. Until 1974 the Camerounian government permitted surplus Mambila cattle to graze within its boundaries during the dry season, since there was a shortage in Mambila. The termination of this arrangement, in combination with a moderate drought in 1977, resulted in Mambila's cattle declining an estimated 20%. Since Nigerian independence, the government has sought to intensify production and sale not only of cattle, but also of agricultural and forestry commodities. The regulations controlling the health of livestock, the location of both wet and dry season grazing, and the demarcation and fencing of farming, grazing, and forestry areas have been extended. Farmers and stock-owners have continued trying to increase the size of areas reserved for their respective types of production. Support for these perceived alternatives has come from the agricultural and veterinary branches of government, to which should be added a third party, forestry officials. Following Independence, the government commissioned two extensive surveys of the area's economic potential (see Bawden and Tuley 1966, and Nigeria 1973), and engaged a foreign firm to draft and help implement a plan to develop all sections of Mambila's economy. One of these programs, a commercial cattle ranch, has recently been inaugurated by the government.

Selective breeding and sale have been used by the pastoral Fulbe to modify the age, sex, and sub-species composition of their cattle. Almost all cattle are now owned by individuals rather than extended families and lineages, although kin- and neighborhood-based cooperative herding continues. Some men, especially *ardo'en*, own from 1000 to 5000 head of cattle. The proportion of the district's cattle which is owned by non-Mbororo'en has also continued to rise, and several now possess more than 100 head each. The herding of pastoral Fulbe livestock is progressively being done by *gainako* from other ethnic backgrounds, and increasingly such labor is being paid for in cash. Several young Mbororo men have withdrawn from animal husbandry, and have moved to towns, where they either become traders or governmental workers, or remain unemployed.

Pastoral Fulbe cattle-rearing since 1961 has been transformed from a primary orientation toward subsistence to one of production for market. Symbiotic exchanges of food between Mbororo'en and non-Mbororo'en have virtually disappeared. Money has increasingly replaced livestock in filling the pastoralists' kinship obligations. The giving of tributes or gifts to lamidate officials has diminished considerably since Nigerian Independence, but gratuities and bribes in cattle or cash have become more common in local politics. Pastoral Fulbe are now using their new income to pay for permanent homes in rural, and sometimes village, areas; for planting commercially valuable eucalyptus trees; and for foods, medicines, clothing, radios, beer, tobacco, horses, motor vehicles, furniture, and other household and luxury goods. A number of *ardo'en* and wealthy traders have also marketed cattle in order to undertake the *hajj* to Mecca.

These changes reflect the dramatic increase in the extent to which cattle are being marketed, as well as the continually expanding margins of profit. The number of cattle markets and volume of trade have grown considerably as the demand for beef has risen both in and out of the montane grasslands. The desire for consuming meat reflects a number of factors, including the growth of urban populations and wage-earners, the rise in Nigeria's gross national income (particularly after the extensive exploitation of oil got underway), and the expansion of its military forces. For about a decade, Nigerian cattle have been unable to fill the almost revolutionary increase in beef demand, hence the government has had to import animals from neighboring nations, as well as meat from overseas. In addition, extended drought conditions throughout most of the savannah and sahel ecozones from 1970 exacerbated this shortage.

The inflation of beef prices has contributed to a widening of the income differentials among Mbororo'en, as well as between them and other ethnic groups. In 1976 Nigeria abolished the *jangali* tax throughout the nation, in order to encourage the marketing of cattle. Beyond the owners' increased profits, it is not clear how this measure has affected livestock production and exchange, in Mambila and elsewhere. The local governments' lost revenues, however, are more than compensated for by the allocations being made by the provincial and federal governments.

Cattle agents and dealers, and to a lesser extent butchers, are no longer solely persons with Hausa or Kanuri ethnic backgrounds. Several Mbororo'en, Town Fulbe, and non-Fulbe have begun to take up these occupations, often on a part-time basis. Most of these men are associated with established long-distance trading networks, and are sub-agents or clients to experienced dealers rather than being fully independent.

The sedentarization of the pastoralists and remission of a portion of *jangali* revenues to the *ardo'en* contributed to generating more pressure for creating new ardoates. By 1976 these had increased to 22, in addition to which there were three village-based areas in which Town Fulbe or Hausa served as *jangali* collectors. At the district and divisional levels of government, before civilian government was suspended in 1966, the majority of the council members were Mbororo'en, Town Fulbe, or Hausa; and a number of the remainder were non-Fulbe village headmen who had converted to Islam (and thereby had changes of title from *arnabe* to *jauro'en*). Essentially the same ethnic composition prevailed in the Cattle Control (or Land Use) Committee, which decided upon the demarcation of land into farming and grazing zones. (In the last decade, the situation has changed considerably, although the District Head [Chief] remains a Pullo; the predominant ethnic group in the district, Mambilas, have attained local political control. The district council of eleven members in 1977 contained only four Mbororo'en and Town Fulbe, two of whom were appointed and two elected.)

The diminished political influence of Mbororo'en in Mambila is related to the political transformation in all of Nigeria, and especially in the northern states, since 1966 (cf. Azarya 1978). The future allocation of the montane grasslands for farming, grazing, forestry, and town and industrial development is likely, therefore, to be affected by the changing ethnic composition of its legislative and executive organs. The increasing penetration of federal agencies, funds, and programs for bringing economic, political, and social changes will also be of growing importance.

Religious, marital, recreational, educational, and ideational changes have also occurred as Mambila has become increasingly integrated into wider spheres of communication and exchange. The Mbororo'en have given up such ceremonies as the *soro*, *gerewol*, and *luggol* marriage; polygyny, lineage exogamy, prostitution, and inter-ethnic marriages have increased. Adherence to Muslim beliefs and practices has become more regular, largely as a result of the influence of the Reformed *Tijanniya* and Shaykh Ibrahim b. Abdullahi Niass of Kaolack, Senegal, but in part because of Mbororo sedentarization and their increased interaction with Town Fulbe and Hausa. However, the elders (*maube*) have resisted the implementation of Koranic inheritance rules with respect to their cattle estates since this would fragment herds and make them less viable for their heirs. These rules have already generated considerable conflict between fathers and sons. Smoking tobacco, consuming commercial beer, and visiting prostitutes have increased noticeably since 1971, particularly among the younger men. The use of Fulfulde as a *lingua franca* is being challenged increasingly by the spread of Hausa and English. The introduction of universal primary education is bringing in new ideas and attitudes which are affecting Mbororo'en and non-Mbororo'en alike. The full consequences of this are not yet clear, but one of the first effects has been on the ethnic and age composition of the cattle-herding labor force.

Independent Cameroun[8]

In 1961 the inhabitants of the Southern Cameroons under British administration voted to federate with the Republic of Cameroun, which had gained independence from France the previous year. A constitutional change establishing the United Republic of Cameroun was approved in 1972. The Mbororo'en in Donga-Mantung Division during the decade of the 1970s experienced somewhat different, but perhaps equally extensive, changes than their counterparts across the border in Mambila. The population of farmers, pastoralists and cattle, which already was significantly higher in Donga-Mantung than in Mambila, continued to grow without interruption. Considerable grazing land was put into crop production, and other areas were settled for the first time by newly-arriving Mbororo'en.

Previously the government had been less insistent on and supportive of Mbororo sedentarization, and only in 1965 did it give them permission to build vegetable and cereal gardens next to their homesteads. By then, most pastoral Fulbe had already become sedentary, although continuing to engage in transhumant movements. Nevertheless, considerable numbers of nomadic Mbororo'en continued, and continue up to the present, to drift or migrate into Donga-Mantung from central Nigeria. (Terminologically, these new families, lineages, and clan-segments are classified as *Aku'en*, but this term is both imprecise and has derogatory implications.) Some of these newcomers were transients, and within a few years moved eastward to less populated areas of the Adamawa Plateau in east central Cameroun and the Central African Empire. (A few of the pastoral Fulbe who arrived in previous decades also relocated in this fashion.) Others shifted from nomadic to semi-sedentary residences within the less verdant portions of Donga-Mantung and adjoining Menchum Divisions, west of the sections in which the earlier arrivals lived. Occupying an ecozone that is lower in elevation, hotter and drier, and has a more savannah type of vegetation, these Mbororo'en raised herds primarily composed of subspecies that are thought to be more resistant to trypanosomiasis.

The British government's active program of demarcating lands into farming and grazing zones fell into abeyance soon after its introduction in the early

1940s, mainly because it imposed a framework of land use and control that did not give sufficient attention to dynamic demographic and economic factors. Since World War II, a veritable agricultural revolution has taken place. Crop production intensified greatly through contouring, intercropping and multicropping, and the raising of cash crops (especially coffee, which has surpassed kola nuts as the chief source of income). The raising of chickens, building of small dams and stocking of ponds with fish, the creation of cooperative milling and marketing societies, and various other community development projects have helped transform the horticultural economy. Competition for access to and control of natural resources has thus become progressively intense—considerably exceeding that in Mambila—and consequently it has generated much inter-communal tension, with subsequent litigation, mediation, and adjudication. One of the principal causes of conflict has been the recurrent practice of farm women entering demarcated grazing areas to open up new farm plots illegally (cf. Kaberry 1960).

These dynamic changes in the agricultural sector have placed quite strong constraints upon livestock expansion, not only by Mbororo'en but also by an increasing number of individuals from horticultural communities. As of 1973, non-Fulbe were reported to own 26% of the cattle, and they were generally reluctant to remove their stock to government-designated dry season grazing areas, arguing that they had plentiful crop residues from which cattle could obtain adequate nutrition. Overall, as grazing land continued to be converted to crop production, the pastoral Fulbe suffered in attempting to maintain or expand the size of their herds.

The Camerounian government's efforts to improve animal husbandry have generally followed the directions initiated by the British, but their impact continues to be limited. Innoculation measures, rotational grazing, and the creation of cattle markets have been augmented, resulting in some measure of success, whereas efforts to improve the quality and quantity of meat, milk, and dairy products have been less effective. A commercial ranch was recently established by the government, using funds partly from the World Bank, to produce more beef for southern markets, but this venture was neither intended for, nor has it had any noticeable impact upon, the local population's system of animal husbandry. Even more recently, the government has introduced a program for making loans to farmers and graziers to increase and/or diversify their production; the effects of this are not yet known, but the plan seems likely to favor wealthier applicants. Legally, the insecurity facing pastoral Fulbe regarding rights of access to natural resources for their livestock continued in 1974. In that year, the government passed an ordinance declaring all grazing areas of the Republic to be 'national lands'.

The Mbororo'en rely considerably upon non-Fulbe laborers to work their gardens and construct their homes. However, because their herds are smaller than those of the pastoralists in Mambila, fewer non-Fulbe *gainako* need to be employed. In addition, it is more difficult to attract them as employees since they are likely to be Christians instead of Muslims, better educated in

Western-secular schools, and to know about—if they have not experienced—living and working in towns, cities, and plantations.

Almost no symbiotic exchanges now occur between Mbororo'en and non-Mbororo'en, and the infrequent giving of livestock as gifts or gratuities to horticultural headmen and chiefs has diminished even more. Among themselves, money has almost entirely replaced cattle in ceremonial and gift transactions. Unlike the situation in both Nigeria and francophone Cameroun, owners still pay *jangali* on their herds annually. Revenues from this source remain a significant, although gradually declining, proportion of income for local and divisional treasuries. The revolutionary change in agriculture, and particularly the expansion of cash cropping, has contributed to the decline in importance of *jangali* receipts. The provincial and national governments, since Independence, have also been increasingly responsible for funding and directing numerous economic and non-economic changes within Donga-Mantung Division.

All Mbororo'en now sell their livestock and livestock products through regular periodic markets. Little demand exists for milk and butter. In contrast, the demand for hides and bones has risen beyond the available supply. The demand for beef has risen steadily since Independence, not only locally but even more in the southern part of the nation and in Gabon and Nigeria. Cattle traders and agents in the grasslands, since they are Town Fulbe, Hausa, Mbororo'en, and Wimbun are less homogeneous ethnically than in Mambila; in turn, they are linked with Bamiléké, Ibo, and others in trade networks that serve distant areas, particularly through markets in Nkongsamba and Kumba.

The inflation in cattle prices has far surpassed the modest rise in tax rates, hence profits for cattle-owners have risen rapidly during the last few years. However, since both the average herd size and the number of Mbororo taxpayers in ardoates are lower than in Mambila, the incomes of the *ardo'en* and larger herd-owners do not reach the level found across the Nigerian border.

Unfortunately, there are no data available to show the comparative incomes of farmers and graziers, but on the basis of impression alone it is hard to discern any substantial differences. The pastoral Fulbe convert much of their income into constructing and equipping their homes, starting or embarking on small-scale crop production, acquiring consumer and luxury goods, and paying for leisure activities. These capital transfers are generally similar to those of the non-Mbororo population, except that the latter invest more in schooling for their children.

As was the case in Mambila, the prestige and income associated with being officially recognized as *ardo* have led to much personal, lineage, and clan-segment competition, fission, and residential mobility. Pastoral headmen, like their counterparts in farming communities, entice Mbororo'en to settle in the territories where they have responsibility for collecting *jangali*. By 1977, the number of *ardo'en* appointed as tax-collectors had risen to 20. (In addition, several non-Fulbe had by then been appointed to collect the tax from villagers who owned cattle, since the latter consistently objected to making payment through a Mbororo collector.)

The pastoral Fulbe have had little formal representation in the political organs of Donga-Mantung, and informally they have exercised minimal influence and power. Mbororo'en have rarely been members of local development committees or held important roles in local branches of the nation's single party, the Union National Camerounaise. Several, however, have served on temporary commissions to investigate and adjudicate disputes between farmers and graziers. However, more and more these disputes are being settled in Magistrates' Courts, and most Mbororo'en view the decisions as generally being disfavorable to them. The government, continuing the practice of the British, has not established any formal Fulbe Council. The *ardo'en*, however, are periodically brought together to learn about dry season grazing assignments and to discuss such matters as techniques of animal husbandry, marketing, and the demarcation of land problems.

Since 1972, when the United Republic of Cameroun was formed, political constraints upon the Mbororo'en in Donga-Mantung seem to have stabilized, and possibly lessened. The Head of State, President El Hadj Ahmadou Ahidjo, was born of Town Fulbe parents in the northern part of the nation (formerly under French administration). Although he has occupied this office since 1958, he seems to have had little influence upon the political, economic, and social position of the pastoral Fulbe in the montane grasslands. More important, perhaps, has been the establishment of a clear policy which asserted that Fulbe in anglophone areas are no longer to be thought of as strangers or denied the civil rights available to all citizens. The 1974 ordinance, which declared all grazing lands to be 'national lands', probably marks a significant turnabout that may increase the economic, if not the political, status of pastoralists throughout the nation. Subsequent measures can be anticipated that will bring cadastral surveys, the registration of plots, and the issuance of deeds or titles (probably of usufruct, rather than *de jure* ownership). Furthermore, since they are fully united with ex-French Cameroun the Mbororo'en in Donga-Mantung are able to interact with and possibly build alliances with Fulbe throughout the country, and with other Muslim communities, such as the Bamum.

Compared with Mambila, the pastoral Fulbe (as well as the non-Fulbe) in Donga-Mantung have undergone less Hausafication and Islamicization, although several of their customary rituals and practices have been abandoned, and the strength of *pulaaku* and the authority of elders has declined. In contrast, Christian and coastal Euro-African influences have grown stronger. Except for lesser attendance by their children in Western-secular schools, the Mbororo'en have acculturated somewhat toward southern Camerounian forms of music, language, recreation, marriage, and participation in national ceremonies, as well as having made significant changes in their food production activities.

Ethnicity and Stratification

In Mambila, the pastoral Fulbe have given up several distinctive customs, but have adopted virtually none of those practised by surrounding horticultural communities. On the other hand, they have progressively accepted many of the beliefs, ideas, and practises generally characterizing Muslim Town Fulbe/Hausa. The prestige and power of this group has spread over a wide area of the central sudanic zone and has been the model emulated by many horticulturalists (including a large segment of the Mambila ethnic group) as well as pastoralists. Mbororo'en also have been the agents of acculturation among horticulturalists, influencing them toward the Muslim Town Fulbe/Hausa way of life, through such means as inter-ethnic employment, patronage, marriage, concubinage, and adoption. Overall, the pastoral Fulbe, and, to a lesser extent, a considerable number of ethnically Mambila persons, have been progressively incorporated or assimilated into the pervasive Town Fulbe/Hausa ethnic category or system.

Among other ethnically Mambila individuals, and certainly among most Yamba and persons of several other ethnic groups residing in the district, the contrary has been true. For them, the acculturative model has been less cohesive or singular, and is tied in with the more Christianized and Europeanized peoples of coastal Nigeria and Cameroun. Rarely, however, do these non-Fulbe serve as agents of acculturation for individuals from pastoral or urban Fulbe and Hausa backgrounds.

Continuities and changes in Mbororo ethnic identity and consciousness have been similar in the Camerounian grasslands, although the relative importance of the two models for acculturation is the obverse of that in Mambila. Distinctive social and cultural differences between horticultural ethnic groups have by no means disappeared, but all are being influenced considerably by the northward spread of Christianity and coastal Euro-African culture. The pastoral Fulbe in Donga-Mantung have become more 'Westernized' in some of their habits, but their ethnic consciousness and identity remain basically intact.

Historically, relations between Mbororo'en and non-Mbororo'en on both sides of the international border have invariably been symbiotic, complementary, competitive, and conflictive. Yet the frequency and strength of these types of relationships have differed over both space and time, as well as the substantive area of life concerned, e.g., production or exchange, governance, or religion.

In Mambila, the Mbororo'en generally came to have higher status than other ethnic groups, chiefly because of the prestige and power of the Town Fulbe/Hausa throughout the central sudanic zone. The protection, privileges, and assistance given the pastoralists generally exceeded that given to farming communities. Interaction between pastoral and sedentary Fulbe and Hausa over a long period of time made it normal for such relationships to continue in the montane grasslands. The pastoralists' willingness to accommodate their religious beliefs and practices to Islam was reciprocated by sedentary Muslims. The rapid and successful expansion of cattle rearing by the Mbororo'en was welcomed by the Town Fulbe/Hausa, for it not only provided additional food but also a major portion of revenue to local and provincial governments.

In Donga-Mantung there were fewer opportunities for the pastoral Fulbe to build political, religious, or social and cultural links with the lamidates/emirates of the savannah zone. Power remained with horticultural ethnic groups at the local level, and with the British (and later Camerounian) officials at higher levels. The newly arrived religion, Christianity, was one foreign to the Mbororo'en and had virtually no attraction for them.

The crucial factors responsible for the differential status positions of the pastoral Fulbe in Mambila and in Donga-Mantung thus appear to have been primarily political, economic, and demographic. Clearly the conditions under which the Mbororo'en in Mambila—and to a lesser extent in Donga-Mantung—came to have much greater wealth than horticulturalists were mainly the product of political decisions about the use of land. On the other hand, a dependency upon cattle rather than crops has inherent advantages for generating wealth, *viz.*: (1) cattle increase in number faster than crops and in terms of labor expended; (2) cattle are more rapidly and more cheaply transportable to markets, particularly when only foot travel is used; (3) cattle, unlike most crops, pose no problem of storage or deterioration, although they require constant nutritional attention; and (4) cattle can be withheld from the market for longer periods, and with less damage, than can most crops, hence the chances of increasing profits are greater. All of these factors allowed for, possibly even encouraged, a more rapid expansion of livestock than crop production. Any consideration of this expansion must note the relative isolation of grassland farmers from markets where a high demand for their products might have existed. Cattle, on the other hand, were less plentiful and productive in many ecozones, and therefore a higher or unfulfilled demand existed for them in non-pastoral areas. The slower and less certain ascendancy of cattle production, and hence the status of the Mbororo'en, in Donga-Mantung seems related to its early and continuing importance as an area able to produce specialized crops (especially kola nuts, but later coffee as well) that were in high demand outside the grassland ecozone.

Thus, until recently, the Mbororo'en in Mambila have been superordinate over the horticultural populations whereas the reverse has been true in Donga-Mantung. The ethnic base which facilitated the birth and maintenance of inter-ethnic stratification has been weakened by changes over time, and it seems correct to say that pastoral Fulbe in both areas have undergone some reversal of status. Not only have political systems been modified, but, as well, the ethnic distinctions in type and scale of production have also changed noticeably, external market prices have affected the size and distribution of incomes, and the public has come to participate more in local, provincial, and national political life.

Particularly important has been the spread of cattle ownership among traditional horticulturalists and townsmen, and the more modest beginning of farming by traditional pastoralists. It appears, therefore, that superordinate-subordinate relations between ethnic groups are dissolving into class-based relations that are founded mainly upon wealth, occupation, and education.

Four status groups seem to be emerging: 1) farmers, 2) cattle-rearers, 3) skilled and unskilled workmen, most of whom receive wages or salaries and live in towns, and 4) administrators, judges, teachers, religious officials and businessmen, most of whom are urban residents also (Frantz 1972a).

The future status relations of ethnic groups will, of course, be the product of the dynamic interplay of several processes. Firstly, a high status position, once achieved, tends to generate reinforcing behavior, e.g., wealth (in cattle) among the Mbororo'en is positively related to the acquisition of more wives and concubines (*sulabe*); to sedentary settlement; to attracting kinsmen and non-kinsmen as dependents, employees, or clients; to undertaking the *hajj*; and to gaining access to loans, political office, and important decision-makers in government. Secondly, the assured access to natural resources used in producing wealth is critical, particularly when equal or greater wealth can be produced by alternate types of productive activity. Thirdly, participation in the distribution/marketing, as well as in the production, of cattle can facilitate the earning of greater profits. Fourthly, a willingness to become sedentary enhances a pastoral group's likelihood of having regular access to natural resources, the market, and political decision-makers. Fifthly, in contrast, if there are areas in which natural resources are not being fully exploited, a willingness and organizational capacity to migrate can be positively adaptive. Finally, to the degree that pastoralists can accommodate to a prevailing religious (and value) system and a government's plans for increasing production, the more likely they are to preserve their collective status in the larger system.

Conclusions and Interpretations

For longer than a century, the montane grasslands straddling the southern border of Nigeria and Cameroun have been a meeting place of two new, dissimilar, and often competing religious *cum* social-cultural systems, one based on Islam and the Town Fulbe/Hausa system of emirates/lamidates in northern Nigeria, and the other based on Christianity and coastal African-European social and cultural systems. The former has had considerable impact on the history of adaptation of the Mbororo'en who settled in the grasslands, particularly in the Mambila area, whereas the latter has been of more importance in the Donga-Mantung area.

In both countries the pastoral Fulbe have successfully occupied ecological niches in West Africa's most unusual ecozone. They and their cattle have greatly increased in number, in parallel with expansions in the horticultural population and in crop production. The Mbororo'en have made an almost complete transition from nomadic to sedentary residential patterns, and a small percentage have even moved into villages and towns. The ending of nomadism has not meant the decline of pastoralism, but rather the contrary. Cattle production has shifted from being basically subsistence-oriented to market-oriented. Pastoral Fulbe have moved from a position of marginal economic importance to one that is crucial both nationally and internationally. Most exchanges involving cattle are no longer symbiotic or by means of barter; now they occur mainly through regular markets and involve the medium of money. The geographical locale of the constantly expanding market demand has shifted over time, mainly in a southerly direction, and partly due to political factors.

Pastoralists and farmers have begun to diversify into the production of new types of food, and all have consciously aimed to intensify their output. The ethnic division of labor has also changed, especially among cattle-herders but also in the realm of traders and governmental employees. Income differentials among Mbororo'en, and between them and farming communities, have become greater, although this is more true in Mambila than in Donga-Mantung. In the latter area, where a veritable revolution in agriculture began in the 1930s, the development of cash-cropping and the widening of the market facilitated a faster rise in the income of farming communities.

As population and production increased among both pastoral and horticultural peoples, some overgrazing and erosion appeared, but other sections of the grasslands have benefitted from improved techniques of husbandry, especially in the agricultural sector. Of greater significance, perhaps, has been the intensification of competition and conflict with respect to access to and the control of natural resources. The security zone established by the town-based Fulbe *lamibe* during the Fombina epoch, together with the combined British-Adamawa system of administration, provided greater opportunities for the Mbororo'en in Mambila than their counterparts in present-day Donga-Mantung. The latter were later arrivals, they came into an area with a denser horticultural population, and their efforts to expand animal husbandry and to obtain permanent rights to land and other resources were more constrained by the economic and political policies of the British.

Politically, the pastoral Fulbe in both Mambila and Donga-Mantung successfully adapted their local organization from one based on lineage to the imposed one based on territory. *Ardo'en* in Donga-Mantung were essentially recognized only for the collection of *jangali*, while those in Mambila had considerably more authority. The former also filled an inconsequential role in local and provincial political affairs, quite in contrast with the ascendant role of the pastoralists in Mambila, who were allied to the Town Fulbe/Hausa of northern Nigeria. The Mbororo'en in both areas have undergone some status reversal in the last two decades, reflecting the differential courses of change in the two national political systems in which they are now citizens. Access to office and political support have come to depend less on lineage, ethnicity, and religion, and more on education, training, and wealth.

In religion, the Mbororo'en in both Mambila and Donga-Mantung have perceptibly shifted their beliefs and practices toward those of Islam, as practiced by the Town Fulbe/Hausa. The presence of two competing religious systems centered on opposite sides of the border, however, has divided the pastoral Fulbe less than have the national political and economic systems. In other aspects of culture, the Mbororo'en in Donga-Mantung are being influenced somewhat more than their cousins in Mambila by 'Westernized' or Euro-African forms of speech, music, dress, consumer goods, housing, and leisure activities, most of which have been moving northward from the Atlantic coast. Only recently have these non-Islamic and non-Town Fulbe/Hausa elements of culture become noticeable in Mambila; and here, particularly with the rapid expansion of universal primary education, it is possible that in the next generation the pastoral Fulbe will become more 'Westernized' than those in Donga-Mantung.

The pastoral Fulbe in both Mambila and Donga-Mantung are not completely integrated into the economic, political, religious, social, and cultural life of the provinces, nations, and the world. Yet the significance of ethnic identification has been modified, and probably diminished somewhat, as translocal systems have progressively affected them. Neither Nigeria nor Cameroun possesses national cultures at present, but both political systems have encapsulated and incorporated the Mbororo'en who live within their boundaries. This trend is likely to increase with the intensification of schooling, literacy, popular democracy, and governmental services.

In economic terms, the pastoral Fulbe in both sections of the montane grasslands are now well-integrated into market systems that extend even beyond national boundaries. Crucial problems concerning land use and land tenure remain to be worked out in both nations, and livestock production is still inadequate to fill either the goals of governments or the demands of consumers. But given the probability of continued high beef prices, and the presence of limited off-take from what will probably be a relatively unchanging amount of land used in pastoral production, it may be predicted that the processes of Mbororo integration into regional and worldwide economic systems are likely to continue without diminution. Even though the pastoral Fulbe now participate in trans-national economic spheres, their future will be greatly affected by the policies and practices of the Nigerian and Camerounian governments with respect to the allocation of land, granting of titles, credits and loans, prices, and improvements in the quality of animals, rangelands, and husbandry techniques. All these measures will increasingly be made, it seems, in the context of local, regional, and national 'development' plans.

In religion, too, the Mbororo'en have become considerably integrated into an international system, in fact one that is even broader geographically than the political and economic systems which embrace them. A large number of ethnically Mambila farmers have converted to Islam, but the majority of the non-pastoralists in the montane grasslands shifted their religious beliefs and practices towards those of Christianity. The introduction and spread of these two competing religions, since they are assoicated with historic differences in ethnic identity and types of production, has serious implications for the future integration of the Mbororo'en (and non-Mbororo'en) into wider religious systems. Such differences might become the main basis of polarization between ethnic groups, an outcome that would be contrary to the combined effect, thus far, of all the processes of integration. Any outcome will, of course, also be affected by governmental decisions and by the informal spread of secular values and 'Westernized' living styles.

In sum, the intrusion and growing acceptance of externally-generated and supra-local political, economic, and religious systems have basically trans-formed the pastoral Fulbe of the montane grasslands, both internally and in their relations with other peoples. Ethnic distinctiveness and complementarity have begun to decline, and class-based social relations are rather quickly being generated. Both national and international factors are likely to become increas-ingly important in shaping Mbororo continuity and change in the future.

Nomadic Thoughts on Ethnicity and Pastoralism in Africa

The present study raises questions of both practical and theoretical import regarding the accuracy and usefulness of the term, 'Fulbe', not only in the montane grasslands but elsewhere as well. Well beyond this locality, a single term has been used to cover individuals and communities who live primarily by pastoralism, by farming, by both, or by neither. This suggests that it may be better of speak of Fulbe simply as a category, and of those who follow dif-ferent specializations in the production and distribution of goods, in gover-nance, and so forth as segments or sections. The substantive or human characteristics of persons who either choose to label themselves, or are labelled by others, as 'Fulbe' is thus so variable that only empirical inquiry can ascer-tain the extent and meaningfulness of the term.

A related problem comes from the fact that labels as well as people migrate, and this takes at least two forms: individuals, and even groups, can shift their ethnic identity with varying degrees of ease and with non-standardized amounts of behavioral change; alternatively, persons can give up a 'traditional' label and assume or develop a new one. Illustrations of these forms are provided by the widespread incorporation of non-Fulbe into Fulbe households, on the one hand; and of sedentarized pastoralists who have come to depend primarily on horticulture, as in the case of the Toucouleur (Curtin *et al.* 1978: 99), on the other. Analagous situations exist elsewhere in Africa with, for example, peoples known as Tuareg, Maasai, Suk or Pakot, and Baqqāra.

Animal husbandry in the montane grasslands has also been taken up in some measure by non-Fulbe individuals and groups (cf. Frantz 1975), and this trend is likely to grow. The long-term consequences of this are that pastoral production need not compel either nomadic movement or an abrupt change in ethnic identity or other aspects of culture. Two implications follow from this: First, scholars should take more cognizance of the increasing presence of a 'livestock factor' in the life of many 'horticultural' societies and village/town communities; and second, officials concerned with development will need to draft and implement plans that do greater justice to the reality of dynamic changes in the degree of group dependence on multiple types of productive activity. The growing competition for access to and control of natural resources

in sub-Saharan Africa thus takes at least three forms: (1) pastoralists competing with pastoralists, as in Niger, Tchad, and the Republic of the Sudan
between Fulbe and non-Fulbe populations, or one Arabic group against
another; (2) horticulturalists competing with horticulturalists, as seen in the
Mambila area between Yamba and Mambila communities, and in Donga-
Mantung between Wimbum and Bansaw settlements; and (3) the widespread
competition between essentially pastoral and essentially horticultural peoples.

It may be suggested, finally, that while the labels, 'Fulbe' and
'Mbororo'en', have never been totally accurate or stable in time, they are progressively losing their value. The ethnic basis of many social relations in the
past are being transformed by the development of new kinds of commonalities
and differences, particularly with respect to the ownership and control of
wealth and the holding of political office. Systems of relations that are non-
ethnic and supra-local, as well as involving many people in a nation, region or
portion of the world, are becoming increasingly determinate of every 'Fulbe'
community, society, and culture.

REFERENCES

ABUBAKAR, S.
    1970   *The emirate of Fombina, 1809-1903.* Zaria: Unpublished Ph.D. dissertation, Depart
          ment of History, Ahmadu Bello University.
    1972   "The establishment of Fulbe authority in the upper Benue basin, 1809-1847",
          Savanna, 1, 67-80.
AZARYA, V.
    1978   *Aristocrats facing change: The Fulbe in Guinea, Nigeria, and Cameroon.* Chicago: University
          of Chicago Press.
BARTH, H.
    1857   *Discoveries in North and Central Africa.* New York: Harper and Bros.
BAWDEN, M. G., and TULEY, P.
    1966   *The land resources of southern Sardauna and southern Adamawa provinces, northern Nigeria.*
          Tolworth, Eng.: Land Resources Division, Directorate of Overseas Surveys, United
          Kingdom Government (Land Resources Study no. 2).
BOUTRAIS, J.
    1974a "Les conditions naturelles de l'élevage sur le plateau de l'Adamaoua (Cameroun)",
          Cahiers d'O.R.S.T.O.M., série sciences humaines, 11, 145-98.
    1974b *Études d'une zone de transhumance: la plaine de Ndop (Cameroun).* Yaoundé: Ministère du
          plan et de l'aménagement du territoire, et Office de la récherche scientifique et
          téchnique outre-mer.
BRACKENBURY, E. A.
    1924   "Notes on the 'Bororo Fulbe' or nomad 'Cattle Fulani' ", *Journal of the African socie*
          ty, 23, 208-17, 271-77.
BRAUKÄMPER, U.
    1970   *Die Einfluss des Islam auf die Geschichte und Kulturentwicklung Adamauas.* Wiesbaden:
          Franz Steiner.
    1971   "Zur kulturhistorischen Bedeutung der Hirten-Ful für die Staatswesen des Zen
          tralsudan", *Paideuma*, 17, 55-120.
BUTTNER, T.
    1964   "Zur Problemen der Staatenbildung der Fulbe in Adamawa", *Wiss. Z. Karl-Marx-*
          Universität. Ges.- und Sprachwiss. Reihe, 13, 223-57.

1966 "Die sozialökonomische Struktur Adamaus im 19. Jahrhundert", *Wiss. Z. Karl-Marx-Universität. Ges.- und Sprachwiss. Reihe*, 15, 603-26.
1967 "On the social-economic structure of Adamawa in the nineteenth century", in *Études africaines*, 43-61. Leipzig: Karl-Marx-Universität.

CARTER, J.
1967 "The Fulani in Bamenda", *Journal of tropical geography*, 55, 1-7.

CHILVER, E.
1961 "Nineteenth century trade in the Bamenda grasslands, Southern Cameroons", *Afrika und Übersee*, 45, 233-58.
1963 "Native administration in west central Cameroons 1902-1954", in K. Robinson and F. Madden (eds.) *Essays in imperial government presented to Marjorie Perham*, 89-139. Oxford: Basil Blackwell.

CHILVER, E., and KABERRY, P. M.
1960 "From tribute to tax in a Tikar chiefdom", *Africa*, 30, 1-19.
1967 *Traditional Bamenda*. Buea: Government Printer.

CURTIN, P., *et al.*
1978 *African history*. Boston: Little, Brown and Co.

DE ST. CROIX, F. W.
1945 *The Fulani of northern Nigeria*. Lagos: Government Printer.

DONGMO, J.-L.
1972 "L'élevage bovin dans l'ouest-Cameroun", *Le Cameroun agricole, pastorale et forestier*, 133, 17-29.

DUPIRE, M.
1970 *Organisation sociale des Peule: étude d'ethnographie comparée*. Paris: Plon.

FRANTZ, C.
1972a "Stratification and ecology on the Mambila plateau, Nigeria", paper read at the annual meeting of the American Anthropological Association.
1972b "Fulbe migration and metropolitan culture in rural Mambila, Nigeria", paper read at the annual meeting of the African Studies Association.
1975a *Pastoral societies, stratification, and national integration in Africa*. Uppsala: Scandinavian Institute of African Studies (Research Report no. 30).
1975b "Contraction and expansion in Nigerian bovine pastoralism", in T. Monod (ed.) *Pastoralism in tropical Africa*, 338-53. London: Oxford University Press.
1978 "Ecology and social organization among Nigerian Fulbe", in W. Weissleder (ed.) *The nomadic alternative*, 97-118. The Hague: Mouton and Co.
1980 "The open niche, pastoralism, and sedentarization in the Mambila grasslands (Nigeria)", in P. C. Salzman (ed.) *When Nomads Settle*. Brooklyn: Praeger. J. F. Bergin Publishers.
1981 "Development without communities: Social fields, networks, and action in the Mambila grasslands of Nigeria", *Human Organization*, 40, 211-20.

FROELICH, J.-C.
1954 "Le commandement et l'organisation sociale chez les Foulbé de l'Adamaoua", *Études camerounaises*, 45/46, 3-91.

GLEAVE, M. B.
1965 "The West Cameroon meat scheme", *Geography*, 50, 166-68.

HAUSEN, K.
1970 *Deutsche Kolonialherrschaft in Afrika*. Zürich: Atlantis.

HAWKINS, P., and BRUNT, M.
1965 *Report to the government of Cameroun on the soils and ecology of West Cameroun*, 2 vols. Rome: United Nations Food and Agricultural Organisation (Expanded Program of Technical Assistance Report no. 2083).

HURAULT, J.
1964 "Antagonisme de l'agriculture et d'élevage sur les hauts plateaux de l'Adamawa (Cameroun): le lamidat de Banyo", *Études rurales*, 15, 22-71.

114   CHARLES FRANTZ

1969-70 "Éleveurs et cultivateurs des hauts plateaux du Cameroun: la population du
         lamidat de Banyo", *Population*, 24, 963-94; 25, 1039-84.
JEFFREYS, M. D. W.
    1962 "The Wiya tribe", *African studies*, 21, 83-104, 174-222.
    1966 "Some notes on the Fulani in Bamenda, in West Cameroon", *Abbia*, 14/15, 127-34.
    1967 "Fulani", *Anthropological journal of Canada*, 5, 1-10.
KABERRY, P. M.
    1952 *Women of the grassfields*. London: H.M.S.O.
    1960 "Some problems of land tenure in Nsaw, Southern Cameroons", *Journal of African
         administration*, 12, 21-28.
KIRK-Greene, A. H. M.
    1958 *Adamawa past and present*. London: Oxford University Press.
McCULLOCH, M.
    1954 "The Tikar of the British and French Cameroons", in M. McCulloch, *et al. Peoples
         of the Central Cameroons*, 11-52. London: International African Institute.
MAFIAMBA, P. C.
    1969 "Notes on the polyglot populations of Nkambe", *Abbia*, 21, 59-90.
MOHAMADOU, E.
    1964 "L'histoire des lamidats Foulbé de Tchamba et Tibati", *Abbia*, 6, 15-158.
    1965 *L'histoire de Tibati*. Yaoundé: Editions Abbia avec la collaboration de Centre de
         Langue Evangelistique.
Nigeria, Federal Republic of. Ministry of Agriculture and Natural Resources
    1973 *Survey of the agricultural productive potential of the Mambila plateau in the context of Nigerian
         economy*, 2 vols. Rome: LI.DE.CO., S.p.A. [Livestock Development Company].
NJEUMA, M. Z.
    1969 *The rise and fall of Fulani rule in Adamawa, 1809-1901*. London: Unpublished Ph.D.
         thesis, School of Oriental and African Studies. University of London.
    1973 "The foundations of the pre-European administration in Adamawa: Historical con-
         siderations", *Journal of the historical society of Nigeria*, 7, 3-33.
PFEFFER, G.
    1936 "Die Djafun-Bororo: ihre Gesellschaft, Wirtschaft, und Sesshaftwerdung auf dem
         Hochland von Ngaundere", *Zeitschrift für Ethnologie*, 68, 150-96.
PRESCOTT, J. R. V.
    1971 *The evolution of Nigeria's international and regional boundaries: 1861-1971*. (B.C.
         Geographical Series, no. 13). Vancouver, B.C.: Tantalus Research Ltd.
REHFISCH, F.
    1955 *The social structure of a Mambila village*. London: Unpublished M.A. thesis, Depart-
         ment of Anthropology, University College, University of London. (Printed as *Occa-
         sional Paper* no. 2, Department of Sociology, Ahmadu Bello University, Zaria,
         Nigeria, in 1972.)
RUDIN, H.
    1938 *Germans in the Cameroons, 1884-1914*. New Haven: Yale University Press.
STENNING, D. J.
    1957 "Transhumance, migratory drift, migration: Patterns of pastoral Fulani
         nomadism", *Journal of the Royal Anthropological Institute*, 87, 57-73.
    1959 *Savannah nomads*. London: Oxford University Press.
STOECKER, H. (ed.)
    1960-68 *Kamerun unter deutschen Kolonialherrschaft*. Berlin: Rütten und Loening.
STRÜMPELL, K.
    1912 *Die Geschichte Adamauas, nach mündlichen Überlieferungen*. Hamburg: L. Friederichsen.
THORBECKE, F.
    1912 "Haussahändler", *Deutsche Kolonialzeitung*, 29, 881-83.
WIRZ, A.
    1972 *Vom Sklavenhandel zum kolonialen Handel: Wirtschaftsräume und Wirtschaftsformen in
         Kamerum vor 1914*. Zürich: Atlantis.

NOTES

1   Fieldwork in Mambila Division (now Sardauna Division) of the North-Eastern State (now Gongola State) of Nigeria was conducted during the summers of 1971, 1972, and 1974, plus ten days in 1977. Intermittently, archival research was done in Kaduna, Yola, Gembu, Ibadan, London, and Oxford. Fieldwork in the Donga-Mantung Division of the North-West Province of Cameroun was carried out from February through July, 1977, and archival materials were read in Buea, Yaoundé, Mankon (Bamenda), Nkambe, and Nwa. Financial support for these investigations has been received from Ahmadu Bello University (Zaria, Nigeria), the State University of New York (Buffalo, N.Y.), and the Research Foundation of the State University of New York (Albany, N.Y.). Permission to conduct research was kindly granted me by Ahmadu Bello University, state and local governmental officials in Nigeria, and the Office National de la Recherche Scientifique et Technique in Cameroun. I am greatly indebted to dozens of citizens and friends who gave me generous and valuable assistance, and wish to thank in particular those who rendered lengthy assistance to me: Mahmoudu Hamman, A. Bobboi Jauro, Salihu Dogo, and Yakubu Haruna Yaro. I am also grateful for the keen insights and other aid extended by Alhaji Mohammadu Toungo, then Grasslands Officer in Gembu, and A. T. Ngala, Chief of the Farmer-Grazier Branch, Ministry of Animal Breeding and Industries (since renamed), North-West Province, Mankon (Bamenda). Access to these multiple sources for data has enabled me to carry out various reliability checks; nevertheless, some errors or misunderstandings must remain, and for these I am solely responsible.

2   Among the major works concerned with the Fombina period, see Barth (1857), Strümpell (1912), Brackenbury (1924), Kirk-Greene (1958), Stenning (1959), Chilver (1961), Jeffreys (1962, 1966, 1967), Büttner (1964, 1966, 1967), Mohammadou (1964, 1965), Njeuma (1969, 1973), Abubakar (1970, 1972), Braukämper (1970, 1971), and Wirz (1972).

3   The principal sources dealing with the montane grasslands during the German period are Strümpell (1912), Thorbecke (1912), Pfeffer (1936), Rudin (1938), Kaberry (1952), Froelich (1954), Kirk-Greene (1958), Stoecker (1960-68), Chilver and Kaberry (1960, 1967), Chilver (1963), Dupire (1970), Braukämper (1970, 1971), Hausan (1970), and Wirz (1972).

4   No study of the Mbororo'en in the Mambila area of the Northern Cameroons was done during the period it was under British administration. The most relevant sources are de St. Croix (1945), Rehfisch (1955), and Kirk-Greene (1958). For materials touching on the pastoral Fulbe in the Southern Cameroons under British administration, see McCulloch (1954), Kaberry (1960), Jeffreys (1962, 1966, 1967), Chilver (1963), Gleave (1965), Carter (1967), Chilver and Kaberry (1967), and Mafiamba (1969).

5   Prescott (1971). Minor boundary adjustments between Southern and Northern Nigeria were also made over 40 years, including those of the Mambila area of Northern Cameroons and the contiguous Bamenda area of the Southern Cameroons.

6   This structural arrangement was similar to that utilized by the French in the immediately adjoining area to the east. See Froelich (1954), Hurault (1964, 1969-70), Mohammadou (1964, 1965), Dupire (1970), and Boutrais (1974a).

7   Other than my own field research, the Mbororo'en in Mambila District/Division have not been studied. See, however, the valuable reports by Bawden and Tuley (1966) and by LI.DE.CO. (Nigeria 1973), a revised copy of which was released in 1977 but has not been available. See also Frantz (1972a, 1972b, 1975a, 1975b, 1978, 1980, and 1981).

8   Aside from my own study, I know of only one published report (Boutrais 1974b) which concerns the Mbororo'en in Donga-Mantung Division; it focussed on the marginal Ndop plain, not the highland area, which straddles the boundary that formerly separated East and West Cameroun. Some useful data can also be found in Hawkins and Brunt (1965), Gleave (1965), Carter (1967), and Dongmo (1972).

Nomadic Pastoral Society
and the Market

The Penetration of the Sahel by Commercial Relations

ANDRÉ BOURGEOT

Centre National de la Recherche Scientifique, Paris, France

THIS PAPER has two aims: It seeks, first, to discover what economic and political factors are favourable to the penetration of commercial trade relations among the nomadic inhabitants of the Sahel. Secondly, it attempts to analyse the effects of the introduction of a new economic rationality based on the logic of free trade. In the course of this study I shall deal with the issue of integrated development in the nomadic regions and will offer a critique of the project of transnational vertical stratification of pastoral production.

Drought and Commercial Trade Relations

The pastoral production of the Sahel had already made its entry into the capitalist market economy when the severe drought of 1969-1974 hit the region. Its integration which was only partial, had two main economic characteristics: The first was the tax levied on livestock by the colonial governments; the second was the injection of investment of capital earned in other fields of economic activity and destined for commercial trading operations oriented toward both interior domestic and export markets.

These investments, derived from private savings from public service salaries or on profits from trade, show the passage from money capital to productive capital invested in the pastoral economy and realized in commercial transactions in livestock.

The chief feature of the entry of pastoral production into the market economy is to be found in the circulation of livestock within the commercial networks controlled by economic agents who are for the most part from outside the nomadic community. But this does not in itself affect the *orientation* of pastoral production and has not fundamentally transformed the internal logic of the traditional economy. What has happened is that new, external technical factors, such as technological innovation, the introduction and intensification of veterinary care, and the hydraulic policies have greatly contributed to the reduction of animal mortality, thereby creating the conditions for livestock accumulation. These new factors, since they were not accompanied by a structural reorganisation of pastoral production, have resulted in over-use of pastures disturbing the organisation and utilisation of pastoral space.

The fast pace of the penetration of market relations in the nomadic world occurred during the 1960's and had become firmly established by the time of the drought of 1969-1974.

If, in the past, one could affirm that periodic and minor droughts in the Sahel constituted an adjustment factor in production, the drought of 1969-1974 took place within a new politico-economic context. The traditional mechanisms of adjustment—loans of livestock and cows in milk, the in-alienability of the herd, religious offerings, etc.—are not solely the product of climatic or epizootic uncertainties; they are profoundly inscribed in systems of mutual aid, the redistribution of goods and the circulation of livestock, as well as in relationships of patronage and protection. But these balancing mechanisms are upset when climatic and economic conditions (droughts, epizootic diseases) go beyond "normal" limits. The human and livestock losses during the last drought were so great that, in most cases, it was impossible to maintain any system for the circulation of livestock, which made clear the diminished capacity of the group to cope with various risks and uncertainties.

The main feature of this drought, which reached its peak in 1973-74, was its transformation into widespread famine. But its *causes* were also different from those of former droughts: it was the result of a mode of exploitation of ecological niches and the conditioning effect of the penetration of capitalist relations of production. In this new political and economic situation, the specific capacities of nomadic societies for dealing with climatic hazards have been profoundly effected. Thus this last drought was unique not only in its consequences but also in its causes—climatic, political and economic. Its dominant character was expressed in its disruption of the conditions of production, where it upset the traditional patterns of pastoralism and thereby revealed the new weakness and vulnerability of these traditional systems. This weakness was evidence of the impact that neo-colonialism had had on these communities yet at the same time was an indication of how capitalism could be more deeply implanted, by extending its sphere of influence to include not only the circulation of livestock but also the level of the production process itself.

The post-drought situation therefore facilitated the penetration of capitalist relationships of production and the emergence of social transformations introduced by both external and internal factors.

Moreover, the drought, considered not as a causal factor in itself but rather as the result of a combination of bioclimatic, political and economic factors, has been influential in changing the economic behaviour of a certain category of stockraisers, namely the rich owners of large herds. It revealed to certain herders that the stocking of animals did not provide an indestructible guarantee of wealth and that, in fact, the best method of "conservation-reproduction" of wealth was to obtain hoardable, nonperishable valuables which could be put to use for the purchase of livestock destined for commercial use.

Techniques of Production and Economic Behaviour

We must distinguish clearly between two types of economic behaviour. The first mode of behaviour is that of pastoral nomads living in accordance with the economic logic proper to traditional socioeconomic structures. The behaviour of this group of producers is not determined by specifically economic ends nor by a desire to maximise production. The notion of profitability (*rentabilité*), as conceived by classical economics, does not enter into the economic strategy of these stock-raisers, whose objective is to satisfy biological and social needs. Commercialised exchange, in transactions of purchase and sale, intervenes only in the procuring of currency for the payment of poll taxes, taxes on livestock and for the purchase of cereals, tea, sugar, clothes, transistors, etc.

The second mode of economic behaviour is that of the wealthy stock-raisers, government employees who may or may not be of nomadic origin and various tradesmen who invest in livestock and whose strategy is clearly influenced by the market orientation and the profit motive. Indeed, some stock-raisers have exhibited capitalistic behaviour for the last 15 years. Herds are increased in *accumulation oriented towards commercialisation*. The decision to partially orient production towards the creation of a surplus governed by the laws of the market thus takes place at the level of pastoral production and management of the herd. This new strategy for the use of livestock shows that the herds tend to be no longer considered only as a means of production and an object of consumption, but have taken on the character of *merchandise* containing a commercial monetary value. For these stock-raisers, the value of their livestock is not in any way contradictory to or competitive with the traditional social forms governing the utilisation of livestock.

One such strategy, which encourages migratory movements of men and animals, has led to the creation of livestock markets and the spontaneous development of new trade networks, both national and transnational.

Moreover, sale prices fluctuate in accordance with local supply and demand and this provokes ever-increasing and widespread mobility in search for a beneficial commercial operation. Thus, in some parts of the Gourma of Mali certain stock-raisers have established a system of emissaries and intermediaries whose function is to find the market where the highest price for livestock is to be obtained, so that the herd can be moved with the utmost speed and efficiency to these locations. A strategy such as this one leads to perceptible changes in the utilisation of space and contributes to the disequilibrium of the already precarious spatial organisation of pastoral society.

These same herders were the first to profit from the lessons of the drought and deduced that:

— the accumulation of livestock reserves was no longer a means of meeting the challenge presented by climatic uncertainties and epizootic diseases;

— livestock is a precarious and perishable good, the destruction of which means an absolute loss;

— money is not perishable and can procure power.

— The orientation of pastoral production towards a marketable surplus presupposes the existence of a degree of specialisation in the techniques of production. Even where it is not utilised for a specifically economic end, such specialisation exists among stock-raisers, notably among the Fulani and the Tuareg of Gourma in Mali, whom I shall take as my example in the remarks which follow.

The best evidence of the efficacy of production techniques is to be found in the composition of the herds and their spatial deployment in salt cure techniques as well as in castration techniques. I shall limit myself to the last two techniques, the most important for my discussion.

1. *Salt cure techniques*

The exploitation of localized salt fields each having specific properties, is the sign of a rudimentary level of specialisation in the technique of livestock production and reproduction. According to stock-raisers, the salt cure has three main functions, which vary according to the category of the animal concerned (large animal or small ruminants) and the nature of the minerals they consume.

The function of lactation is served by a soil rich in natron and therefore of higher acidity.

The function of fattening and therapeutics is served by certain "banco" salt fields which, when exploited in combination with particular winter pastures, have fattening properties. The animals store up the calories liberated in the consumption of these grasses, thus creating energy reserves which "insulate" them against the cold. Some of these fields have special curative properties, notably in the treatment of "streptothricosis" or "dermatophisosis", a bacterial skin disease which affects the area from the base of the tail to the beginning of the hump on bovine animals. These fields help cure cutaneous lesions such as *streptothricosis* which appears frequently in the pasture-lands of "Burgu" (*Echinochloa stagnina*). The "Burgu" also favour certain parasitic diseases such as "destomatosis", caused by fluke-worm, which the Kel Tamacheq call "liver burn"; "coccidiosis", which usually strikes young calves and is characterised by diarrhea with traces of blood, caused by the presence of the "coccides" in the large intestine; "echinococcosis", the symptom of which is the presence of one or more oozing cysts.

The function of reproduction is served by "banco", the consumption of which necessitates a climb up to the pasture-lands of the Niger River, particularly by the large animals. The function of reproduction is confirmed by the fact that certain Tamacheq and Fulani stock- raisers, who control large herds, take only their milk animals up to the river, thus underlining the tendency towards specialisation as well as the importance attributed to milk production and hence to reproduction.

This type of strategy is implicit also (although not clearly systematised) in the mode of competition (indeed opposition) for access to pastures where the grass is reputed to be favourable to milk production. The *graminaceae* most favourable to milk production in winter pasture-lands are the *Cenchrus biflorus*, that covers sandy areas, the *Aristida mutabilis*, found in colluvial zones, the *Blepharis*, which is associated with the presence of pit water, and so on. Like these grassy pasture-lands, high pastures, too, are favourable to milk production.

This brief description clearly shows that there exists a specialisation in the eco-system; however, it would be a fundamental error to want to increase this process of specialisation within an ecological niche, a specialisation that results in augmented milk production. The development of this process to the end of integrating dairy production into commercial networks creates the conditions of more intensive competition for access to natural resources, resulting in the transformation of competition into opposition, implying the development of class dependency relations.

This transformation of competition into struggle simultaneously provokes an inevitable overstocking of desirable pastures (producing irreversible degradation) and profoundly modifies the form of appropriation of natural resources, automatically favouring those herders who were already in a strong position and transforming migratory patterns and grazing rights.

In a social and political terms, such a transformation would create conflict and even antagonism among stock-raisers.

2. *Castration techniques*

The Kel Tamacheq have two techniques for castrating bovines:

— *"Anakad"* (to cut): a method causing profuse bleeding, the chief drawback of which lies in the difficulty of stopping the flow of blood.

— *"Udich"* (to crush): a method which consists of crushing the testiculary funiculus with a stick.

The first technique (*anakad*) is much older and is more generally practised than the second (*udich*). The age for gelding varies as a function of different social categories and the goals to be achieved, and is thus an indication of the manner in which the livestock will be used (the ultimate aim of the process of production). Thus, warrior tributaries castrate their males at the age of from 5 to 10 months. This practice at such an early age is justified by their desire to obtain an animal socially perceived to have aesthetic value. These tributaries (the *imghad*), formerly warriors, practise the cutting method of castration on young animals, knowing that the youth of the animal is protection against severe hemorrage. But the aesthetic argument is pertinent. In effect, these tributaries have a relation to the herd which consists of the accumulation of animals in order to fulfill the traditional social rules (for gifts, loans, inheritance of herds in accordance with religious rules of succession: the *ebetikh* goods). In other words, livestock tends to be less commercialised (in the capitalistic sense of the term) in these groups than among the other categories of the Gourma population. On the other hand, former slaves (*iklan*), the *Ibogheliten* (mixed social categories), the *Kel Antassar* (the el Faqiten priestly minorities), and the *Kel Agays* (priestly groups) geld their animals from the age of 2 to 3 years, their main concern being to fatten them up, which shows a certain tendency towards commercialisation, most notably among the *Kel Antassar*, who sell their cattle at the age of 4 to 5 years.

These practices, which are still extremely widespread, now tend to exceed their original social function and occur at all levels of society. In effect, the techniques of castration and salt cure which formerly were carried out only among certain social categories of stock-raisers have now been generally adopted by all stock-raisers, irrespective of their social standing. Former captives, freed from the political and economic constraints imposed by their masters, here constitute the most dynamic and innovative element, particularly now that the Gourma is no longer cut up into zones of political influence. In the final analysis, it is these former slaves who form, among the stock-raisers, the group which is best-equipped to adapt itself to a system of production based on the development of commercial trade relations.

Modes of Exploitation of Labour

The management of large herds requires a labour force organised either on the basis of salary or on that of the traditional social structure with its intrinsic system of values. The organisation of a salaried labour force being relatively well known, I shall concentrate on the manner in which labour is exploited for capitalist production using as its basis the norms and categories of traditional society. In this process unpaid herdsmen are used, the value of whose labour is defined in the form of prestations in kind (livestock, derivatives of pastoral production, tea, sugar and clothes), codified in a customary agreement corresponding to the biological and social needs of the herdsman. In other words, the livestock owner realises a surplus profit based on the surplus labour (*surexploitation*) of the herdsmen. To summarise this description, it appears that the economic behaviour of the entrepreneur is oriented towards capitalist accumulation of goods without there being *a labour market organised in the capitalist fashion and without application of the law of value to the labour supplied.*

This system of capitalist accumulation permits owners to simultaneously gain both absolute surplus value and additional surplus value, thus engendering the process of social class formation which adheres to the values of capitalism.

There is an absolute surplus value because the herdsman usually has to look after his own herd as well. In a given set of ecological conditions and with certain techniques of herd management, the herdsman can only assume responsibility for so many head of livestock, obliging him to appeal to manpower recruited from among his kin in order to free himself from prolonged hours of work. Yet in essence this corresponds to an increase in work hours, camouflaged by the utilisation and intensification of kinship ties. There is, moreover, a constant increase in the amount of labour required for herding because, since the drought, ecological niches are spaced further apart and this

requires an additional expenditure of energy, notably in lengthier herd migrations and in digging new pools and wells or deepening the old ones.

There is an additional surplus value because the unit value of livestock
merchandise becomes inferior to its *social* value. In effect, the absence of salary
relations between the owner and his herdsman (or men) makes it possible to
obtain a cost of livestock production which is well below the average cost both
for traditional stock-raisers and for those who use a salaried labour force. In
this case, there is already a degree of *specialisation* coming into play at the level
of production (that is to say, the raising of livestock for commercial purposes)
which facilitates the rise of "pastoral productivity". This limited and non-
generalized specialisation already constitutes a disruption, a pioneering practice of considerably increasing supplementary working hours, or to put another
way, labour time without compensation. This yields enormous profits for the
owner, who in return for regular hours of work gives only low-cost allowances
in kind. While it is the regular hours of work which determine its unit value,
the livestock merchandise is sold on local markets or exported to the Sahel-
Sudanian countries or to the countries along the coast at a price which corresponds *not* to its unit value but to its social value.

This exploitation of traditional labour relations makes it possible to realise
an enormous percentage of surplus value because there is a large gap between
the cost of labour and its productivity. Moreover, the extra surplus value
stimulates the introduction of new production techniques. A typical example of
this is the readiness of these stock-raisers to adopt the salt-cure technique in
place of the salt lick, augmenting productivity, while reducing the area of
transhumance, and thus facilitating the concentration of livestock-capital. Furthermore, since the drought, measures for herd protection have been intensified in response to the recrudescence of predators, especially felines, up to the
point that since 1974 herds of larger domestic stock are no longer left unguard-
ed. This increased control has made possible an increase in animal productivity, notably by making it possible to collect milk which formerly was wasted. At
the same time, it has also created an increase in the amount of labour required
which carries with it the risk of a new division at the heart of the labour process. This strategy cannot help but engender social inequalities favourable not
only to capitalist accumulation but also to the *concentration* of capital.

Thus we can note the co-existence of several contradictory—indeed an-
tagonistic—economic rationalities within the same socio-economic formation.
This co-existence permits, at least for the time being, the reproduction of the
former relations of production. They are incorporated into and are utilised by
new relationships of production, everywhere gaining ascendency, and becoming part of the relations of exploitation which in this case correspond to and
may be identified with class relations.

To sum up then, this capitalist strategy, based on the process of accumulation and concentration of capital, has not yet led to the creation of a labour
market organised in a capitalist manner. It has not yet transformed the value of
the labour-force into a merchandise, limiting itself for the present to the

maintenance of its value. It is perhaps these special circumstances which have encouraged that appropriation of extra surplus value which is characteristic of a social-economic formation in transition.

Drawing my conclusions from the remarks put forward in the above three paragraphs, I would stress that the imposition of taxes and the passage from money-capital to productive capital were not sufficient to bring about the integration of great domestic herds into the capitalist economy. It is not the taxes, a necessary yet insufficient means, that will overcome the traditional system of gifts, loans and redistribution of goods, but rather the pressure of a capitalist monetary system which has created the conditions for the transformation of an entire system of economic rationality. It has achieved this by changing the means of production (in this case, livestock) into merchandise and by permitting the realisation of local capitalist accumulation.

Specialisation and Development Projects

Organisations specialising in Third World development encourage the specialisation of pastoral production, as a point of departure for the promotion of specialisation throughout the entire eco-system (vegetable, animal, human). The aim of specialisation is justified by the notion of "range management", a concept founded on capitalist economic theory, which when applied to pastoral land and herds amounts to a structural reorganisation of pastoral production.

As applied to the land used in herd migrations, specialization involves the choice of those ecological zones in which the vegetative composition is adapted to a form of specialised production, conceived as a transnational project of vertical stratification. This "stratification" is based on the division of territory into different zones determined by agrostological and climatic criteria. The choice of these criteria clearly reveals the priority given to natural, ecological factors over specifically economic determinants. Not only has this type of approach already proved its incapacity to solve or even suggest solutions to these problems, but it is based on assumptions which date to the beginning of this century.

These projects relate to the zone of nomadic pastoral specialisation within the geographical area of the Sahel, i.e. the zone between isohyets 100 mm to 400 mm and therefore including both the Sahel sub-desert (isohyet 100 to 200 mm) and the regular Sahel (isohyet 200 to 400 mm).

The Sahelo-Sudan zone (isohyet 400 to 600 mm) as well as the Sudan proper (isohyet 600 to 1,500 mm) corresponds to a zone of informal peasant "backyard fattening" (embouche-paysanne) and finishing through the installation of ranches (involving modification in the appropriation of pastures, privatisation and specialisation of ecological niches with salarisation and in this case the proletarianisation of herdsmen transformed into workers). The agrostological possibilities of the Sudanese-Guinean zone are practically identical, and they could therefore be used to the same ends.

The forest and forest hinterland (isohyet 1,300 to 1,000 mm), consisting mainly of the countries along the coast (Senegal, Ivory Coast, Ghana, Togo and Nigeria, all countries lacking stock-raisers), would provide the consumers for the livestock raised and produced in the two other zones.

The logic of specialisation in pastoral production, through the intermediary of vertical stratification, risks changing the Sahel into a meat-producing area for the profit of other countries, notably the deficient coastal nations whose production is oriented towards the cultivation of a single crop for export. And, if the countries of the Sahel, *stricto-sensu*, should be unable to supply this demand, or should lack the political and/or economic means of resisting the outside pressure put upon them, they would be in danger of being left on the periphery under the pretext that they were unable or lacked the political will to become involved with a capitalist-style economy. What is more, this policy of stratification reduces the nations of the Sahel, that is, the poorest nations (Mali, Niger, Haute-Volta, if we consider only West Africa) into productive zones where the cost of production is very low, while the consumer zones, that is, the countries along the coast, are offered conditions favourable to the accumulation and concentration of capital. The aim of this policy is very clear: It consists of developing capitalist accumulation, where conditions are most favourable, so as to facilitate more widespread reproduction of capital. At one pole, production; at the other, the concentration and intensified circulation of capital thus developing the influence of those countries most involved in capitalism, notably Senegal, Ivory Coast and Nigeria, at the same time creating the conditions of a labour market organised in the capitalist manner and reaching out to include intra-African migratory processes and networks.

It is evident that this whole state of affairs, founded on the imperatives of capitalist production, is destructive of an already precarious equilibrium which has always existed, despite periodic difficulties, within traditional pastoral production—an equilibrium between the objectives of consumption and the possibilities of production. The implementation of vertical stratification, together with more widespread commercialisation not under the direct control of immediate producers, lays the foundation for an ''industrialised'' form of pastoral production, to the detriment of its subsistence form.

There is a risk in this operation of repeating the same mistakes that were made in agriculture where capitalism developed ''industrialised'' export crops to the detriment of basic food crops, whose absence was most severely felt during the recent drought period. It must be emphasized that industrialised cultivation has not improved the standard of living of the immediate producers but has on the contrary been the cause of their increasing impoverishment. In effect, the profits from the expansion of industrial cash cropping, in terms of the total amount of money in circulation, have not been adequate and, in fact, have served only to aggravate the life conditions of the farmers. In addition, the industrialisation of agricultural production has increased their work-time.

One of the consequences of this development has been the reinforcement of social inequalities and the emergence of social classes originating from the neo-colonial states. In effect, these states have been used as the instrument for the realisation of capitalist accumulation and as the training ground for the formation of a "national" bourgeoisie.

In the neo-colonial states it is sufficient to note the total subjugation of the Plan to development considerations. I will take the example of Mali (there are many others), where the 1970 3-year plan, drawn up by French experts and more than 80% financed by foreign resources, envisaged doubling the production of industrial cash crops (cotton and peanuts) giving the monopoly on production operations to the CFDT and the BDPA and expropriating the peasants of Segou, Bamako, Kayes and Sikasso. In stock-raising, this plan allowed for a $ 14 million investment by the United States in order to raise livestock for leather; this represented a source of currency for the Malian government. But just who benefited from this currency? Certainly not the producers.

Clearly a transnational project of vertical stratification in pastoral production can only be implemented if there is direct support from the neo-colonial states involved. They are neo-colonial in the etymological sense of the term, for whether it is in their conduct or in their utilisation of the state, the influence of businessmen, national and/or foreign, rests on the same foundation, that of the power of territorial governors or the Governor General of French West Africa. The principle is the same, for the state becomes the crucible in which social classes are formed. One thing among others which seems to me to be characteristic of the colonial system is that it succeeds in penetrating an economy and dominating a country only by means of the commercial trade of large companies which are supported by a highly centralised administrative hierarchy.

But these states are not only neo-colonial, they are also becoming capitalist, in large measure through the activity of national private enterprises in the fields of trade and transport. These enterprises, particularly those which are concerned with transport, intervene directly in the productive sector, for transport constitutes a stage in the production process insofar as it bridges a gap, providing an intermediary between the finished or unfinished product and its desired destination. In the final analysis, ownership of means of transport is a sure way of realising surplus value. The ownership of the means of exchange, which characterizes the commercial sector, is not a special feature of these states that have become capitalist, for in the neo-colonial states, this sector is already in the hands of national and foreign businessmen.

The centralisation of the administration, and its organisation into a hierarchy, seems to me to play a role similar to that of colonialism, albeit adapted to the new political conjuncture. Thus the government is constantly wavering on the problem of what measures should be taken with regard to rich tradesmen who practice smuggling. Sanctions will sometimes be imposed on all, and sometimes the policy will be complete *laisser-faire*, in accordance with political fluctuations. This practice nonetheless permits the encouragement of a class base for the state insomuch as it facilitates the emergence of a commercial bourgeoisie. Thus, rich livestock traders, such as the Dioulla and the Marka, are habitual smugglers of imported consumer goods and organise the slaughter and clandestine export of livestock on-the-hoof. The profits they realise in this fashion are invested abroad. It is estimated that these investments of clandestine origin amount to about 15 million francs in Mali. This development of the traditional smuggling trade, which is not taken into account in official economic plans, is not only tolerated but actually encouraged and thus a sort of "livestock bourgeoisie" has come into being as a political support of the state. At the time of independence, there was no opposition to the big French companies on the part of these same businessmen for the excellent reason that they picked up a share of the companies' profits. It is interesting to note that neither during the colonial period nor at the time of independence did these businessmen provide their struggling countrymen with either a political leader or a progressive ideology. And yet they now tend to present themselves as the political backbone of the newly-created states.

To return to pastoral production and the transnational stratification project, it can already be predicted that the present phase of the penetration of capitalistic market relations, with privilege given to industrial pastoral production, will be followed by the development of food production, for the necessary economic and political conditions will have been created for the transformation of food produce into a form of *merchandise*, just as the logic of stratification, specialisation and commercialisation, transforms livestock, a means of production, into merchandise.

But this economic logic can only be widely implemented by the transformation of the property structure, that is, by engaging in a process of privatisation of ecological niches. The beginnings of this can already be seen in the development of ranches which are by nature in direct contradiction and in competition with the traditional system of production.

They are in contradiction with it because they are based on a different economic rationality, that of the law of the market and of profit, and in competition with it, particularly on the level of vegetation, for each appropriates for its exclusive use dozens of hectares of pasture-land. This process pushes small stock-raisers to the periphery of the best pastures and tends to settle them into the poorest ecological zones. Moreover these ranches are the centre for the innovation of new production techniques (salt licks, utilisation of milk and hides, etc.). It seems clear that by bringing about the liquidation of pasture-lands and herds, these ranches, guaranteed by the State (the government grants substantial loans which is evidence of the intervention of the state in pastoral production by means of investments taken from public funds) diminish but have not yet eliminated the capacities of existing social-economic systems to reproduce themselves.

REFERENCES

BONTE, P., BOURGEOT, A., DIGARD, J. P., LEFEBURE, Cl.
1979 In *Tropical grazing land ecosystems*, a state of knowledge report prepared by UNESCO/

UNEP/FAO, Natural resources research, XVI, Chap. 8, Part 5, Human occupation: Pastoral economies and societies; 655 p., p. 261-302.

BOUDET, G.
1975 *Manuel sur les pâturages tropicaux et les cultures fourragères.* IEMVT. Ministère de la Coopération, 254 p.

BOUDET, G., BOURGEOT, A., COULOMB, J., FERGUSON, D. S., VANDEMAELE, F.
1976 Interim report of the feasibility study on the management of livestock and grazing rights to combat the population drain in the Sahelian-Sudanian region (SOLAR-UNEP). *Stratification of Livestock in Arid Regions*, 72 p. 21 annexes, bibliogr.

BOURGEOT, A.
1979 "Class structure, political power and territorial organisation in the Touareg country". In: Group for the study of the Ecology and Anthropology of Pastoral Societies. *Pastoral Production and Society*. Cambridge University Press/Editions de la Maison des Sciences de l'Homme, 1979.

1978a "Etude de l'évolution d'un système d'exploitation sahalian au Mali". Rapport de July mission "Etude socio-économique" *Comité de Lutte contre l'Aridité en milieu tropical.* D.G.R.S.T. Paris Roneo 44 p. cartes H.T.

1978b "Pastoralisme et développement au Mali". In: *Nomads in a Changing World.* An International Conference, June 7th, London. Forthcoming in P. Salzman & J. Galaty, ed., Philadelphia: ISHI Publishers.

1978c "De quoi meurt le Sahel?" *Témoignages Chrétiens* No. 1774, Jeudi 6 juillet.

1978d "Le développement des inégalités". In: *Bulletin Production Pastorale et Société*: Supplement to MSH-Information No. 2 Eté 1978. Maison des Sciences de l'Homme.

COPANS, J. (ed.)
1975 *Sécheresses et famines au Sahel (I and II)*, Paris, Maspéro, Dossiers africains 1975, I, 155 p., II, 143 p., bibliogr.

Comité d'Information Sahel
1975 *Qui se nourrit de la famine en Afrique?* Paris, Maspéro, 197 p.

DESSAU, J.
1976 "Le Mali: une expérience partielle de l'indépendance économique". In: Bernis, G. de, Dessau, J. etc. in *L'Afrique de l'indépendance politique à l'indépendance économique*. Paris, Maspéro, Presses Universitaires de Grenoble, Collection Textes à l'appui/Economie, p. 173-197.

ECKHOLM, and BROWN, L. R.
1978 "Spreading deserts: the hand of man". In: *Bulletin of the Atomic Scientists*, Chicago, January, p. 10-51.

GALLAIS, J.
1975 *Pasteurs et Paysans du Gourma. La condition sahélienne.* Paris, CNRS, Mémoire du CEGET, 239 p., Cartes H.T., bibliogr.

JOUVE, E.
1977 "Le Mali, de 'l'option socialiste' au gouvernement des militaries (1968-1976)". In: *Revue Française d'Etudes Politiques Africaines*, Février 1977, 134 (12), p. 24-49.

MARX, K.
1973 *Le Capital*, livre 1er, tomes II et III. Paris, Editions Sociales.

SWIFT, J.
1973 "Disaster and a Sahelian nomad economy. Report of the 1973 Symposium". In: *Drought in Africa*, Centre of African Studies (SOAS) London, p. 71-78.

SAN FIE
1978 "Le spectre de la famine". In: *l'Economiste du Tiers-Monde* No. 23, Mars-Avril 1978.

Bedouin and Social Change
in Saudi Arabia

DONALD P. COLE

The American University in Cairo, Cairo, Egypt

Introduction

THE AIM of this paper is to examine and explain the socio-economic situation in which pastoral nomads, the Bedouin, find themselves in present-day Saudi Arabia. To do so requires a brief description of the main characteristics of the mode of production operative in the interior parts of Arabia prior to the creation of the modern state known as the Kingdom of Saudi Arabia in 1932, the subsequent emergence of the oil industry there following the discovery of oil by Americans at Dhaharan in 1938, and the economic boom that has been occurring in Saudi Arabia since the increase of oil prices during and following the Ramadan (October) War of 1973 AD, to the effects of which special importance should be given.

The works of Ibn Khaldun (1958), Samir Amin (1976), Talal Asad (1973), my own ethnography of a highly traditional section of the Āl Murrah Bedouin (Cole 1971; 1975), and a sociological survey of four groups of Bedouin by Saad Eddin Ibrahim and myself (Ibrahim and Cole 1978) have been drawn upon to describe the basic features of the particular mode of production characteristic of pre-modern Arabia.

The paper, however, is not mainly concerned with the traditional socio-economic-political structure of the area. Saudi Arabia—within a very brief period—has experienced a revolution in the structure of its economy. This is common knowledge, but the basic structural features of the newly-emerging economic system have been little studied and there has been almost no systematic analysis of the present-day mode of production that is emerging there. In order to raise this as an issue for scientific discussion, I have relied mainly on statements published by the Saudi Arabian government in *The Second Development Plan for 1395-1400 AH—1975-1980 AD* (Kingdom of Saudi Arabia, Ministry of Planning 1976) and a draft statement by the Saudi Arabian Ministry of Planning (1978) on *The Strategies for the Third Development Plan for 1400-1405 AH—1980-1985 AD*. I have also relied on personal observations and conversations with a wide range of Saudi Arabian government officials during the course of visits to the Kingdom during 1977 and 1978.[1]

Concrete evidence on the present-day socio-economic position of the Bedouin in Saudi Arabia is drawn mainly from the already mentioned sociological survey conducted by Professor Saad Eddin Ibrahim and myself in 1977 on a sample of 208 Bedouin males from four major tribal groupings in four different regions of the country—the Āl Murrah in the Eastern Province, the Dawasir in southern Najd, the Beni Zayed in the Qunfudah region of the Tihama, and the Harb near Madinah (Ibrahim and Cole 1978). The other major source of data is an unpublished anthropological survey I conducted during the summers of 1977 and 1978 in the Arabian Shield-South, an area of some 202,000 square kilometers in the inland part of southwestern Saudi Arabia, where the major Bedouin tribes are the Subay', the Qahtan, the Shahran, and the Bani Yam.[2]

The Traditional Mode of Production and Nomadic Pastoralism in Arabia

The mode of production under which traditional Bedouin society operated is well described by Ibn Khaldun in a chapter of the *Muqaddimah*, entitled "Bedouin Civilization, Savage Nations and Tribes and their Conditions (of Life)". He accurately notes at the beginning of the chapter that

> It should be known that the differences of condition among people are the result of the different ways in which they make their living. Social organization enables them to co-operate toward that end and to start with the simple necessities of life, before they get to conveniences and luxuries (II: 249).

He points out correctly that Bedouin social organization is intimately interrelated with economics. As we will observe later on, his concept of the evolution of simple, basic societies (e.g. the Bedouin) into more complex ones enjoying a higher standard of living is not automatic as he sometimes seems to imply. Indeed, as I shall argue, the mode of production under which the Bedouin operate does not allow them to evolve into more complex societies.

Ibn Khaldun goes on to state that

> Some people adopt agriculture...Others adopt animal husbandry, the use of sheep, cattle, goats, bees, and silkworms, for breeding and for their products. Those who live by agriculture or animal husbandry cannot avoid the call of the desert, because it alone offers the wide fields, acres, pastures for animals, and other things that the settled areas do not offer...Their social organization and co-operation for the needs of life and civilization, such as food, shelter, and warmth do not take them beyond the bare subsistence level, because of their inability (to provide) for anything beyond those (things). Subsequent improvement of their conditions and acquisition of more wealth and comfort than they need, cause them to rest and take it easy (II: 249).[3]

He juxtaposes the conditions under which the Bedouin live and work with those of the "sedentary people" who take pride in the finer things of life, luxuries such as fine cuisine, splendid clothes, and fine houses. The sedentary people according to him are

> the inhabitants of cities and countries, some of whom adopt the crafts as their way of making a living, while others adopt commerce. They earn more and live more comfortably than Bedouins, because they live beyond the level of (bare) necessity, and their way of making a living corresponds to their wealth (I: 250).

Ibn Khaldun's acknowledgement that there is nothing in Bedouin social organization that leads to the production of anything beyond the bare necessities of life and that when they do obtain more wealth and comfort than they need, they rest and take it easy is very important and accords well with general observations I have made in contemporary Saudi Arabia. It shows us that the mode of production under which the Bedouin operate is one that does not lead to expansion or increase in at least the material side of things. Other parts of the *Muqaddimah* provide evidence that *al-assabiya*, kinship, can lead to bigger and bigger socio-political groupings because of the nature of segmentation. But the mode of production under which the Bedouin operate does not lead to increased production of anything beyond the bare necessities.

Although Marshall Sahlins does not refer to the Bedouin, his concept and his description of the domestic mode of production in his *Stone Age Economics* seem completely relevant in describing traditional Bedouin socio-economics:

> Constituted on an uncertain household base, which is in any case restrained in material objectives, stinted in its use of labor power and cloistered in relation to other groups, the domestic mode of production is not organized to give a brilliant performance (1972: 99).

That traditional Bedouin economy and society are based on the patrilocal household is well-documented in the ethnographic literature and it is unnecessary to describe this in detail here. Suffice it to note that in Saudi Arabia, herds, the major property of nomadic Bedouin, and date palm farms, the major property of sedentary Bedouin, are owned and managed by the household and their products almost exclusively consumed by the household. Ibrahim and I found in our study of a sample of 208 Bedouin from four different tribes in Saudi Arabia that only six percent raise animals for selling only, whereas 37.7 percent raise them for domestic use only and 54.3 percent for domestic use and selling (1978: 21). However, most of those who report raising animals for both domestic use and selling in fact irregularly sell only an occasional animal or two when a bit of extra cash is needed or when a Royal Prince or the King happens to fancy a fine racing camel.

The same obtains for the Bedouin in our sample who admitted to some engagement in agriculture (53.4 percent). Of those who practise agriculture, 67.8 percent use the products for domestic consumption only; 3.5 percent for selling only; and 28.7 percent for both domestic use and selling (1978: 27).

According to Sahlins, labor power in societies organized according to the principles of the domestic mode of production tends to be under-utilized to a significant degree. This is clearly the case among the Bedouin in Saudi Arabia. According to my observations, a camel herd of one of the most highly mobile and long distance camel herding groups in the Arabian Peninsula requires the attention of two full-time and one part-time herders. According to my calculations for the Āl Kurbi minimal lineage of the Āl 'Azab of the Āl Murrah (nine households and herds with a total population of 64 adults), the full-time attention of only 18 people and the part-time attention of nine is required for herding their camels—their sole productive activity. Herding itself thus requires the attention of only 42 percent of the adult population, a third of whom are part-timers—or if calculated on a full-time basis, 33 percent. Actually, in 1968-70, the Āl Kurbi employed 20 full-time herders, all of whom were under 30 years of age and most of whom were unmarried males between the ages of about 18 and 22. Nine people, all boys between the ages of about 6 and 18, were employed as part-time herders (cf. Cole 1975b: 3-4). In the Arabian Shield-South, my observations in 1977 and 1978 indicate that one adult male, one woman, and one other person—either a young boy or girl—are sufficient to tend to all herding and household activities presently practised by these Bedouin.

In our study, which included both long-range and short-range nomadics, Ibrahim and I found that the average household among the Bedouin (which equals a herding unit) includes six full-time residents. Yet, households range in size "from two persons to as many as fourteen (1978: 12)". There is thus obviously a significant degree of excess labor power in traditional herding units (households), especially since they do not engage themselves in any other productive activities.

At the same time, herding does not now and probably never has provided nomadics with enough return for their basic subsistence. In 1968-70, I found that eight out of the ten households I studied had at least one male in the Reserve National Guard of Saudi Arabia. In return for going to the unit's headquarters for one or two days each month to collect it, he received enough money to buy all articles desired or needed by his household (other than milk which they produced). Ibrahim and I found that one third of our 208 respondents said that at least one member of their household worked for the government and 36 percent admitted to receiving some other form of cash from the government, though we suspect that a much larger percentage in fact receives cash from government sources (1978: 28-29). Many Bedouin also easily obtain loans from government banks for buying material and equipment (such as trucks and water tankers) which hardly anyone, at least at present, seriously expects them to fully repay.

In the past, the Bedouin took what they needed or wanted by force. As Ibn Khaldun claims, this is due to the fact that desert life requires the Bedouin to "provide their own defence and not [to] entrust it to...others (I: 257-58)". Moreover, their life in the desert requires them to be brave and courageous (something which sedentary life does not require, according to Ibn Khaldun). As he claims, "since desert life no doubt is the reason for bravery, savage groups are braver than others. They are, therefore, better able...to take away the things that are in the hands of other nations (I: 282)".

What I am arguing here, essentially, is that because of the characteristics of their domestic mode of production, the Bedouin, have never been able through herding to create anything more than a bare subsistence for themselves. Yet Ibn Khaldun claims that "Bedouins are prior to sedentary people. The desert is the basis and reservoir of civilization and cities (I: 252)".

Man seeks first the (bare) necessities. Only after he has obtained the (bare) necessities, does he get to comforts and luxuries. The toughness of desert life precedes the softness of sedentary life. Therefore, urbanization is found to be the goal of the Bedouin...Through his own efforts, he achieves what he proposes to achieve in this respect. When he has obtained enough to be ready for the conditions and customs of luxury, he enters upon a life of ease and submits himself to the yoke of the city...Sedentary people, on the other hand, have no desire for desert conditions, unless they are motivated by some urgent necessity or they cannot keep up with their fellow city dwellers...Evidence for the fact that Bedouins are the basis of, and prior to, sedentary people is furnished by investigating the inhabitants of any given city. We shall find that most of its inhabitants originated among Bedouins dwelling in the country and villages of the vicinity. Such Bedouins became wealthy, settled in the city, and adopted a life of ease and luxury, such as exists in the sedentary environment (I: 252-53).

Nonetheless, the domestic mode of production of the Bedouin does not allow them to produce surplus goods which would provide them with the bases for creating cities. They may drift into cities and become urbanized but they are incapable of creating them so long as they practise herding organized according to the principles of the domestic mode of production.[4] Historically, they have if anything, probably been more responsible for the destruction of urban-based civilization and highly productive agriculture, as witness their activities in North Africa from the eleventh century AD onwards (cf. Amin 1970: 14-21).

Ibn Khaldun's error, and I think the error of many others engaged in the study of Middle Eastern culture and society, is to concentrate on the disparate elements of the culture and society (Coon's "mosaic" approach) and to consider them as separate entities which can be fully understood on their own terms and in isolation from other elements of the total socio-cultural framework. We can only fully understand the dynamics of Bedouin social organization and economic activities, in the past or the present, by examining them within the context of the wider system within which they operate.

To understand the Bedouin in the pre-modern Arab World, the recent work of Samir Amin (1976), entitled *La nation arabe: nationalisme et luttes de classes*, is instructive. According to Amin, precolonial Arab civilization was essentially associated with cities which were trading centers dealing mainly in long distance trade. According to this argument, we can only understand the precolonial Arab World

in its setting, which is that of a region of passage, a central meeting point between...the three zones of agrarian civilization: Europe, Black Africa, and Monsoon Asia. The Arab World filled commercial functions, linking agrarian civilizations which were ignorant of one another. [Accordingly] the social formations on the base of which its civilizations flowered were mercantile formations...[for] *the decisive surplus on which its major cities lived at their peaks did not generally and principally come from the exploitation of the rural sector*, but from the profits of long-distance trade (translated in Ibrahim and Hopkins, eds. 1977: 10; emphasis added).

Pastoral nomads, the Bedouin, played a special role in this mercentile system, especially as they became involved in transportation. According to Amin,

Islam was born in Arabia, among a population of nomads who were organized as a function of the long-distance trade between the Eastern Roman Empire and Persia on one hand, and South Arabia, Ethiopia and India on the other. The profits drawn from this trade allowed the survival of the urban merchant's republics of the Hejaz...The pastoral subsistence economy of the nomads was juxtaposed to mercantile activity to which it furnished men and animals, *but the mercantile classes did not extract any surplus from it* (translated in Ibrahim and Hopkins, eds. 1977: 11; emphasis added).

In his discussion of the Bedouin as a military force in the history of the Arab World, Talal Asad also stresses the involvement of the Bedouin in trade. In sixth century Mecca, for example, he shows that there existed "a sedentary group of merchants basing their power on a co-operative trade enterprise involving bedouins but managed by the merchants (1973: 64)". He sees that this "trade involvement was complementary to pastoralism (e.g. the selling of animals) and in part an alternative to it (e.g. the provision of animal transport or service as paid militiamen, or full-time commercial activity (1973: 65)". As he correctly points out, "the problem of 'surplus men' available for activities other than full-time pastoralism [is related to] the kinds of property and work arrangements obtaining in a pastoral society (1973: 65)".

In conclusion, there is evidence that the traditional household mode of production under which the Bedouin operated their herding activities allowed mainly for a surplus of men—i.e. the major surplus they produced was men not products, although they apparently sold some animals occasionally to merchants as they do nowadays. Because they were part of a wider socio-economic system, this human surplus was sometimes mobilized in the service or in the interests of the wider socio-economic system when it needed them—in trade operations and warfare mainly. During periods when the wider socio-economic system declined or collapsed, usually due to events outside the region, as Samir Amin would argue, the Bedouin went back to herding and their bare subsistence.

Much the same is true in present-day Arabia. Then, as now, one can only understand pastoralists within the context of the wider socio-economic context. What is perhaps most different today is that the wider socio-economic context within which the Bedouin operate is itself related to the wider international world of capitalism of which it is a peripherial or marginal appendage.

Socio-economic Development in Present-day Saudi Arabia

If it is true that we can only fully understand the Bedouin within the wider socio-economic framework, then we must sketch out the essential features of that wider socio-economic context. This section of the paper then is devoted to a brief overview of what seems to be the way in which development has been taking place in Saudi Arabia in recent years, especially as gleaned from a review of selected Saudi Arabian government documents and from conversations with a number of relatively young Saudi Arabian government officials.

The fundamental long-term strategic goals of Saudi Arabia's development have been stated in the Kingdom's *Second Development Plan for 1395-1400 AH—1975-1980 AD*. These include the following seven objectives: to maintain the religious and moral values of Islam; to assure the defence and internal security of the Kingdom; to maintain a high rate of economic growth by developing economic resources, maximizing earnings from oil over the long term, and conserving depletable resources; to reduce economic dependence on the export of crude oil through diversification of the economic base; to develop human resources by education, training and raising standards of health; to increase the well-being of all groups within the society and to foster social stability under circumstances of rapid economic change; and to develop and utilize the physical infrastructure to support the achievement of the above-mentioned goals.

Indications from the Ministry of Planning are that these objectives are still valid and will govern the direction of *The Third Development Plan for 1400-1405 AH—1980-1985 AD*. However, the Third Plan is expected to put greater emphasis on the utilization of the physical infrastructure than on its development in company with an increased emphasis on the development of human and economic resources, and a continued emphasis on the well-being of citizens and the stability of society.

At present, mid-point in the period of the Second Development Plan, Saudi Arabia's economy is essentially dualistic, consisting of two interacting systems which might be called the "modern" and the "traditional". The modern economic system includes some industry, elements of large-scale modernized agriculture, financial and other services, capital intensive trade and government. The oil industry is an obviously important element in the modern economic system. Other important elements are the country's very large foreign reserve holdings, probably the greatest in the world, the fact that it is the largest single provider of new investment funds flowing into the world's economic systems and has one of the world's largest foreign aid programs. It is also a vital supplier of funds to international lending and development agencies. At the same time, it is a very significant consumer of the exported goods and services of industrialized nations. Because of its felt responsibilities and the tasks of managing its oil reserves and production and because of the felt need to protect and manage its extensive and growing overseas investment holdings and aid programs, a very significant amount of top quality Saudi Arabian managerial manpower and ministerial time are required.

Alongside the modern economic system, which mainly operates from metropolitan centers, is the traditional economic system prevailing in rural areas and small towns and even in parts of the metropolitan centers. This system is based on peasant subsistence agriculture, nomadic pastoralism, petty trade, and various services which support and supply these activities. The Ministry of Planning estimates that some 35 percent of the Kingdom's labor force (excluding nomads and all women) is engaged in the low growth, low productivity, and low wage sectors of agriculture and personal and community services.[5]

More or less straddling the traditional and modern economic systems are the construction sector and the traditional service sectors. The construction sector draws manpower from the traditional system and employs it in the development of the modern system. Many of the service functions of the modern systems, especially trade and transportation, are provided by enterprises from the traditional economic system using labor-intensive, low capital, small-scale, and relatively inefficient ways, yet receiving great cash income because of the high demand from the modern system. Both the construction sector and the traditional service sectors essentially draw manpower out of the traditional productive sector of agriculture (and pastoralism)[6] without transmitting it into modern productive sectors. Instead it is kept in economically inefficient but relatively well-paid employment. Some 57 percent of the Kingdom's labor force (excluding nomads and women) is estimated to be engaged in government, construction, transport, and trade—all throughput rather than productive output sectors. This leaves only eight percent of the Kingdom's labor force to be engaged in productive output sectors.

As already mentioned, the traditional economic system is mainly operative in rural areas and small towns while the modern economic system operates out of metropolitan centers. This has led not only to a general rural-urban imbalance in development but to the creation of regional imbalances as well. Infrastructural development has tended to have an urban bias up to the present and rural areas have been, relatively speaking, neglected. Also, industry has tended to concentrate in the so-called "central corridor" of Saudi Arabia (Jeddah-Mecca-Taif-Riyadh-Hofuf-Dammam) with Jubail, Yanbu, and Madinah as outposts. As a result, migration into the central corridor cities is very high. Meanwhile, the north and the south of the Kingdom risk a probable depopulation and decline.

One of the major goals of development stated in the Second Development Plan is to reduce economic dependence on the export of crude oil through the diversification of the economic base. Very much related to this is another stated goal of developing human resources by education, training, and by raising standards of health. As Saudi Arabia seeks to diversify its modern economic system, it is essential that its own human resources be developed in such a way as to significantly contribute to and benefit from the development of the modern economy.[7] Although the diversification of the modern economic system may require a heavy input of foreign labor and expertise, at least during the short run, it is essential that Saudi Arabian human resources be trained and fully incorporated into the modern system. Otherwise, the Kingdom runs a very strong risk of having the dualistic division of the economy into traditional and modern systems solidify or, alternatively, having the traditional productive system replaced with a non-productive sector of the population that will have to be supported by welfare. That the emergence of a significantly large non-productive sector is a potential threat is given support by a recent manpower study by the World Bank. This study projects an oversupply and consequent unemployment of uneducated and unskilled Saudi Arabians (excluding nomads) amounting to eight percent of the total Saudi Arabian labor force.

The best way, probably the only way, to achieve a well-balanced development of the modern economic system *and* thus to guarantee the increased well-being of all groups in the society is through full incorporation of all groups into the modern economic system. This obviously implies the disappearance of the traditional system. Yet coincident with an oversupply of unskilled and uneducated Saudi Arabian labor there will exist, according to the World Bank, a critical shortage of skilled, professional, and managerial manpower—a shortage that can only partly be met by foreigners available for employment in the Middle East after 1980.[8]

The Bedouin in Contemporary Saudi Arabia

The Bedouin are singled out for special consideration in the Second Development Plan for 1395-1400 AH—1975-1980 AD, a fact that shows that the government is cognizant of and concerned about the Bedouin's situation. According to the Plan, the life and economy of the Bedouin in Saudi Arabia have the following characteristics:

— Low per capita income in comparison to the national average.

— Heavy reliance on raising livestock as their basic source of income while producing the major share of domestic meat supplies.

— Almost total dependence on clement weather for the survival of flocks and herds.

— Rapidly deteriorating range lands in most areas due largely to overgrazing.

— Lack of immediate access to most social, educational, and other services.

— Significant migration to urban areas resulting in an estimated net annual decrease of 2 percent per year in the nomadic population.

The Plan goes on to explain that

The Bedouin have a complex and highly developed social, economic and legal system that has adapted to change over many hundreds of years. Nevertheless, the pace of change in the rest of the Kingdom has recently been so fast that the economic and social gap between the Bedouin and the population is widening; consequently special programs, based on realistic appraisal of the needs and changing social and economic role of the Bedouin, are required to improve the life of this segment of the population (Ministry of Planning 1976: 422).

So far, however, well past the mid-point of the period of the Second Development Plan, no specific programs aimed at rectifying and improving the position of the Bedouin have been initiated except for one—the development of an animal subsidy program whereby people receive a cash subsidy based on the number of animals (sheep and camels) they own. On the other hand, sedentarization programs, such as the massive King Faisal Settlement Project at Haradh, have been abandoned. That project, which was originally intended to be the nucleus for the settlement of 1000 Bedouin families, has now been turned over to a foreign (Irish) company to run as a highly capital-intensive modern farm on a profit-sharing basis with the government. In other areas, such as the Wadi Dawasir, agricultural development is being implemented by foreign firms in collaboration with the Saudi Arabian Ministry of Agriculture and Water. These farms utilize highly capital-intensive methods and rely on a foreign labor force (often European or North American) and have essentially no interaction with the local population, although the overwhelming majority of settled, semi-settled, and nomadic Bedouin in the area are interested in expanding and improving agriculture in what they consider to be their own Wadi.

The substandard socio-economic conditions of the Bedouin, at least in comparison with those prevailing among the rest of the Saudi Arabian population, are easily documented. In the Arabian Shield-South, an area of 202,000 square kilometers in the interior part of southwestern Saudi Arabia, 72 percent of the total employed population is engaged in traditional agriculture (including pastoralism). Construction and transportation employ five percent of the labor force. The remainder are primarily engaged in traditional retail and service activities. Professional workers account for only three percent of the labor force, clerical workers four percent and managerial workers only 0.2 percent.[9] The percentage involved in the traditional labor force is well above the national average mentioned earlier but is representative of the situation in rural areas in general.

According to the 1974 *Population Census* (Ministry of Finance and National Economy 1974), this area has a total population of 727,432 people, approximately ten percent of the total national population. People enumerated at waterpoints (almost all nomadic Bedouin) account for 33 percent of the total population of the Arabian Shield-South. Villagers (among whom are included a large number of sedentarized Bedouin) account for 48 percent of the population while those enumerated in emirate capitals (often no larger than villages) account for 20 percent of the population. The area thus has a higher percentage of Bedouin than the national average which is estimated at 25 percent.

The highest degree of illiteracy is found among those enumerated at waterpoints—96 percent of all people 10 years and older are illiterate as opposed to 80 percent of all villagers 10 years and older and 54 percent of all people in the same age category in emirate capitals. Also, only two percent of children ages 6 through 9 at waterpoints were enrolled in schools while 50 percent of children in the same age category from villages were in schools and 57 percent of those in emirate capitals were in schools.

Ibrahim and I found a somewhat better situation among the 208 Bedouin we interviewed: only 62 percent claimed that no one in their households was literate. This figure was higher, however, for long range nomadics, among whom 72 percent said that no one was literate in their households (1978: 62-63). I observed no change in educational status among the Āl Azab Āl Murrah I revisited in 1977 after a seven year absence; none of these long distance camel nomads have gone to schools, nor have they sent any of their children to schools, nor do they have any plans for doing so. On the other hand, the young sons (now about 11 or 12 years old) of a nephew of the paramount amir of the Āl Murrah (himself illiterate) already have more formal education than their father at about 27 when I first knew him. Nonetheless, it is obvious that nomads have by far the lowest educational status of any sector of the Saudi Arabian population and it does not seem that any special efforts are being made to rectify this situation, at least not among the average Bedouin pastoralists in the desert ranges.

Yet the Bedouin say they believe strongly in the value of schools—95.2 percent of our sample said they would like their children to be in school. The reasons given are various. Many (16.3 percent) said the primary reason for wanting their children in schools was to learn more about religion. Almost as many (15.3 percent) said to learn about practical subjects. A much smaller percentage (9.1) said in order for them to have a better occupational career. A few more (12.0 percent) said in order to make more money. Just over a fifth (21.2 percent) said to learn about religion and all the other reasons mentioned above. Thirty-six percent, however, gave only vague reasons for wanting children in schools (Ibrahim and Cole 1978: 68). However, when we asked about the usefulness of education for the Bedouin themselves, we found that only 89.1 percent of the semi-settled and short range nomads and 79.1 percent of the long range nomads generally felt that education was useful for them so long as they remained Bedouin. Yet, about 96 percent of the semi-settled and short range nomads said they would definitely settle for the sake of their children's education while only 74.6 percent of the long range nomads said they would settle. Over 90 percent of all of them said that nomadism itself was the major impediment to schooling (1978: 69).

It thus appears that the Bedouin are themselves ambivalent about the usefulness of modern education. Many of those interviewed felt that education was of no practical use for full-time Bedouin—i.e. there was nothing, in their view, that modern education could contribute to the herding enterprise. At the same time, they recognize that nomadism itself is the major impediment to obtaining an education and large majorities of both the semi-settled and short range nomads and the long range nomads said they would definitely consider settling so that their children could obtain a modern education. This contradiction suggests two major conclusions. One is that a majority of Bedouin consider Bedouinism and herding to be old-fashioned, traditional, and/or backward and that it does not require any modern education to be practiced. Secondly, the fact that a majority believes that modern schooling is nonetheless a good thing, and that most said they would consider settling to allow their children to obtain an education suggests that they realize that, at present, socio-cultural-economic improvement or upward mobility in Saudi Arabia revolves around their abandoning nomadic pastoralism as a primary activity in favor of other occupations.

As mentioned earlier, Saudi Arabia is experiencing a rapid change in its economy and cities are the major foci for this change. Accordingly, as in the past, the Bedouin are migrating to the cities and are contributing a significant part of their male population to the modern and semi-modern labor force. In the Arabian Shield-South, in 1974, there were 26,286 fewer males than females present in rural areas (from waterpoints and villages). Since the majority of these males were between the ages of 20 and 39, it is obvious that they are employed in activities outside traditional herding and agriculture. These absent males represented 5.2 percent of the population enumerated at waterpoints and 4.68 percent of that at villages. In fact, a higher percentage of males are probably engaged in outside activities than these figures show, since many work part-time and are thus part-time residents in their tents and villages.

Ibrahim and I found that 33.2 percent of our sample reported that at least one member of the household worked for the government (1978: 29). If we add private enterprise and self-employment in sectors such as transportation, an even higher percentage of Bedouin males could be said to work in non-pastoral activities. Yet, if we consider that an oversupply of uneducated labor is projected, the Bedouin who remain uneducated are likely to find themselves without job opportunities in non-pastoral sectors.

Generally speaking, the career aspirations of the Bedouin for their children are not particularly high. Ibrahim and I found that 32.7 percent said anything they choose or whatever God grants. Only 21.6 percent had what one might consider high level occupation aspirations—these include engineers, officers, pilots, and top level bureaucrats. More than one third (37 percent) opted for subprofessional careers requiring only secondary school or equivalent education such as elementary school teachers and government clerks. Low-level occupations such as janitors, drivers, and herding and agriculture were the career aspirations of a minority of 8.7 percent (1978: 66-67).

In fact, the majority of Bedouin employed outside of herding work in low-level occupations. My own observations of oil camps and geological survey camps show that the majority of Saudi Arabians employed as unskilled laborers are young Bedouin working to obtain money for such things as bridewealth or to buy a motor vehicle. A large part of desert transportation is in the hands of Bedouin but more sophisticated highway hauling is being done by non-Bedouin with an increasingly large number of young Europeans, Australians, and New Zealanders working as drivers. Most of the soldiers in the National Guard are Bedouin and some serve in the Police Force and Army. Only a small handful have ever obtained high level government posts—e.g. there is only one deputy minister who was originally a Bedouin and whose father is still a Bedouin herder. There are also a few relatively well-off merchants who were originally Bedouin but these are a minority among the merchant class in Saudi Arabia.

The only significant avenue at present which provides special training programs and potentially leads to high-level careers in the modern sector of society is the military. The Vinnel Corporation, an American concern under contract to the Saudi Arabian government, for example, provides English language training, Arabic literacy classes, and training in modern military science to members of the National Guard, all of whom are from Bedouin tribes. Those who are chosen to be officers usually spend a period of up to several years in special training programs abroad, usually in the United States. Similiar programs exist for the Police, the Army, the Air Force, and the Navy—although people from sedentary backgrounds as well as Bedouin may be included in these programs. The wide majority of Bedouin in these programs marry Bedouin girls who remain at home in the desert with the herds—their husbands visiting them on week-ends and during vacations. Outside of the military and security forces, however, very few Bedouin ever receive advanced training in modern subjects, since there are almost no desert-based Bedouin youth in universities either within the Kingdom or abroad.[10]

Although I have used literacy and education as the major criteria for suggesting the present place of the Bedouin in contemporary Saudi Arabian society, there are other criteria which can be applied to show their generally low contemporary social status. These include housing and health conditions and practices. A vast majority of the Bedouin live in tents, straw huts, or shacks that are overcrowded and lacking in water, kitchen, and toilet facilities. A majority of our sample (88 percent) expressed the need for new housing—mostly for permanently built housing in one settled community (Ibrahim and Cole 1978: 47).

Concerning health, suffice it to say that 71.7 percent of the Bedouin Ibrahim and I interviewed said they would go to a modern doctor or clinic for treatment but most (59 percent) would have to travel a considerable distance to another community to obtain modern medical services. It is, additionally difficult for them to obtain regular medical service. If they go to a doctor or clinic in case of illness, it is only once and there is seldom any follow-up treatment. Doctors we interviewed in the field unanimously expressed the opinion that the Bedouin suffer from malnutrition and anaemia and often have eye diseases. In general we found that the Bedouin were quite receptive to modern medicine and one of their most emphatic requests was for conveniently located hospitals, clinics, mobile medical units and/or in-residence paramedics (1978: 84-91).

Contemporary Herding Practices of the Bedouin

The herds of camels, sheep, and goats that are owned and managed by Bedouin households represent a significantly large element in the non-oil based or derived wealth of Saudi Arabia. Animal censuses that have been done until recently are generally believed to be unreliable but it is hoped that recent aerial surveys may give an accurate account of the total number of animals on the desert and semi-desert ranges of the country.

In recent years, the government of the Kingdom has come to recognize that livestock, most of which is owned and managed by Bedouin households, is a major resource of the nation and that the livestock sector of the economy should be encouraged and developed (cf. Al-Saleh 1976). The major program the government has initiated in this regard is a cash subsidy program administered by the Ministry of Agriculture and Water whereby the government annually pays 30 riyals (about $ 9) per sheep and 50 riyals (about $ 17) per camel. This program was initiated following the severe droughts which occurred during the 1960's, which resulted in the mass starvation of animals. The subsidy program was intended to help and to encourage the Bedouin to rebuild their herds and flocks. Government loans through the Agricultural Bank on extremely easy terms are also available to individual Bedouin to purchase water tankers.

The cash value of the sheep and camels owned by the Bedouin is extremely high. The cash value of a one-year-old sheep is a minimum of 300 riyals (about $ 90) and is more likely to be in the range of about 600 riyals (about $ 180). The minimum price for an average full-grown milk camel is 3000 riyals (about $ 900) and prices as high as 20,000 riyals (about $ 6666) are quoted for both racing camels and very fine, pure-bred milk camels. However, the Bedouin do not regularly sell their animals, as mentioned earlier in this paper. Instead of consuming any significant part of meat raised on its own ranges, Saudi Arabia as a nation imports most of its meat (other than chicken). This is so despite the fact that the local mutton is the prefered meat of a majority of the increasingly large urban population. Thus the modern cities of the area, as described by Amin and Asad for earlier periods, do not consume any significant surplus production that emanates from the Bedouin sector of the population. The supplying of meat and other animal products to the cities seems never to have been a traditional activity of the Arabian Bedouin and this continues to be the case to the present.

For the past, it could be argued that the vagaries of weather and disease among the animals did not allow them the potential to produce a large enough surplus to regularly supply a large urban population. In addition, raiding and tribal warfare often diverted their attention from the business of herding. Today, however, increasingly large numbers of animals are being kept on the ranges by the Bedouin, with consequent serious over-grazing and destruction of the rangelands.

Several major changes have occurred during the past three decades that are related to herding practices. One of the most important has been the conversion of all rangelands to Public Lands by a Royal Decree issued in 1953. This Decree made the *hema* system illegal and thus abolished the rights that tribes had traditionally (and by their own military strength) held as exclusive grazing rights to certain areas. All rangelands thus became open to any who wanted to graze them, a right which was and is upheld by the national government through its own police forces.

Another major factor that has contributed to more intensive use of the ranges has been the development of water resources—first through the drilling of modern State-owned wells throughout the desert, including remote areas, and more recently, through the acquisition of pick-up trucks by almost all the Bedouin and water tankers by many of them. Thus no longer are the Bedouin restricted to grazing areas where they have traditional tribal rights to water resources. Finally, the generalized use of motor vehicles to transport animals and households to grazing areas has meant that the Bedouin and their herds have become much more mobile than in the past.

The consequence of these modern innovations is that as soon as rains fall in any particular area vast numbers of Bedouin, without regard to tribal origin, descend on that area with their herds and graze the area intensively until news comes of another area which has received rain, at which time they load their herds and households on Mercedes trucks (for hire usually, with a Bedouin as driver) or on their own pick-ups and move on.

The only remnant of traditional herding or migration practices that still holds partly true is that most households and herds return to their tribe's traditional home territory, where their traditional tribally owned wells are located, during the summer. However, they less often cluster around wells as in the past but keep their animals and households dispersed on the grazing areas and truck water to them.

What appears to have happened is that unplanned, spontaneous, and partial efforts at modernization by both the government and the Bedouin is leading to the potential destruction of rangelands as a result of overgrazing and vehicular traffic, without the nation having even benefited from a short-term increase in its domestic meat supply.

The Royal Decree that made all rangelands Public Lands and declared *hemas* illegal was part of the government's effort to displace customary law with Islamic Sharia law throughout the nation and for all citizens. The general intention at the time was to bring an end to the armed tribal conflict that resulted when tribes enforced their claims to specific grazing areas and reserves by their own military prowess. The aim was to remove one of the major reasons underlying the endemic warfare and feuding characteristic of Arabia before the consolidation of the present nation-state of Saudi Arabia. Although it was not the intention of the law-makers at the time, this Decree paved the way for open and uncontrolled use of ranges throughout the Kingdom.

The development of modern water resources has also been seen by both the Bedouin and the government as a major way of improving the Bedouin standard of living and of giving them the benefit of modern technology. In similar fashion, the granting of subsidies and easy loans to purchase tankers is seen as a way of distributing some of the Kingdom's cash reserves to a segment of the population that tends to have a very low per capita cash income while at the same time offering the Bedouin encouragement to improve their herds.

What no one in the government expected, however, was that these innovations would lead mainly to an explosion in the intensity of rangeland use by the Bedouin without their contributing much of their dramatically increased surplus of animals to the national economy or for the benefit of the society at large which much prefers local lamb and mutton to any of the various imported varieties.

Generally speaking, the Bedouin are not happy with the way in which the present state of affairs affects their economic activities as Bedouin herdsmen. They want to improve their own level of production, they say, to be able to depend primarily on their own efforts without having to be too dependent on government bureaucracies which they find difficult to deal with. Interviews and discussions with Bedouin on the rangelands of the Arabian Shield-South have revealed a number of their thoughts on the characteristics of the Bedouin economy at present and how they would like to change it:

— First, they say that all of the Bedouin are receiving subsidies from the government for their sheep and camels although many complain about delays in receiving them and some doubt that all of the money allocated ever reaches the hands of the Bedouin themselves.

— Second, since the subsidy program began, the herds of sheep have about tripled in size. They say that a herdsman who had 100, now has 300 and one who had 300, now has 900.

— Third, they have not noticed any major changes in the state of the ranges as a result of the increased number of animals. They say that no species of plants have disappeared. They readily agree that if there are more animals, more plants will be eaten by them. But the Bedouin say that the major determinant factor in the state of the ranges is not the number of animals on them but is rainfall and that is according to the will of God.

— Fourth, if there is no rain, they say they have to try to feed their animals *hab*, a traditional form of wheat, and dates, for they claim these are the only things their animals know how to eat. But feed is not readily available in the remote desert ranges, although automobile spare parts and gasoline and a wide variety of imported consumer items are readily available in the small desert villages and towns that dot the map of Arabia and are regularly frequented by most of the Bedouin. But even if they can find feed conveniently near-by, it is expensive. Therefore, if there is a severe drought, they say they would let the animals die.

— Fifth, they say that they are aware of and fully agree with the fact that there is a meat shortage in the cities. They also agree that they are the ones who own most of the animals in the Kingdom. Yet, they admit that they rarely sell their animals on a regular basis or in large numbers. They say that they do not need to because they are receiving money from the subsidy program and from other activities (jobs, etc.) and they are not generally in need of extra cash at present. They say they often let their animals die rather than sell them. Also, they complain that the marketing process is difficult and they claim that they can seldom market animals and make any money. They would not mind selling if the marketing process were easier and less haphazard and if they could be sure of maintaining a minimal core herd in spite of drought and disease. They often moan that they are weak, that their situation is very precarious and that their survival depends on things they have no control over—drought and diesease. Their major traditional means of combating drought and disease is to have herds as large as possible.

— Sixth, they say that each has to fend for himself and he who rests or is lazy will be eaten up by others. Thus one is strongly encouraged to utilize the ranges to the fullest because if one does not use them, someone else will.

According to the Bedouin, a solution to their problems and to the cities' meat shortage would be a project by which the government helps the Bedouin to develop agricultural plots.[11] They say they need water, machines to plow the land and labor. Once the wells are dug and there are easy ways to irrigate and when the major work for preparing fields has been completed, they believe that the Bedouin can do most of the labor if they have machines. The Bedouin stress that the government should provide the complete package—the whole system: wells, an irrigation system that works, machines, their spare parts, and mechanics who can fix them. They say there is no use in giving things in bits and pieces, as has happened in the past.

The Bedouin also say that the government should give this package to individuals. Many have already staked claims on land they would like to have developed for them. They would like the government to help them out and give them title to the land but they also admit that the government should have the right to make sure people actually use the land. No one wants any joint tribal-based projects to be arranged because they say that people would only end up fighting among themselves "as even brothers do when they jointly own a piece of property". It should be noted here that this individualistic attitude of the Bedouin is a continuation of and manifestation of their socialization into the domestic mode of production. As such, it runs counter to the government's idea for major agricultural development in Saudi Arabia (essentially capital intensive agri-business operations). It is also counter to the few private agricultural development efforts in Saudi Arabia which have achieved any significant degree of success in increasing production and selling in the local markets. These, too, have been capital-intensive agri-businesses.

Aside from helping them develop small-scale agricultural plots, the Bedouin say that the government could register the animals an individual owns and then require him to sell a given proportion of the young animals each year, in an organized fashion and for a guaranteed minimum price. This requirement they say should be part of the deal for receiving government aid for developing agriculture. The Bedouin should grow alfalfa and other feed products for fattening their animals and to use as feed during years of drought. The overall goal of such projects should be to make the Bedouin strong and more secure so that ultimately they do not have to depend on government aid or outside employment.

Conclusions: The Bedouin Socially and Economically in a Modernized Saudi Arabia

The general aim of this paper has been to draw attention to the Bedouin of Saudi Arabia within the general context of the total society in which they exist. Several points remain to be made concerning their position within the changing world in which they find themselves and to point out briefly some avenues of directed change that might be explored to improve their present position and to incorporate them more fully and with opportunities equal to those of other citizens in a more fully modernized Saudi Arabia.

First, as Ibrahim and I concluded,

Quantitatively, the Bedouin are a significant group. Their socio-political import is even more impressive. For one thing, the present ruling elite in Saudi Arabia, the Al Sa'ud, descends from one of the major Bedouin tribal confederations of Najd, the 'Anazah, a kinship affinity of which they are conscious and proud. The moral fabric, the social order, and the value system of Saudi society today cannot be fully comprehended without an understanding of its Bedouin component.

Economically, the significance of the Bedouin in Saudi life has undergone dramatic change in recent decades. Owners of huge herds of camels, sheep and goats, the Bedouin in pre-oil times accounted for the greatest wealth of the nation. This important economic role, however, has been eclipsed in the last quarter century by the wealth derived from oil. Also, in terms of manpower, the Bedouin are far from being incorporated into modern economic sectors. Their economy is still based on subsistence-oriented herding and their herds are more like fixed assets than transactional market commodities. Thus, despite their numbers and the absolute value of their animal wealth, the Bedouin are marginal to modern Saudi economy. Their non-utilization as manpower, moreover, constitutes a most serious problem in a country like Saudi Arabia which is experiencing an immense labor shortage (1978: 3-4).

Secondly, the importance of the tribe as a socio-political-economic unit in Saudi Arabia has lost a great deal of its meaning as a result of the way the present national society and culture are emerging. Tribal control of grazing and migration patterns has been largely eclipsed by the 1953 Royal Decree which legally opened all rangelands to anyone who wished to use them without regard to tribal affiliation and by the development of modern State-owned water resources and by the Bedouin's almost universal acquisition of motor vehicles, which allows them much more mobility than ever existed before.

Also, the tribe has declined in political significance because the government administers the area on the basis of localities rather than on tribal divisions. The rural areas where the Bedouin live are administered by government amirs who are employees of the Ministry of Interior. Most of these men have a tribal background but seldom come from shaikhly families in their own tribes. They are almost without exception from a different tribe from that which predominates in the locality they administer. Most of their duties are related to maintaining law and order and seldom have anything to do with modernization efforts. Nowadays the traditional tribal leaders themselves mainly form a kind of social elite within their own tribes and are more actively engaged in their own economic improvement and in securing their sons in positions as officers in the National Guard rather than in promoting general tribal politics or in leading modernization programs among their own fellow tribespeople.

One result of this is that all tribes together are coming to be seen as forming a single category in Saudi Arabian society. Tribalism and Bedouinism have tended to replace tribes as such in the basic fabric of Saudi Arabian social life. This phenomenon merits much more attention than can be given to it in this paper. Essentially, however, it means that the fact of tribal origin still conditions aspects of behavior in the emerging national society—e.g. type of work one will follow; whom one can marry—and it is a way of categorizing people socially. What is more significant now, however, is to say that one is of tribal origin rather than from any one particular tribe. All people from tribes are more like each other in terms of behavior and social identity than they are like other sectors of Saudi Arabian society—e.g. those of former slave status, those of traditional sedentary background living in villages, those who are merchants, or those who are members of the royal elite.

It should also be noted that the position of people of tribal origin, essentially the Bedouin, in the social hierarchy of Arabia is ambivalent. Some, especially some powerful elements of the Royal Family, consider them to be very high. Most people, nowadays, consider them to be of quite low status because of their inability to have achieved anything significant in the modern society. They are generally seen by the more modernized urban elements as the one major group in Saudi Arabian society which has not taken advantage of the new opportunities that have developed and who are increasingly seen as a kind of pariah group in the contemporary society—no matter how high their status may have been in the past.

This leads naturally to the question of what avenues might be opened up for them, if they are to be incorporated into the modern society on any kind of an equal footing with others. One way is through the modernization of livestock production whereby some Bedouin continue to practise their pastoral skills but not as subsistence-oriented producers. They would become market-oriented producers of meat for the national market. This would probably involve at least the following elements, which can only be mentioned in passing: 1., a reduction in the total number of both Bedouins and animals and herds; 2., controlled grazing practices; 3., the development of feed supplies and the provision of veternarian services throughout the rangeland areas to obviate the effects of drought and animal diseases; 4., the development of regular markets, feed lots for fattening and finishing, and slaughter houses at appropriate locations to secure the smooth and regular distribution of meat to the wider public.

The second way—and this must accompany the above—is through the development of special programs to train the Bedouin to work and participate successfully in the modern sector of the economy. This is essential if the livestock sector is modernized because it is generally believed that many fewer Bedouin would need to be employed in that sector if it were developed on a more market-oriented basis and less on a household mode of production basis, as is still typical of the situation at present. It is also essential that the Bedouin be trained to participate in the modern sector of the economy if that sector is in fact to fully develop, as envisaged in the Kingdom's Development Plans. The Bedouin represent a sizable proportion of the indigenous population—as much as 25 percent—and their participation in an active way and not just as more or less passive, part-time, unskilled laborers and drivers is essential if the economy is to become significantly more modernized. A more diversified economy will reduce dependence on the export of crude oil, which is essential if the country is to achieve any significant degree of real economic and political independence within the context of international economic and political systems. The Bedouin and other rural groups who are increasingly subsisting on welfare and traditional low-scale productive activities must be trained and incorporated into the modern economy and society.

Many hundreds of years ago Ibn Khaldun commented that

Bedouins are unable to settle in a city with a large civilization (population). The reason for this is that luxury increases in a city with a large civilization...The needs of the inhabitants increase on account of the luxury. Because of the demand for (luxury articles), they become customary, and thus come to be necessities. In addition, all labor becomes precious in the city, and the conveniences become expensive, because there are many purposes for which they are in demand in view of the prevailing luxury and because the government makes levies on market and business transactions. This is reflected in the sales prices. Conveniences, foodstuffs, and labor thus become, very expensive....The income of the Bedouins, on the other hand, is not large, because they live where there is little demand for labor, and labor is the cause of profit. Bedouins, therefore, do not accumulate any profit or property. For this reason, it is difficult for them to settle in a big city, because conveniences there are many and things to buy are dear. In the desert, (the Bedouins) can satisfy their needs with a minimum of labor, because in their lives they are little used to luxuries and all their requirements. They are not, therefore, obliged to have property.

Every Bedouin who is attracted to city life quickly shows himself unable (to compete) and is disgraced. The only exceptions are such (Bedouins) as have previously accumulated property and obtained more of it than they needed and therefore achieved the amount of tranquility and luxury that is natural to civilized people. They, then, may move to a city, and their condition, as regards customs and luxury, can blend with that of its inhabitants. This is the way the civilization of cities begins.

God "comprises every thing" (I: 279-280).

Ibn Khaldun's comments sound almost as if they were a description of the current situation in Saudi Arabia. It is hoped, however, that a situation will evolve whereby the accumulation of property will not be the major prerequisite for Bedouin to successfully settle without being disgraced. Hopefully, a situation will emerge whereby some can go to the cities armed with modern skills that will allow them to compete and to contribute to the development of their own country and whereby some others can make the rangelands more productive for the total society and for themselves.

REFERENCES

AMIN, Samir
1970   *The Maghreb in the Modern World.* Middlesex: Penguin Books.
1976   *La nation arabe: nationalisme et luttes de classes.* Paris: Editions de Minuit.
ASAD, Talal
1973   "The Bedouin as a Military Force". In: Cynthia Nelson, ed., *The Desert and the Sown: Nomads in the Wider Society.* Berkeley: Institute of International Studies, University of California.
BARTH, Frederik
1973   "A General Perspective on Nomad-Sedentary Relations in the Middle East". In: Cynthia Nelson, ed., *The Desert and the Sown: Nomads in the Wider Society.* Berkeley: Institute of International Studies, University of Calif.
COLE, Donald P.
1971   *The Social and Economic Structure of the Al Murrah: A Saudi Arabian Bedouin Tribe.* Ph. D. Dissertation, University of California, Berkeley.
1975a   *Nomads of the Nomads: The Āl Murrah Bedouin of the Empty Quarter.* Chicago: Aldine.
1975b   "Local Organization Among Camel Nomads and Supralocal Power Institutions in a Radically Changing Society: The Āl Murrah in Saudi Arabia". Paper presented at American Anthropological Association Meetings, San Francisco.

Ibn Khaldun
    1958   *The Muqaddimah: An Introduction to History*. Translated from the Arabic by Franz
            Rosenthal. New York, Pantheon.
Ibrahim, Saad Eddin and Donald P. Cole
    1978   *Saudi Arabian Bedouin: An Assessment of their Needs*. Cairo, American University in
            Cairo Press.
Ibrahim, Saad Eddin and Nicholas S. Hopkins, eds.
    1977   *Arab Society in Transition: A Reader*. Cairo, American University in Cairo Press.
Kingdom of Saudi Arabia, Ministry of Finance and National Economy
    1974   *Population Census 1394 AH—1974 AD*. Riyadh.
Kingdom of Saudi Arabia, Ministry of Planning
    1976   *The Second Development Plan for 1395-1400 AH—1975-1980 AD*. Riyadh.
    1978   *The Strategies for the Third Development Plan for 1400-1405 AH—1980-1985 AD*.
            Manuscript.
Sahlins, Marshall
    1972   *Stone Age Economics*. Chicago: Aldine.
al-Saleh, Nasser
    1976   *Problems in the Modernization of the Livestock Sector in Semi-Arid Regions: A Saudi Arabian
            Case Study*. Ph.D. Dissertation, University of Durham.

NOTES

1   These visits were made in my position as an anthropological consultant to the World Bank
    (1977) and as a Senior Anthropologist on a team to study the Arabian Shield-South for
    agricultural and water development under the general auspices of the Saudi Arabian
    Ministry of Agriculture and Water. I would like to express my gratitude to these institutions
    for their co-operation; the ideas expressed here are my own.
2   This study has been carried out as part of the study mentioned in note 1 for the Ministry of
    Agriculture and Water.
3   This statement, which is an interesting early development of the idea of ecological adapta-
    tion, clearly shows that Ibn Khaldun did not believe that the Bedouin themselves were
    capable of producing complex civilized societies although his general notion of evolution of
    societies from simple to complex often gives the implication of the opposite.
4   This argument runs counter to that advanced by Barth (1973) who seems to believe that
    nomads in the Middle East are capable of creating a surplus which allows them to dominate
    much of the rest of the society.
5   It should be noted here that this dualistic division of the economy into modern and tradi-
    tional systems may seem similiar to the structure of pre-modern Arab socio-economics
    discussed earlier. However, the modern urban sector is clearly increasingly tied into the
    international capitalist system, which would seem to be a difference in kind from the system
    in which the pre-modern mercantile trade of the past operated. Also, the rural sector
    nowadays is more dependent on the urban sector which itself is in an essentially dependent
    position vis-a-vis the developed capitalist world.
6   The Ministry of Planning and most Saudi officials seldom consider the nomads as an ele-
    ment in the economy—traditional or otherwise. They are seen by them more as a social
    phenomenon that merits little consideration when discussing the economy of Saudi Arabia.
7   Although I believe this to be a sincere desire on the part of the government, many of the best
    trained Saudis opt to live and work abroad.
8   Both references to the World Bank manpower study were conveyed to me verbally.
9   These figures are all based on calculations I made from figures presented in the 1974
    Population Census.
10 It should be added that occasionally some youth are sent abroad for advanced technical

training related to the oil business. An example is one youth from the Al Murrah who was sent to study in Michigan by ARAMCO.

11 A major goal of the Bedouin at present is to have a small date palm farm with a permanent house. This reflects their notion of improvement at present and fits in with their traditional organization based on the household mode of production. They are not so much interested in developing viable new communities as in obtaining a small farm to complement their household-organized herding operations.

Pastoralism and Class Differentiation among the Lakenkhel

ASEN BALIKCI

University of Montréal, Montréal, Canada

IN A RECENT PAPER on the alleged equality of nomadic social systems Talal Asad draws attention to the necessity of perceiving pastoral groups from the outside and examining closely their historic position within global society. Asad argues that the social conditions of the pastoralists' existence are reproduced by this total system. Pastoral nomadism is a technical activity, "un genre de vie", expressive of certain forces of production which can be found in combination with different relations of production in specific historical settings. The crucial questions then refer to the formation and appropriation of surplus by pastoralists, the manner in which pastoral accumulation emerges from specific relations of production and how these are integrated into a dominant mode of production prevalent at the level of global society. More specifically Asad asks how, in each case, a determinate historical pattern of social division of labour comes to acquire class characteristics among pastoralists (Asad, 1979).

With these questions in mind I shall examine the case of the Lakenkhel of Northeastern Afghanistan, a Pashtoon group located in Baghlan province. At the time of the field research in 1975 most Lakenkhel were fully sedentarized; pastoral activities, however, were vigorously pursued in one lineage. The points illustrated here concern the dynamic interdependence of the two main production activities (pastoralism and agriculture), the contractual relations within the pastoral sector and the resulting historic emergence of class stratification differentially affecting specific Lakenkhel lineages.

Until the 1880's the Lakenkhel were established as pastoralists in the area north of Ghazni which they recognize as their traditional homeland. They suffered greatly during the Ghilzai revolt, when their flocks of sheep were destroyed and their leaders severely punished by Abdur Rahman. Following this disaster they moved to the Kohistan region (the southern slopes of the Hindu Kush) as dependent laborers. There they slowly reconstructed their flocks and opportunistically benefited from the newly-established peace and the opening of Northern Afghanistan, by engaging in caravan trade between Peshawar and the bazaars along the Oxus River valley. Their caravan route passed along Narin valley north of the Hindu Kush which was populated by semi-nomadic Uzbak who combined transhumance with dry farming. The Lakenkhel saw the opportunity of acquiring land in the valley, which they did with the help of the government. Eventually the Uzbak were crowded onto the nearby dry plateaus and increasingly larger sections of Narin valley were brought under cultivation with the help of a tight network of irrigation canals and ditches. This initiated a long historic process of sedentarization for the Lakenkhel. At present the three Lakenkhel lineages (Baramkhel, Radirkhel and Salamkhel) occupy three distinct yet almost contiguous villages. Sub-lineages also behave as residential clusters. But nowadays, pastoral activities are primarily concentrated in one sub-lineage, namely the Baramkhel, while the others remain almost completely sedentary following the loss of their sheep at different times in recent history. There are two types of agriculture in the area: irrigated fields yielding two crops, with fertilizers crucially important to the success of the second crop; and dry fields, with productivity varying enormously from year to year according to precipitation.

The pastoral year begins in spring with the establishment of a lambing camp in the lowlands of Gerdau near the Kunduz River. These pastures are protected by the government and have been regularly used by the Lakenkhel and other Pashtoon nomadic groups for about two generations. In recent years following rapid demographic increase, neighbouring villagers have persistently tried to bring these pastures under cultivation. These encroachments have led to open fighting and hesitant government intervention. In 1976 the Lakenkhel considered these pressures as a danger to the pastoral entreprise and moved to another spring location.

Around early May the lambs are strong enough to undertake the move to the high mountain pastures. Flocks and caravans travel separately. The flocks move slowly around mountain slopes where grazing is available while the caravans travel quickly on the roads at the bottom of the valleys and stop frequently. At the stop in Narin the camels are loaded with summer supplies and the caravans enlarged by the addition of numerous cattle and horses to be fattened at the high mountain pastures. Around early June flocks and caravans reach the Daraykhar valley, at an elevation of about 3000 meters, in the heart of the Hindu Kush. There, the Lakenkhel have traditional grazing rights. According to custom these pastures belong to the Tadjik villagers established in the lower valley who primarily own goats which are better adapted to the bushy vegetation of lower altitudes. These villagers are the subjects of a powerful local chieftain and it is to him that the Lakenkhel pay tribute, the amount of which is renegotiated every year.

The Lakenkhel remain at the green pastures of Daraykhar until the middle of August when the male lambs are sold to related Lakenkhel traders who reside on the southern slopes of the Hindu Kush. Once back home the Lakenkhel pastoral families behave as sedentary villagers, completely separated from the flocks which graze throughout winter on wheat stubs and dry grass in the hills around Narin valley.

Lakenkhel migratory patterns reveal an unstable process of ecological adaptation. At the spring lowland pastures agriculturalists and pastoralists compete directly for land. This is a long historic process well understood by both groups. Demography and modern technology (utilisation of tractors) favor the agriculturalists and present government policy can only delay the final outcome. It is thus untrue to state that these pastoralists occupy an empty ecological niche that no other group could exploit. At the upper end of the migration treck the situation is reversed. Two generations ago a very large number of Lakenkhel exploited the Daraykhar pastures. At present the small pastoral segment of the Lakenkhel is faced with an over-abundance of summer pastures. This favorable situation, however, is due to the Lakenkhel's ability to retain their preferential grazing rights in the area.

The instability of Lakenkhel pastoralism is further influenced by certain purely environmental factors. A survey of the reasons for flock loss among two Lakenkhel lineages revealed the prime killer to be heavy snowfall in conjunction with persistent cold during late winter, when the sheep are particularly weak. Frost affects the various flocks differentially depending on their precise location, on the shepherd's technical abilities and on the application of rescue measures by flock owners. It is clear that Lakenkhel pastoral adaptation does not fit an equilibrium model (Bonte 1978, p. 18) but is rather a dynamic process in response to a variety of social and environmental pressures.

What are the basic organizational forms of Lakenkhel pastoralism? Sheep are owned individually except in the case of fraternal joint families where an alignment of brothers exercises joint ownership. Flocks vary greatly in size, from about 50 to over 500. According to local preferences, 500 sheep is an optimal number although a flock comprising 300 to 500 sheep is considered a good flock. It is said that a flock of this size moves at a good grazing speed while a smaller flock travels too fast and a larger flock is difficult for a single shepherd to control. It is impossible to relate flock size to household size because flock management is accomplished by the owner and hired hands (the shepherd and his assistants) without the necessary intervention of additional household members. Considering further that there is no limitation on individual access to pastures, an owner should be capable, in principle, of increasing his flock indefinitely. This is clearly not the case.

What then are the factors limiting flock size? First the obvious historic catastrophies: various sheep diseases, predation by wolves, losses due to snowfalls, etc. Second, structural factors specific to inheritance practice: at the time of marriage or later a son (or sons) may ask for his share of the flock in order to establish himself separately, thus initiating the break-up of large flocks. (In a sense the process of fission in the developmental cycle of the family is projected onto the flock. Fissive tendencies are stronger in polygynous households and in the presence of very large flocks.) Third, personal factors may be important, as for example the varying managerial abilities of flock owners.

The functions of the shepherd are crucially important in flock management. Although he is supervised by the owner and generally takes important decisions only in continuous consulation with him, the shepherd is still the person mainly responsible for the flock's welfare. Shepherds are hired on a one year contract in two phases: six winter months they are paid a global salary of up to 8,000 afghanis while for the six summer months they receive 1/6 of the newborn male lambs and 1/20 of the newborn female lambs. (It is obvious why shepherds prefer large flocks.) A shepherd is a trusted individual with high prestige usually selected by the flock owner from among his relatives. He is always assisted by a salaried servant.

In order to manage their flocks, small flock owners are obliged to join forces and establish an association. Members of such associations are always relatives (*hpil* meaning related people in general or more specifically *uragiray/sakanayi tirbur*-distant/close cousins). The owner of the largest share (*djamdar*: holder of the totality) is responsible for flock management and selecting shepherds. The manager and associates share in the expenses of flock management on a pro rata basis depending on the number of sheep owned by each. In case an associate's family is not present in camp the manager has the right to milk his sheep. Despite frequent quarrels among partners such associations have an average life span of four years.

The management of a single owner flock implies simple dyadic contracts between a superordinate and a subordinate party. This type of contractual arrangement is certainly not specific to pastoralism, but, is as a matter of fact extremely common in other economic sectors, particularly agriculture. As for the joint flock, here again the partnership among equals is an arrangement frequently adopted in a form of trading called *djelapi*: two or three traders bring together unequal capital shares for the purchase and resale of animals and share the benefit on a pro rata basis according to individual capital investment. From an organizational point of view, Lakenkhel pastoralism does not exhibit any novel or specific forms.

What are the economic objectives of Lakenkhel pastoralists? It is worth noting again that Lakenkhel pastoralism is absolutely and fully part of a monetized market economy. All male lambs are sold in summer in toto in a single transaction to a single trader while the sale of old and barren sheep is a continuous activity throughout the year in a variety of circumstances. The sale price of the male lambs is directly determined by national and international markets. (The Lakenkhel are quite frequently informed about sheep prices in the various bazaars of Northern Afghanistan.) The sale price of the male lambs follows the *baybala* practice—the trader is charged an overprice for delayed payment, this to take the place of interest on cash loans which is forbidden in Islam. Again it should be noted that *baybala* payments are used in all sectors of the economy. The Lakenkhel rigorously avoid killing sheep for their own consumption. So strong is this attitude that even sick or wounded sheep killed prior to natural death are sold to neighbouring villagers at a low price. The Lakenkhel consider their sheep as capital on hoof, to be exploited in the most rational way possible. Clearly Lakenkhel sheep represent a "valeur d'change" and not a "valeur d'usage" as P. Bonte assumes (Bonte, 1978, p. 10). Milk products, however, remain outside the market economy, and are strictly for domestic use, since it is considered degrading to sell any.

Two additional activities are closely related to Lakenkhel nomadic sheep-breeding. The first is the breeding of a substantial number of cattle, camels and horses which follow the caravan on the migration treck. These are fattened at Daraykhar valley and later sold to villagers and in the bazaars. Thus the availability of the rich Daraykhar pastures has allowed the Lakenkhel to extend their breeding activities to other species. The second activity is trading. This is a continuous and exuberant activity carried out all along the migration trek and in camp. In a sense, any pastoralist, rich or poor is primarily a trader. The propensity to trade is so strong that practically anything (animals, carpets, guns, etc.) can be bought or sold provided that the price is right.

The pastoralists' first and immediate objective is to complete successfully the annual migration without losses, then to sell the lambs and old sheep and obtain milk products. The second and medium range objective is to increase the size of the flock over a number of years through proper management. Now all Lakenkhel pastoralists own agricultural land in the Narin area and the produce obtained covers family needs as well as frequently providing a marketable surplus. Within the household the following arrangement is typical. A fraternal joint family consists of two married brothers and their descendants. The first brother is fully sedentary and will spend all his time in agricultural activities while the second brother is devoted to the care of the sheep.

Clearly Lakenkhel economic arrangements differ from those among so-called ''pure'' nomads who exchange sheep against grain for food. Among the Lakenkhel, sheepbreeding leads to net capital formation resulting into both sheep sales and flock increase. With fresh capital the Lakenkhel acquire agricultural land or engage in trading ventures. It is clear, therefore, that while the immediate objectives of Lakenkhel pastoralists are centered on the flock, the long range objectives of pastoralism fall outside sheepbreeding, and belong to other economic sectors. This process is similar to the Basseri situation described by Barth (Barth 1961, p. 110) with an important difference: in the Basseri case only rich flock-owners transfer capital into the agricultural sector while among the Lakenkhel practically all pastoralists, whether they own 50 sheep or 500, are engaged in this transfer process.

What is the influence of pastoralism on the emerging class structure among the Lakenkhel? At present the Lakenkhel recognize five socio-economic classes among themselves defined mostly in terms of wealth. *Der mur* and *mur* are the rich land and flock owners, *guzarani* are self-sufficient without debts, *kampagala* are dependent upon the rich for work and do have debts while the *miskin* are hopelessly poor and stand no chance to better their position.

Both pastoralism and class affiliation are unequally represented among the three Lakenkhel lineages. The Salamkheli abandoned nomadism over half a century ago and class differentiation has been determined among them by processes exclusively within the agricultural sector and best expressed in the process of land accumulation with no apparent influence from pastoralism. The

Badirkheli on the other hand are recently sedenterized. For unknown reasons several of their rich flock owners did not acquire agricultural land, at a time when this was easily possible. The Badirkheli say today that their elders had decided to "hang on the tail of the sheep". In a succession of harsh winters they lost most of their sheep, since they were unable to provide them with fodder at the critical moment. Following these disasters they sold their remaining sheep and abandoned nomadism. Today there are no rich individuals among them, and the bulk of the Badirkheli are indebted sharecroppers or remain hopelessly poor, mostly employed by the affluent Baramkheli.

A further structural element may explain Badirkheli neglect of pastoralism after a crisis situation. In his study on Swat Pathan leadership forms, Barth has described the complex local patterns of competition and dominance comprising a system of dyadic relations between one superordinate and one subordinate person (Barth, 1959, p. 42). This complex pattern of intense and continuous rivalry (*siali*) comprising a series of interlocking dyads is prevalent in all sections of Lakenkhel society although more visible among the rich. In the field, it was possible to observe that pastoralists were continuously comparing the size and quality of their flocks in an agonistic manner. It was as if one's flock existed mainly in relation to the neighbour's flock. The implication is that after repeated sheep losses and the elimination of rivals, the *siali* pattern was broken among the Badirkheli and the owners lost the will to struggle and compete.

This process did not take place among the Baramkheli. Among them emerged a leader. This entreprising and opportunistic individual had already begun acquiring land a half a century ago and passed on the impulse for land acquisition to his rivals. At the same time he continued intensive sheep-breeding while maintaining various trading activities. Following the *siali* pattern his rivals tried to imitate him and catch up with him. The result was the emergence of an upper class of vigorous agriculturalists-pastoralists among the Baramkheli who stand in sharp contrast with the fully sedenterized segment of the lineage. This process of class differentiation developed as follows. As noted already the Baramkheli, with the initial cash proceeds of sheep sales, acquired some agricultural land. This provided the families with produce and made sheepbreeding into a capital producing activity. In case of impending disasters (heavy snowfalls, for example), these households, because of their agricultural holdings, had ample fodder to feed the starving sheep. Further, with increased cash income they were able to hire the best shepherds and improve the management of their flocks. Additional cash proceeds and capital increase from sheepbreeding were continuously transferred to the agricultural sector. During the initial phases of sedenterization agricultural labour was difficult to obtain but with the settling down and increased pauperization of the Badirkheli, abundant agricultural labor became available. At the same time, the rapid population increase in the Narin valley restricted the availability of irrigated lands. Taking advantage of the opportunity, the Baramkheli transferred their fresh capital to dry farming and new trading activities. This process was made possible by sheepbreeding, with the flocks serving as an expanding supply of capital. Most Badirkheli remained an agricultural proletariat at the lower level of the class structure while the Baramkheli pastoralists established themselves at the top. From this it is easy to see the dialectical relation between pastoralism and agriculture and the function of pastoralism in the process of Lakenkhel class differentiation. This very process explains sufficiently the continuation of pastoralism among the Baramkheli.

We have indicated that active leadership played an important role in this process—a role that is best evidenced in a contemporary crisis situation. When encroachments by agriculturalists at the lowland lambing camp became very difficult to oppose, the leader negotiated grazing rights with a tribal chief in a different area, thus opportunistically renewing an old alliance. Similarly at the highland pastures the leader mobilized his followers to oppose intruding nomads with guns in hand and renegotiated grazing rights with the powerful Tadjik chief. The community of Baramkheli pastoralists would not have been able to face this conflict situation without its leader and would have lost its pastures and would probably have abandoned pastoralism. The community of pastoralists remained a functioning unit because of its leader.

Lakenkhel pastoralism is a technical activity, "un genre de vie partiel", rather than a total way of life, and its importance has been decreasing during the last decades both in absolute terms and in reference to the other sectors of tribal economy. At present it is a partial activity within a more diversified household economy.

Structurally, Lakenkhel pastoral nomadism lacks originality in the sense that there is not a single contractual relation specific to the pastoral sector; all relations of production within the pastoral sector or linking the pastoral sector to the regional economy are found in the other economic sectors as well. Lakenkhel pastoralism remains firmly integrated in the regional and national economies and its organization is a reflection of forms prevalent in a much wider area. Considering this lack of structural originality, Lakenkhel pastoral nomadism cannot be defined as a specific mode of production.

To conclude, Lakenkhel pastoral nomadism is not a simple subsistence activity since it does not provide the pastoralist-sheep owner with critical subsistence income. It is essentially a capital generating activity, a supplemental strategy within the household economy. It can be included as part of a form of "primitive capital accumulation". Here, the term primitive refers to the simple and immediate process of capital accumulation directly from the technical activity. The same process is visible in the local agricultural sector. The labour of sharecroppers, herders and other hired hands acting contractually and directly on technical activities generates a surplus immediately appropriated by the landowner—sheep owner. This surplus is sold to markets and allows for capital accumulation. This process determined the emergence of a specific class structure which for historical reasons affected the Lakenkhel lineages differentially. It is clear that the contractual relations constitute the central element of this form which qualify it to be considered tentatively as a mode of production under the heading of "primitive capital accumulation".

The final objective of analysis identified by Asad is the precise determination of the mode of production operating at the level of global society, with a description of the manner in which it affects the pastoral sector. The exact determination of a mode of production in a transitional society like Afghanistan which comprises strong tribal formations, emergent capitalist forms and scattered feudal vestiges is a difficult task and falls outside the scope of this paper. But the fact that we, as anthropologists, are primarily trained in the description of small-scale societies should not deter us from the future analysis of larger forms of society. Indeed, this essay pursued the task of explaining the perpetuation of transhumance and pastoral activities among the Lakenkhel, which has been seen to result from political and economic forces related to the larger market and regional context, as well as the dynamics of local level pastoralism.

REFERENCES

ASAD, T.
  1979   "Equality in nomadic social system? Notes towards the dissolution of an anthropological category". In: *Pastoral Production and Society*. Cambridge University Press.
BARTH, F.
  1959   *Political Leadership Among Swat Pathans*. London: London School of Economics Monographs on Social Anthropology No. 19.
  1961   *Nomads of South Persia*. Boston: Little, Brown and Company.
BONTE, P.
  1978   *L'approche marxiste des sociétés d'éleveurs nomades dans les pays occidentaux*. Forthcoming in: *Nomadic Peoples in a Changing World*, conference. P. Salzman and J. Galaty, eds., Philadelphia: ISHI press.

Afterward: On Some General Theoretical Issues

PHILIP CARL SALZMAN

McGill University, Montréal, Canada

I AM AN EMPIRICIST. I so call myself in spite of the fact that the term "empiricist" has become a pejorative term in anthropology, a term of disapprobation. An empiricist, it is said, is someone who believes that knowledge is based upon observation alone and that reason plays no part; who thinks that general understandings can be generated by inference; who is concerned only with physical phenomena and overt behavior and so ignores mental life and meaning; and who sees only surface patterns without exploring the underlying springs from which those patterns derive. The empiricist is thus atheoretical, literal-minded, and superficial.

Naturally, I admit to none of these accusations in my identification with empiricism. It is true, of course, that numerous scholars, past and present, and irrespective of self-identification, could be faulted for one or more of these shortcomings. But, I would argue, the above-mentioned offenses are not necessarily implications of empiricism, nor do they encompass the most important sense of empiricism as represented in the classic texts or in the best of current practice. This most important sense of empiricism, which I take to be the core meaning, is the demand for evidence in support of assertions, the requirement that arguments not be self-validating, the expectation that ideas will be critically examined in the light of independent information. In short, the empiricist is one who has not made up his mind *a priori*, who is investigating rather than proselytizing, who wishes to know what the case is rather than wishing to show that the case is what he knows. For the empiricist, ideas and arguments must ultimately prove themselves in risky tests where the possibility exists that emerging evidence will show the ideas and arguments to be incorrect.

An empiricist, then, is concerned first, whether an idea or argument is formulated in such fashion that it can be challenged by evidence, and second, whether and to what extent evidence has in fact been brought to bear in evaluation. These questions should be addressed in the normal course of discussion to the constructive and provocative arguments that are emerging in work on change and development in nomadic and pastoral societies, such arguments as these: that in pastoral societies cattle play to a substantial degree the role of money (Schneider); that pastoral specialization results in a considerable increase in the productivity of pastoral labor (Bonte); and that some pastoral systems produce as a surplus, not cattle, but men (Cole), to mention but three of the theses presented in this volume. That the question of risky tests and further evidence is raised here is not to suggest that the authors of these hypotheses are unconcerned about evidence, or that they would not concur with my general methodological sentiments (whatever they may think about the label "empiricist"). Rather, the question of independent evidence and risky tests is raised for two reasons: First, to do justice to these and other provocative and valuable hypotheses, it is necessary for those of us working in this field to follow up by putting them to the test systematically and critically. It is not enough for us to cite, either pro or con, the arguments of others, and to examine how they do or do not fit with our own theories. If we are to synthesize a more general knowledge, and to be confident that it is firmly based, we shall have to collectively attend to our past and emerging collective resources, that is, the insights and theories and hypotheses of all of us working in this field. Let me be a little more specific. With few exceptions, each of us works among certain peoples in a particular region, and each of us draws most heavily from his or her own research in formulating his or her general ideas. So when different researchers have different ideas, one question which immediately comes to mind is whether the peoples with whom they have worked are in fact different, which would account for the differences in ideas, the problem then being generalization beyond the appropriate populations. (Specific examples of such questions are mentioned below.) Should this be the case, further attention must be given to defining parameters, to baseline conditions. Alternatively, different arguments and conflicting positions about peoples whom we have good reason to believe are fundamentally similar, cry out for risky tests to generate evidence, for a confrontation profound enough, through the use of independent evaluation, to provide a good basis for deciding correctness. With such conflicting arguments, we must give attention to equivalence of terminology, to the empirical referents of terms, to the kind of evidence that would be regarded as decisive.

What I am suggesting here is certainly orthodox enough, even prosaic. But while the position is prosaic, the tasks indicated are more often recommended than carried out, the objectives more often spoken of than achieved. Making the best use of the ideas and arguments presented in the preceding chapters means not taking them as given, not just using them as the basis for further theoretical elaboration, but carrying out close, systematic, and critical evaluation using independent evidence, so that provocative arguments can be developed into grounded and supported theory.

The second reason that the question of tests and evidence is raised here is that in the remainder of this discussion I intend to discuss some general theoretical issues raised in the papers. Much of the following will be at a fairly high level of abstraction, and there will be little occasion to come down the ladder of abstraction to empirical referents or to adduce evidence in support of one or another position. In this context, even a programmatic statement such as I have made about the empirical imperative is worthwhile if there is a reinforcement of the notion that abstract theoretical discussion is by its non-empirical nature inevitably partial and incomplete.

At the same time, it is theory which gives meaning to facts. Facts cannot speak for themselves, and it might not be too extreme to argue that facts do not exist in themselves; it is theory that designates what counts as facts, and having done that, speaks for them, specifies their significance. The selective function of theory which designates some bits of existence as relevant and therefore facts, and the explanatory function of theory which indicates the meaning of facts, do not present a problem for the empirical imperative, but rather provide the parameter within which this engagement with the "objective world" takes place. While the empirical test may keep us from holding incorrect theories, only creative theories can direct us toward valuable understandings.

One major theoretical issue is the nature of economic action in general and the nature of pastoral production in particular. As regards economic action, the crux of the argument is the extent to which pre-capitalist pastoralists are "economic men", calculating, accumulating, maximising economic value. One view, represented by Bourgeot in this collection, is that pre-capitalist pastoralism is primarily a "simple form of pastoral production for food-provision", the aim of the stock-raisers being "to satisfy biological and social needs" and the herds "considered only as a means of production and an object of consumption". From this perspective, production is oriented to the finite goals of human nourishment and subsistence, and the means of production, livestock, are indeed means to achieving those goals rather than values in themselves or means to achieving a specifically economic goal, such as accumulation of wealth. A contrary view, represented by Schneider in this collection, is that pre-capitalist pastoralism is oriented not toward producing food *per se*, but rather toward producing wealth, for "foodstuffs, like...other types of goods, are probably not viewed by any people out of context of the general system of supply and demand they face, but rather as an asset which can be eaten or traded, depending on which brings the best return". Livestock, according to this view, "play the role of...money; media of exchange, stores of value, standards of value, liquid reserves, standards of deferred payment and means of deferred payment"; thus, " 'food' is not food but wealth, an asset to be manipulated in whatever way will bring the best return". From this perspective, wealth and the pursuit and maximization of wealth are features of all pastoral societies; precapitalist pastoralists are engaged in calculation and accumulation, and to this extent can be seen as "economic men".

There are several comments—other than my initial one about the need to devise empirical tests—that I would make about these contrary views of economic action in pastoral society. First, it is not obvious that there is a contradiction between the pastoralists' "aim to satisfy biological and social needs" (Bourgeot) and processes of calculation, maximalization, and accumulation; indeed, even if some "natural" limits to biological and social needs are assumed, it might well be that calculation, maximalization and accumulation are an integral part of the action required to satisfy those needs. Second, I would argue that "biological and social needs" are culturally constituted and do not prescribe any inherent limit to the use of wealth. Is there so obviously a limit to the "need" for things into which wealth can be converted: allies, prestige, security, wives, religious credit? Third, the livestock wealth that Schneider discusses is wealth because it can be converted into values which are culturally defined. Consequently, accumulation of wealth is significant not in itself, but insofar as it is converted—into more fertile fields, into wives, into political ties, into food (Schneider). Fourth, wealth and its pursuit and accumulation have different significance in different societies because of the different values into which it is converted. What is critical is whether its disposal for conversion rests with individuals or collectivities, and whether it is converted into intensive or extensive ties, and whether these conversions are oriented toward welfare and security, political alliance, religious credit, or direct consumption. Fifth, the distinction between a pre-capitalist, natural subsistence economy and a capitalist economy seems to me overly simplistic. Markets and commercial exchange have existed long before capitalism, and pastoralists, in particular, have been engaged with them to one degree or another throughout many ages and in many parts of the world. And in recalling that pastoralism is only one stream in a mode of production, that transport, carpet making, smuggling, military service, and cultivation, singly or in combination, play major parts in the economies of "pastoralists", we remind ourselves of other ways in which such peoples have been deeply involved in pre-capitalist non-subsistence economies. In the Middle East, for example, pastoralists have been engaged with markets and commercial exchange from the earliest times, and the profound changes in the lives of Middle Eastern pastoralists in recent times owe more to advanced military, medical, and communications technology than to any direct impact of capitalism. Sixth, on a less technical note, one notices occasionally the implication that competition and conflict, expropriation of resources and degradation of the environment, inequality, oppression, and greed and violence arrived initially with capitalism, or at least was evolved to an especial high state of perfection and applied with particular enthusiasm under the auspices of capitalism. And while we undoubtedly should make it part of our task to establish the grave human costs in the systemic processes of capitalism, historical naivity about the evils of non-capitalist systems hardly adds to our credibility in carrying out that task.

The second issue is the nature of pastoral production, in particular the productive capacity of pastoral systems and the place of labor in that capacity. There are two divergent arguments, one of which stresses the productive capacity of pastoral systems and their potential for expansion, and the other of which stresses the limitations of productive capacity. Bonte, in this volume, emphasizes the importance of labor in tapping the productive potential of pastoral systems: "Pastoral specialization is accompanied by a considerable increase in the productivity of pastoral labor". And this leads to "an increased accumulation for the community as a whole". In contrast, Cole, in this volume, argues that Bedouin pastoralism, in spite of its high level of specialization, is characterized by a low productive capacity: "...the mode of production under which the Bedouin operate is one that does not lead to expansion or increase in at least the material side of things. ...does not lead to increased production of anything beyond the bare necessities". Bonte attributes the productive capacity he sees in pastoral societies to communal organization, and the need to transform inequalities in accumulation among domestic units of production into an increased accumulation for the community as a whole. Cole attributes the limited productive capacity to the characteristics of their domestic mode of production within which much available labor is unapplied in the pastoral sphere.

In attempting to resolve these two divergent views, several questions come to mind. First, are we quite sure that using the same precise criteria Bonte's East African and other pastoralists are more productive than Cole's Arabian Bedouin? Assuming that the difference is firmly established, we can ask, second, what are the differences in mode of production? In what sense do Bonte's pastoralists have a "communal" mode of production and Cole's Bedouin have a contrasting "domestic" mode of production? If there are differences, why should this be so? Is there no imperative among the Bedouin to transform inequalities in accumulation among domestic units of production into an increased accumulation for the community as a whole? Third, assuming the differences described, do the environmental conditions under which the two sets of pastoral systems operate have any part in the differences? Even if we accept that the investment of human labor contributes to increased productivity and accumulation, the non-human factors cannot be ignored. Of these, two are paramount: One is that livestock reproduce themselves, and under good conditions can increase geometrically. The other is that pastoralism is often carried out in difficult circumstances, in marginal environments, under far from good conditions. To what extent do environmental conditions in Arabia constrain pastoral productivity, even with increased labor input, such that the parameters of productivity are substantially different from those of the groups described by Bonte?

Another major theoretical issue is the relationship between economic factors and political factors in the determination of social forms and the direction of social change. While there is general agreement that economic processes and political processes are often interwoven, frequently set parameters for one another, and usually have a significant impact upon one another, opinions do differ substantially as to degree of interdependence and directionality of influence. Simply stated, the difference on the question of directionality of influence is between those who argue that economic processes, more often than not, influence and even determine the nature of politics, and those who argue that political processes more often than not affect economics. The emphasis in favour of the influence of economics is often seen in "mode of production" analysis, and often expressed in the identification of economics with the "base" and politics with "superstructure". In such a view, processes of ethnic politics, party politics, social control, and the like, are viewed as epiphenomena of economic processes and relations. An emphasis in favour of the influence of politics is often seen in perspectives which take the quest for power, the necessity for social control and defense, and the operation of primordial or interest groups as constituting the conditions under which economic processes must take place. It is not uncommon for the emphasis upon economics to be characteristic of studies with a Marxist theoretical base, and for the emphasis upon politics to be characteristic of non-Marxist orientations. However, two papers in this collection present an intriguing reversal of this tendency; Bonte points to political constitution as the mainspring of social change, whereas Schneider stresses economic factors as the determining influences upon political structure. Bonte argues, as indicated above, that the equality of households with a communal political structure is contradicted by variations in household production. In order to maintain the political structure, the production and accumulation of the society as a whole must increase. This is achieved by a change in the economic structure, in the mode of production, from a less pastoral to a more pastoral system, from a less nomadic to a more nomadic pattern, with associated changes in the division of labor, in inheritance practices, and so on. Thus, for Bonte, political imperatives determine economic processes and economic change. In contrast, Schneider argues that degree of domination is largely a function of the economic situation. The key economic factor is this: In a volatile and dynamic process of the expansive growth of wealth, no one is able to gain monopoly of the sources of wealth, and thus no one is able to build a political hierarchy based upon control of wealth. This process is seen in pastoral societies, where wealth in livestock reproduces itself. Thus heavily pastoral societies have a strong tendency to be egalitarian. In this fashion, according to Schneider, economic processes determine political forms.

There are, in my view, some difficulties in attributing primary determinative power to economic factors. One major point is that there are political "needs" and goals which exist in their own right aside from economic processes and goals. These political "needs" and goals are security and order, and are manifested in arrangements for defense, for social control, and for the formation of public policy. And while these political processes are important aspects of the operation of the society, it is worth stressing, for it is a point often ignored or denied, that usually, in the ordinary course of events, people are deeply concerned about security and order, about the protection of life and limb, about regularity and dependability in daily life, about safety, about the maintenance of peace. This being the case, political goals and political events have a dynamic and a significance of their own, and are not reducible to economic processes and goals, either in terms of their meaning or the bases of their generation. The other major point is that the monopoly of wealth, which Schneider points to as the primary basis of political hierarchy, is not the only factor that must be taken into account. As well and crucial to an understanding of the basis of political process and organization are control of the means of coercion and control of the means of administration. The concentration of coercive ability plays a central role in political hierarchy. And as coercion can directly affect the control and distribution of wealth, this political factor constitutes the nature of economic processes. It is here that the importance of nomadism can be seen to be greater than suggested by Schneider's account, for nomadism can operate as a political mechanism. Schneider argues that there is a straightforward correlation between number of cattle per person and egalitarian political structures. But it is also true that greater concentration upon pastoralism is correlated with mobility. Wealth in the form of livestock is mobile, and in most pastoral societies technology and social organization facilitate mobility. What this means is that mobility can be used to avoid the application of coercion or at least to increase greatly the difficulty of using coercion effectively. Furthermore, the technology and social organization of mobility are usually highly concordant with military capacity throughout the population at large. All of these factors militate against the effective use of coercion against nomadic peoples both from within or from without. (It would be instructive to do a statistical analysis of political structures and pastoral emphasis along the lines of Schneider's analysis, but with nomadism as a "control" variable, and, as a complement, an analysis of political structures and nomadism, with pastoral emphasis as a "control" variable.) Thus, it seems likely that both a volatile, expanding economy that militates against monopoly of wealth and a full and flexible mobility which militates against the application of coercion tend to inhibit the development of political hierarchies and tend to generate egalitarian systems.

The final theoretical issue that I wish to raise is the causal efficacy of different factors in social life and in processes of change. The question is a very general one and extremely controversial, and different answers to it are central elements in conflicting theoretical stances, for example, in the debate between materialists, who argue that ultimately if not immediately such factors as adaptation, population, production, and power determine the nature of social life and the direction of social change, and non-materialists, who argue that all aspects of human life are constituted by categories, models and meanings and energised by values, commitments and cathexis, so that psychic and symbolic processes provide the base upon which any material concern rests. A cross-cutting dimension of this issue is the extent to which causality is seen in monistic terms, as basically one type of factor, or is seen in pluralistic terms, as the result of several independent factors of interaction.

The issue of causal efficacy is brought up in Hjort's discussion, in this volume, of ethnic transformation in northern Kenya. The Ilgira (a section of Samburu constituted by Turkana), who have given up Turkana identity and lifeways, exemplify the way in which cultural transformation can be a means of gaining access to desired resources. Here, then, is a case of material need outweighing cultural influences. Or is it, in fact, quite as simple as this? Are "needs" simply material facts, or are they largely culturally defined? Can one discuss the "insufficiency" of various productive techniques, the "viability" of households, the desire for "needed or attractive resources" and the pressures which "force" households to migrate, without taking into account the cultural criteria of evaluation? There are, in short, many "material facts", but is not their significance defined culturally? People may pursue "material" goals, but goals are symbolic constructs. Similarly with the means for achieving "material" goals, as Hjort points out: "Keeping the relevant cultural factors in mind it seems obvious that one effect of the development process...is...increased emphasis on ethnicity. Hence, rather than a class formation, the cultural systems give rise to efforts to mobilize ethnic ascription as a means to secure a particular mode of survival". Here Hjort is pointing out that processes of change which clearly involve the striving to achieve material goals (access to resources) and which clearly involve modification of major cultural commitments (ethnic identity and practices) can only be understood as heavily influenced and directed by cultural categories, frameworks, and models (ethnicity as a schema for classifying people). In short, one cannot understand the development and nature of social change without taking into account the cultural impetus and cultural constraint.

At the same time, the development and nature of the Ilgira can only be understood if various non-cultural influences are taken into account. Turkana have come under pressure from several kinds of factors: the recurring, cyclical environmental elements of climate and disease, demographic shifts, external constraint upon traditional adjustment mechanisms, e.g. warfare, and externally based competition from alternative land use practices, e.g. subsistence and commercial farming, tourism, commercial ranching, and wildlife reserves. These are "non-cultural" influences because they are not part of, generated by, or controlled by Turkana culture. They are "influences" because they have an important impact upon Turkana trying to carry on life according to their own lights, that is, according to their culture.

The situation of many Turkana was not viable in terms of their own criteria as a result of the various impinging influences. Their difficult situation led some of them to take the initiative, to make innovations, to take chances, to engage in self-transformation in order to better their situation. That some significant percentage of Turkana did so suggests that the personality characteristics among the Turkana population were of a type (or frequency distribution) which made possible individual independence, flexibility, and daring.

Therefore, in accounting for the emergence of the Ilgira, it is necessary to do so in terms of the conjunction of cultural influences, non-cultural influences, and personality characteristics. Each one of these is, of course, the residue of previous conjunctions of all three factors, thus illustrating the ongoing interaction of the three while at the same time recognising their continuing independent influence. There are thus, in my view, a multiplicity of interacting influences, interacting not only in terms of dialectical opposition but also in conjunction and various degrees of cross purpose. This being the case, sound, substantive generalizations are more likely to take the form of middle range statements—about the consequences of change in a certain factor, given the presence of a number of other specified factors—than the form of grand theoretical statements explaining all and every case. Of course, it is middle range formulations that are more amenable to empirical research and testing, upon which we must rely if we wish to move beyond rhetoric and opinion, to find out what is the truth of the matter.

CONTRIBUTORS

ASEN BALIKCI received his Ph.D. in anthropology from Columbia in 1962, and has since taught at the Université de Montreal, where he is now Professor of Anthropology. His research has focused on the cultural ecology of arid zones and includes work in the Canadian Arctic, Ethiopia and Afghanistan. He has worked extensively in cinematic anthropology and has made a number of ethnographic films.

PIERRE BONTE received his Doctorat de Troisième Cycle in Ethnology from the Université de Paris in 1971. He is associated with the Centre National de la Recherche Scientifique (CNRS) and the Laboratoire d'Anthropologie Sociale, and has carried out research missions in Niger, Algeria, Mauritania, Tunisia and Upper Volta. He is a founding member of the Equipe Ecologie et Anthropologie des Sociétés Pastorales at the Maison des Sciences de l'Homme, and a member of the Secrétariat of the Commission on Nomadic Peoples.

ANDRÉ BOURGEOT is associated with the Centre National de la Recherche Scientifique, the Laboratoire d'Anthropologie Sociale and the Ecole des Hautes Etudes en Sciences Sociales in Paris, France. He received his Doctorat de Troisième Cycle in Ethnology, and has carried out research projects with the Tuareg of Algeria, Niger, and Mali on socio-economic aspects of pastoralism. He is a member of Equipe Ecologie et Anthropologie des Sociétés Pastorales at the Maison des Sciences de l'Homme.

DONALD COLE received his Ph.D. degree from the University of California at Berkeley in 1971. He teaches at the American University in Cairo, where he is now Associate Professor. He has carried out research on the social and economic structures of the Bedouin of Saudi Arabia, and on policy-related issues pertaining to social change.

CHARLES FRANTZ received his Ph.D. degree in anthropology from the University of Chicago in 1958, and is now Professor of Anthropology at the State University of New York in Buffalo. He has carried out research among Fulbe peoples of West Africa, with particular emphasis on those in Nigeria and Cameroun and is interested in topics of ecology and politics.

JOHN G. GALATY who is a co-editor of this volume, is Assistant Professor in the Department of Anthropology at McGill University and serves as Secretary of the Commission on Nomadic Peoples of the I.U.A.E.S. He received his Ph.D. in anthropology from the University of Chicago in 1977, after carrying out research among the Maasai pastoralists of Kenya. His primary interests are in the symbolic and ideological aspects of pastoral society and processes of change and development.

ANDERS HJORT is associated with the Department of Anthropology at the University of Stockholm, where he received his Ph.D. degree in 1979. He has carried out research among the Samburu of Kenya and the Beja of the Sudan and has collaborated on a comparative study of pastoral domestic economy. His interests include the regional social and economic relations of pastoralists and the role of small towns.

PHILIP CARL SALZMAN, who is a co-editor of this volume, is Professor of Anthropology at McGill University, and Chairman of the Commission on Nomadic Peoples of the I.U.A.E.S. He received his Ph.D. degree in Anthropology from the University of Chicago in 1972. He has carried out research among the Baluch of Iran, and is interested in political, ecological and ideological aspects of nomadic society.

HAROLD K. SCHNEIDER received his Ph.D. degree from Northwestern University in 1953. He has held the post of Professor of Anthropology at Indiana University since 1970. His research has been carried out among the Pakot of Kenya and the Turu of Tanzania. His research interests focus on the comparative study of East African pastoral economics.

INDEX